I0866878

Dreaming Down the Track

Dreaming Down the Track

Awakenings in Aboriginal Cinema

William Lempert

MINNESOTA

UNIVERSITY OF MINNESOTA PRESS
MINNEAPOLIS • LONDON

The University of Minnesota Press gratefully acknowledges the financial assistance provided for the publication of this book by Bowdoin College.

All photographs, unless otherwise specified, were taken by the author.

Published by the University of Minnesota Press
111 Third Avenue South, Suite 290
Minneapolis, MN 55401-2520
http://www.upress.umn.edu

Available as a Manifold edition at manifold.umn.edu

ISBN 978-1-5179-1826-2 (hc)
ISBN 978-1-5179-1827-9 (pb)
ISBN 978-1-4529-7337-1 (Manifold)

A Cataloging-in-Publication record for this book is available from the Library of Congress.

Printed in the United States of America on acid-free paper

UMP BmB 2025

For Mark

This book contains names and images of deceased people that may be sensitive for some families in Aboriginal communities in Northwestern Australia. It also includes references to suicide. Please seek appropriate guidance before sharing these materials with people in and from these communities.

Contents

INTRODUCTION

Awakenings

Dreaming is about the future.
It's about going back to Country and waking it up.

—Mark Moora

What lives in the spaces between dreams and apocalypse? What are futures made of amidst specters of annihilation? In dire circumstances, how can filmmaking salve old wounds, catalyze political transformation, or perhaps foster something else entirely? These are the questions that animate this book and the years of fieldwork it is based upon. In most stories there is a turning point, when the narrative shifts in a way that permanently alters the trajectory of the characters' relationships and goals. It is there that I start, not at the beginning or the end, but in the middle, at the turn.

With a population of approximately four hundred, Wirrimanu Aboriginal Community—better known as Balgo—is one of the largest in Western Australia and can be reached by land or air. If you found yourself driving down the dusty corrugated Tanami Road, you would keep an eye out for the body of a bright pink Toyota Land Cruiser set beneath an arrow sign that reads WARLAYIRTI ART CENTRE BALGO. If you turned due west, the community would slowly emerge along the horizon, its eggshell water tower rising out of the desert. If you were flying south from the town of Halls Creek, the mail plane would trace the Tanami Road, which would appear from above as though etched through the Earth like a chisel through sandstone. Before landing, the plane would circle Balgo to announce its arrival. Looking down, you would see neighborhoods radiating outward from the center sports oval, orienting families toward their Country. Just before landing on the pebbled runway, the monumental scale of the "pound" overlook would

FIGURE 1. Shell of a Toyota Land Cruiser (troopy) and the sign to Balgo on the Tanami Road.

become apparent, formed when the Wirrimanu (Kingfisher) traveled through this place.

Bureaucratically, Balgo lies at the eastern edge of the Kimberley region of Northwestern Australia (the Kimberley), though it is culturally and ecologically embedded within the Great Sandy Desert, halfway between the continental center of Alice Springs and the turquoise tides of the Indian Ocean. It was here that this narrative turn unfolded on an unassuming day in 2015 when I ran into Mark Moora, a Kukatja man I had come to know through two expansive film projects in as many years.

It is a quiet desert evening as I drive past the rust-hued sandy oval. Three teenagers kick a faded yellow Australian rules football, each impact followed by a burst of dust that catches horizontal sunbeams. Through the rolled-down window, I notice Mark. He is sitting at one of the steel and wood picnic benches underneath the front canopy of the community store. His left elbow supports a relaxed posture as he takes a drag from his Winfield Red. I squint to see him against the crimson backdrop of the setting sun as a smoke plume rises from underneath his leather cowboy hat. As I park the sun-bleached white Toyota Land Cruiser (troopy), he gives me the hand sign for "What's happening?" With my right arm through the open window, I respond with the sign for "Just saying hi." He nods as I walk over and sit down next to him, then asks, "So what now? We finished that *Tjawa Tjawa* film. It was a good one. A true story."[1] After a pause, I think out loud, "Well, I'll be here in Balgo for a few months, and we have film equipment and a troopy. So, if you like, we could make other films."[2] Mark takes a breath and responds, "Ah, more Dreaming stories and Songlines?"[3] "They can be about anything at all," I reply. "Anything?" he asks, a bit surprised. "Sure, anything." He muses on this for a long moment, as he finishes the end of his cigarette. Standing up to walk home, he finally states, "I'll have a rest and think about it."

At daybreak, again I see him sitting in front of the community store, only this time the morning sun lights up his face. Displaying an uncommonly carefree smile, he gestures to convey "Hey, let's talk." He stands up and walks over to the end of the store's long awning, past several groups absorbed in discussions that flow between Kukatja, English, and signs as they wait for the store to open. With his right hand holding his left arm behind his back, Mark moves with his characteristic quiet confidence and proud posture. "Oh, good morning!" he greets as we sit down cross-legged. Suddenly deep in thought, he rubs his expansive beard. It appears white from a distance, though up close a deeper undercurrent of its original dark color reveals itself. "I had a think about it. Let's make a film about going back to Country, about the future. Let's make the real film."[4] After pondering this, the only thing I can think to say is "Sounds good. When do you want to start?" Turning his head, he focuses his one good eye south along the horizon toward his Country of Mangkayi, and with resolution declares, "Tomorrow, first thing early morning."[5]

Dreamings and Awakenings

A turn creates a narrative fracture between its before and after. However, at the time, this moment seemed relatively ordinary within the

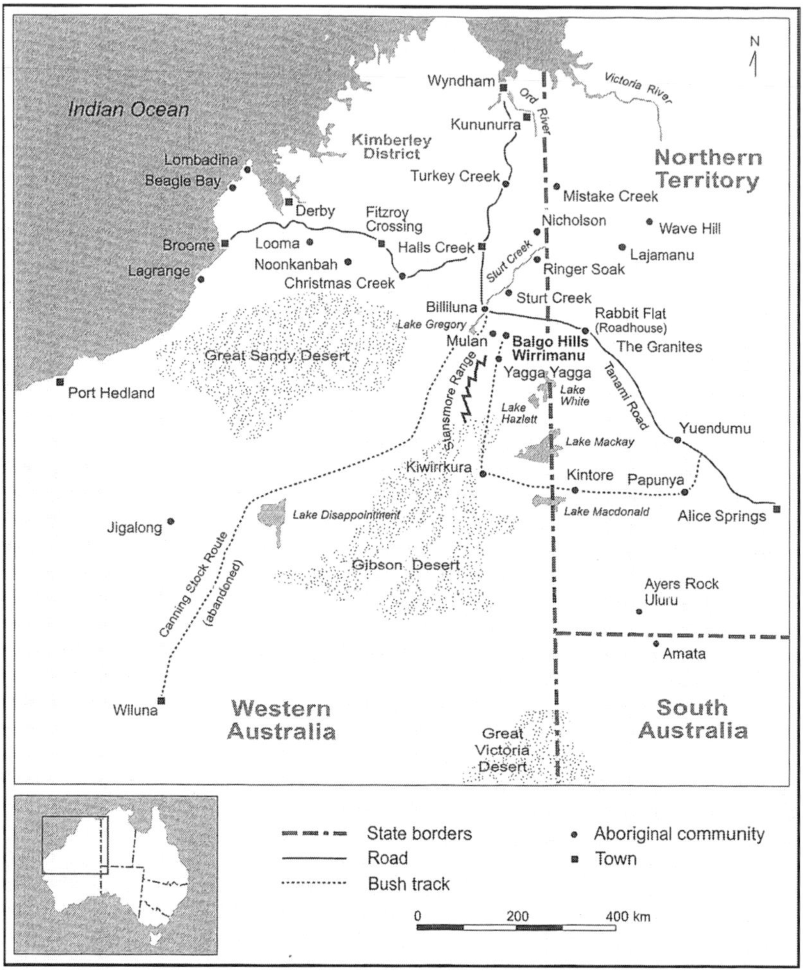

FIGURE 2. Map of Balgo and its surroundings within the Kimberley region. Map courtesy of Sylvie Poirier, 2005.

frenetic realities of fieldwork. As when shooting a documentary, it is often only in hindsight that significant moments become apparent. The daily rhythms of life quickly filled my mind as this powerful statement faded for some time. Looking back at my field notes weeks later, I noticed that I had underlined three phrases in Mark's statement: "Let's make a film about going back to Country, about the future. Let's make the real film." Over the subsequent months and years, I have returned to this moment again and again. What *did* Mark mean by "going back," "the future," and "the real"? Why had his previous ambivalence to film been overtaken by a sense of great purpose and promise? At the time I did not understand this, and in some ways, perhaps I still do not.

What I do know is that this moment was an awakening for Mark. At its heart, this book aims to understand this and other awakenings that he conveyed as we made films together over several years. "Awakening" seems appropriate here in light of its dual meaning as both waking from sleep and a moment of sudden awareness. For Mark these were intertwined, as his awakenings tended to begin with the seed of an idea that gestated overnight into morning's clarity. As he often described, these realizations were woven into his sleeping dreams and into the Dreaming, or Tjukurrpa. While awakenings manifest as sudden shifts, they are the culmination of longer processes that crystallize within a moment.

The relationship between dreams and films has long been discussed and yet remains in some ways ineffable. As Anand Pandian describes it, "From the very beginnings of cinema, films have felt like dreams. Bodies at rest in the darkness of some space, plunged into reverie by a fragmentary stream of images" (2015, 21). Every dream is followed by an awakening, whether it is formative, forgettable, frightening, or otherwise. Over the course of years I witnessed firsthand how the dynamic process of filmmaking could catalyze profound awakenings within its creators. Due to the legacy of *terra nullius* and the continued lack of treaties between Indigenous Australians and the settler state, the existential futures of Aboriginal communities also depend on awakenings in others—including politicians, policymakers, and the general public. Mark increasingly came to believe that this was possible through media-making. It was in relation to awakenings by Mark and other media makers that the central argument of this book emerged: the process of cinematic envisioning transforms how Aboriginal filmmakers imagine and actualize community futures during apocalyptic times.[6]

The next morning, as I arrive at Mark's house just after dawn, he is sitting outside on his concrete patio ready to go. He secures his hat and stands up before I even come to a stop. Pulling himself into the front passenger seat, he glances into the back to confirm our supplies between the troopy's two side benches, mentally cataloging the camera, car jack, crowbar, water containers, and cardboard box filled with food and tea. "Spare tire?" is all he asks. After I reply "Two," he nods and points down the road to pick up Larry, a fellow Elder that Mark has been close to all of his life. When we arrive, without speaking I get out and climb back in through the back double doors of the troopy, while Mark moves to the driver's seat with Larry to his left. Shifting into first gear twice to get the feel of the transmission, Mark turns due south onto the corrugated road toward his Country and away from Balgo.

Retracting my pindan-stained arm inside as we scrape past a bush, the handheld video camera barely misses the shrapnel of twigs. I adjust my footing for the upcoming terrain, pushing my boots against the cooler along the opposite bench seat, as Mark and Larry discuss the best path to a water hole they had last visited decades ago. That night, we angle our three canvas swags (all-in-one camping bedrolls) around a central fire and plan for the following morning. Mostly we sit in silence, chewing kangaroo tails cooked that afternoon in an underground oven, as we gaze at the Milky Way's expanse of stars flickering above us in the Great Sandy Desert. This silence is not an absence of words or respite between them, but a space unto itself. I move the powdered milk container-turned-teapot off the fire with a banana-peel handle, as they roll cigarettes and speak in language about their Country, explaining to me not only the English translations but also the Kukatja words and pronunciations.

On the first night of this and future trips we camped in Yagga Yagga, an abandoned smaller community a few hours south of Balgo. Visiting was bittersweet for Mark, as this was the once-thriving outstation community he led before its decline several years before.[7] It was a place of haunted pasts and promised futures that conjured both desolation and dreams. There in Yagga Yagga, near the sacred site of Mangkayi, Mark planned a renewed home for his family's future.

In documentary film projects, the camera's presence is often a distraction or a cause of self-conscious anxiety. With Mark, however, the opposite seemed to happen. The introduction of the camera focused his purpose, providing a portal for his messages to be heard across time and space, from Parliament in Canberra to his future great-grandchildren in Mangkayi. After years of practice on previous film projects, the process had already become second nature to him.

Knowing we have limited battery time left, Mark quickly adjusts the radio mic out of his beard, then looks and speaks not to me, but directly into the lens, beginning with, "I've got words for you about why I'm making this film, because people have been asking me for a better life out here. That's what I'm trying to do. That's why I'm talking to you." He introduces himself and titles the film *Mangkayi Calling*, as an extension of his broader project by the same name. He describes Mangkayi as more than a place, and "Calling" as more than a metaphor in his plans for returning along old pathways to Country in new ways.[8] He details why and how it will integrate solar panels, satellite phones, websites, new media, camel tours, youth drug rehabilitation programs, acrylic painting, and tribal Law.[9] He discusses a deeper purpose of the film, emphasizing the importance of living in small family groups in one's own Country, as practiced before colonization and missions. The more he speaks the more animated he becomes, and he seems to visualize this future community fully formed, through a coalescence of memory and imagination, fusing past and future within this moment and through this place. As the red light of the camera finally fades, I give the hand sign for wiya (nothing). His index finger responds with palya (good one), and we begin packing up for the ride home.[10]

Irreconciliation

State frameworks for Indigenous relations carry profound implications for the limits and possibilities of sovereignty. "Reconciliation" has found global purchase in settler states in recent decades, becoming the overarching Australian state policy theme for engaging Indigenous people.[11] While in other contexts the term is used to refer to restorative and healing relationships within and between communities, it is wielded by settler states to render "consistent Indigenous assertions of nationhood with the state's unilateral assertion of sovereignty over Native peoples' lands and populations," which has the further effect of "undermining the realization of the previous two forms of reconciliation" (Coulthard 2014, 107). Glen Coulthard's analysis of reconciliation in the Canadian context is further heightened in Australia by the absence of any treaties.

The reconciliation era was initiated by the 1991 Council for Aboriginal Reconciliation Act, passed in the wake of investigations into Aboriginal deaths in custody. The early 1990s was a watershed era for Aboriginal politics that included the 1992 case *Mabo v. Queensland*, which finally delegitimized *terra nullius*,[12] as well as the 1993 passing of the Native Title Act, which began a process for limited land rights.[13] Taken at face value, the reconciliation process aimed to acknowledge past injustices and the traditional ownership of Country, while attempting to reduce racism through broad education about Aboriginal people. However, Indigenous leaders have often challenged the deeper purpose of prioritizing reconciliation. For example, at a conference I attended through the National Centre for Indigenous Studies in Canberra, a prominent Aboriginal scholar rhetorically asked, "How can there be reconciliation when there has never been conciliation in the first place?"

Leanne Simpson (Michi Saagiig Nishnaabeg) describes how reconciliation processes tend to emerge out of a focus on suffering, enabling ways in which "Indigenous grief can be managed, exploited, and used by the state to placate Indigenous resistance." Examining the track record of such state policies, she observes that "these mechanisms have never brought about accountability for Indigenous peoples because they are *processes* that are partly designed to uphold the structure of settler colonialism" (2017, 238). Simpson (2011) asserts that any meaningful reconciliation must be founded within a radical resurgence of Indigenous politics, language, and life. Reconciliation presumes that forgiveness is good and anger is bad, regardless of context (Coulthard 2014, 108). This dynamic is particularly stark in Australia, where reconciliation is promoted in the absence of treaties.

Reconciliation discourse simultaneously flattens and amplifies cultural difference. In her wide-ranging critique of "recognition"—a key focus of Australian policy that is subsumed within the reconciliation framework—Elizabeth Povinelli (2002) describes the cunning ways in which this language enables a liberal multiculturalism that collapses difference.[14] The impulse to resolve differences within such dominant frameworks often results in destructive Aboriginal policies, including wide-scale programs that propose to "close the gap" between Aboriginal and Australian quantitative metrics of well-being. Under the guise of equality, reconciliation implicitly catalyzes the very assimilation that undermines sovereignty and Aboriginal community life.

At the same time, reconciliation fosters tropes of Aboriginal people as inconceivably different others and casts them within a mythological past or ever-suffering present. Journalists and other commentators often do not express surprise when gap-closing policies are deemed unsuccessful. An ongoing undercurrent message is something along the lines of "It would be great to make Aboriginal people equal, but it is unlikely because of how different they are." In some ways, Aboriginal and non-Aboriginal ways of understanding, being, and living *are* incommensurable (Povinelli 2001).[15] However, emphasizing radical differences can quickly become objectifying and depoliticizing, rendering Indigenous people as intellectual fascinations or as beyond the scope of Western understanding.

In an attempt to avoid both under- and overstating difference, I frame discussions of Indigenous sovereignty through "irreconciliation," which I approach as (1) a politics of refusing reconciliation policies, (2) a conceptualization for engaging difference, and (3) a critical reflection on the limitations of ethnographic understanding. I am inspired by Joseph Weiss's (2025) articulation of irreconciliation as a productive framework for resisting settler desires for closure and for "push[ing] away from any such promises of closure, whether in the triumphant liberal or equally triumphant critical mode." Crucially, Weiss emphasizes that "different forms of Indigenous anti-colonial work make colonial erasure impossible, both materially and symbolically, and that they are, thereby, inescapable for settler Canadians" (12). So, too, does the Australian state desire the impossible goal of concealing genocidal pasts and dispossessive presents.

I also build upon Nayanika Mookherjee's articulation of irreconciliation as providing a "vigilance against impunity" that settler states often attempt through the performance of public redress (2022, 28), as well as Ronald Niezen's work on irreconciliation within Canada's Truth and Reconciliation Commission on Indian residential schools. As Niezen describes, reconciliation implies collective guilt that paradoxically "cannot be forgiven and for which no punishment is possible," whereas irreconciliation rejects that stalemate toward the purpose of "rebuilding the world anew" (2022, 89).

Indigenous reconciliation is confounding in the context of a history without conciliation. However, its prominence in Australian policy becomes more intelligible when reimagined through settler state desires to perform its own reconciliation: attempting to synthesize a proud national identity while the brutal colonial violence and dispossession has become increasingly visible (largely due to the work of Indigenous activists and media makers). This is a seemingly impossible task, though if the state can give the impression that it has reconciled with Indigenous people, it justifies settler colonialism in two crucial ways. First, it implies that justice has been achieved not only in the present but also in the past. It performs the magic trick of seeming to forgive the unforgivable through a rhetorical penance that alleviates national guilt. Second, it reimagines history so that meaningful sovereignty is no longer required, while allowing national origin stories that connect early settlers with Aboriginal people and Country to remain intact. Asserting irreconciliation provides a form of what Audra Simpson (Kahnawake Mohawk) (2014) describes as a "refusal" to accede to settler state frameworks that provide false choices. Irreconciliation refuses the whitewashing of colonization that subverts Indigenous sovereignty.

As with the legal language of divorce, where differences are often described as irreconcilable, I center this analytic because it emphasizes the relationship *between* differences, rather than their nature or scope, as well as the pragmatic steps for appropriate decoupling. While reconciliation makes little sense in a failed marriage, settler state reconciliation with Indigenous people is even less coherent, as it lacks the precursor of a consensual union. In this analogy, divorce entails Indigenous nationhood, while compelled reconciliation represents its denial. Irreconciliation gestures toward the framing of Indigenous sovereignty as being in the long-term interests of everyone involved, "moving the center" from the state's assimilatory priorities to those of Aboriginal people and communities (Ngũgĩ 1993). It also provides settler states with a more forthright path to confronting colonial legacies. Avoiding these historical realities harms not only Indigenous people but also settler life, within which colonial hauntings lie just beneath the surface, in various states of sublimation and rupture (Franks 2023; Lepselter 2016, 55).

The irregular and patchwork reality of fieldwork is itself difficult to reconcile. While some aspects of fieldwork become clearer over time, others that once seemed clear can become translucent, or even opaque. My goal is to remain transparent about the things that, although important, remain irreconcilable for me. Over time, I have come to understand some of the moments that I initially viewed as fieldworker failings rather as inescapable aspects of delving into the messy realities of human life, where irreconcilabilities abound.

Sitting with Irreconcilable Differences

Upon our return, Mark was filled with excitement and possibility as rough desert tracks gave way to the silence of Balgo's smooth streets. However, this sentiment was quickly extinguished when a family member explained to Mark that his truck had been in an accident. While no one was injured, its bent frame was unrepairable, and it sat now as a monument to immobility in front of Mark's house. There had been an abrupt shift in the community in the three days since we had left. For months there had been rumors of the state government defunding Aboriginal communities. Now, however, a Western Australia document known as "the list" had been leaked, shared in Balgo as five printed pages folded into quarters. It implied plans to defund—and in effect, close—most Aboriginal communities in Australia's largest state, encompassing a third of the continent. With a lack of treaties, these hundreds of communities were built in a way that made them dependent on fossil fuels and constant infrastructural maintenance. In other words, a sudden lack of state funding would render many of them as practically uninhabitable in the close future. This list ranked communities into three categories, with Balgo slotted into the middle one, which suggested that it would probably stay funded. However, even if it did, under this plan Balgo would likely become a refuge community for the region, since many nearby smaller communities were in the bottom tier, which was implicitly slated for defunding. And just like that, dreams of filmmaking were overcast by the dire urgency of the moment.

This list presented an existential and apocalyptic future for Aboriginal communities in Western Australia, though it was hardly without precedent. It was only the most recent of a long list of state actions going back centuries, including the previous defunding of outstation communities such as Yagga Yagga. For Mark, the planned closing of small communities was heartbreakingly familiar. After his momentary shock, the list seemed to imbue more vitality into his burgeoning interest in filmmaking. He noted that this policy plan only affirmed his vision—that building communities *independent* of governmental funding was the most viable long-term path forward, not only for Yagga Yagga but across Indigenous Australia. Later that day we watched the trip footage at the computer in the community radio station, which faced the Balgo store. Mark reviewed it with care and at the end smiled, declaring, "Ah, I know where we will go next time, my birthplace in Emily Springs. Yuwai [Yes]."

This juxtaposition of inspiration and dejection was not unusual in Balgo, but rather represented a typical feature of daily life. To varying extents, all of the media projects I collaborated on were characterized by levity amid a backdrop of peril. In light of such stark contrasts, I often wondered if anyone, myself included, could communicate this in a meaningful and dignified way. Is it possible to make comprehensible the incommensurable? Irreconcilable contrasts permeate Aboriginal representations across multiple realms. Policies are animated by broadly shared national imaginings of Aboriginal communities. These are amplified through popular films and books depicting either a dreamy mythological past or a dreary suffering present. In anthropology this has manifested through vacillations between what Michel-Rolph Trouillot (1995) describes as the "savage slot" and what Joel Robbins (2013) mirrors as the "suffering slot." This tension has more recently manifested through disciplinary discussions on ethnographies focused on darkness versus desire. As Sherry Ortner (2016) argues, "dark anthropology" highlights tragedy and can inadvertently reinforce negative portrayals of the already marginalized, while "desire-oriented" (Tuck 2009) research emphasizing the "anthropology of the good" (Robbins 2013) runs the risk of promoting optimism while understating crucial challenges. Undergirding this tension is a historical pattern of Indigenous people being cast as pawns within broader social debates, going back at least as far as Hobbes's and Rousseau's classically opposing brutish versus noble states of nature, two sides of the same dehumanizing coin.

This pervasive polarity in Aboriginal representation across time and space seems to be exacerbated by an impulse toward assuredness—the desire to arrive at something solid, rather than the shifting tensions between aspiration and desperation, joy and anguish, light and dark. As ethnographers well know, it is within the unstable places between that people live, and where we are most likely to stumble upon the irreconcilable, and something like the truth. I do not pretend to have in any way transcended these challenges, nor do I intend to downplay the many ethnographies and other works that powerfully portray Aboriginal life in its vivid complexity. I simply wish to highlight the danger of certainty and the certainty of danger in a project such as this.

While the act of sitting tends to be portrayed as a lethargic absence of action, this belies its reality in Aboriginal relationships with their Country. Often self-described as "sitting on Country," this is an active assertion of being with and of a place, which has been practiced since time immemorial. In the context of Aboriginal political movements, it has taken on an additional resonance. From sitting in town center ovals, to the ongoing Aboriginal Tent Embassies at "The Block" in Redfern and across from the Old Parliament House in Canberra, sitting on Country in conspicuous places has become a potent form of refusal—in this case regarding legacies of *terra nullius* that continue to paper over a lack of treaties. Sitting on Country asserts existence despite all efforts of annihilation and inverts "homelessness" as a dominant framework for understanding Aboriginal people in their own Country. Similarly, when engaging questions of irreconcilability and paradox, instead of aiming to solve them, it is worth considering the value of simply sitting with them. While such enigmas may lack resolution, they do not defy understandings that live within and between tensions.

I pull up to Mark's house at dusk. In the week since the first shoot for *Mangkayi Calling*, we have completed a second trip and are planning more. As I am about to knock on his weathered ruby metal door, Mark opens it and nods. As he often says, he is clearer in the morning than at night, having kept stockman hours since his youth. However, this late hour seems particularly difficult for him. I am not sure why and I know enough not to ask. He gestures down before sitting on his concrete porch. I join him in the warm wind and fading soundscape of the setting desert sun. As we sit, a diesel truck sputters in the distance and a conversation next door lingers just out of reach.

Looking out from the edge of his front door, I am reminded that Mark lives at a literal and metaphorical crossroads. At the edge of "bottom camp," his house forms a nexus of three tracks. West leads to the Old Balgo Mission, where he spent much of his childhood. East joins with the corrugated Tanami Road toward the towns and coasts of his early adulthood. South moves through Yagga Yagga toward his Country, toward Mangkayi. Unusually, he lives alone, though is surrounded by family, with his two daughters and other extended relations in larger houses flanking his. Mark rolls a cigarette and stares north into the middle distance. As the sun disappears over the horizon, he breaks the silence as he often does, with a drawn-out "I was thinking . . ." After a short pause, he continues, "Next trip we should bring young people. We should take them back to their Country. Otherwise, they might forget it. Yuwai."

The Visibility Paradox

During my fieldwork a specific form of irreconcilability increasingly emerged, which I have come to think of as a broader "visibility paradox" of Aboriginal representation. On the one hand, the recent era has bolstered an unprecedented expansion of the Australian Indigenous media sphere. This has occurred in both remote and mainstream media, including the rise of multiple national TV networks, numerous regional video and radio hubs, online streaming services, and Aboriginal content within major studio systems, such as the Australian Broadcasting Corporation and Screen Australia. The films I collaborated on were supported by this proliferation. On the other hand, this same period has been characterized by a resurgence in policies of cultural destruction. This included a renewed wave of drastic funding cuts for Aboriginal communities and organizations across the continent, of which the planned closing of most Western Australia communities was only one component.

What is the relationship between the flourishing of Aboriginal media and state policies of annihilation? Is the funding of these media a smoke screen for furthering colonial dispossession? Do Indigenous media serve as a revolutionary refusal, bolstering public support to prevent what would otherwise result in even more devastating state actions? Are these simply coincident, or related in another way altogether? As I would come to find out, the answers to these and related questions lay not on firm ground but in the unsteady spaces between steps. As Eric Michaels wrote, media in Aboriginal communities is "both a blessing and a curse . . . the instrument of salvation or of destruction" (1994, 121). As Donna Haraway (2016) suggests, in such murky waters, perhaps "staying with the trouble" is enough—holding on tightly as a weathered troopy bounces over rocky terrain with a single spare, keeping trust in the vehicle and its guide. In this book, Mark is your guide as well as my own, and these pages are a conduit, as best as I could manage: the vehicle that hopefully holds together enough to make the journey and return home with a story worth telling.

Envisioning Aboriginal Futures

In the eight hours of his spoken footage for *Mangkayi Calling,* Mark uttered "future" well over a hundred times. The future also emerged as a central theme in several other media projects in Balgo. This was surprising, since "the future" lacks a close translation or conceptualization in Kukatja, due to distinctions regarding how time itself is understood.[16] It is not the case that the Kukatja language lacks a sense of temporality, but rather that it encapsulates an ontological framework that is "not concerned with the representation of time, as such, but rather with principles of transformation that are intrinsically linked to *Tjukurrpa,*" which has always been, always will be, and is also present within the here and now (Poirier [1996] 2005, 57).

Many in Balgo suggested to me that the use of the term "the future" seemed relatively new and that as recently as a decade before it would have rarely been used. What seems to have changed in this period is an unlikely convergence of the bureaucratically banal and the politically imaginative. In previous years there had been various Closing the Gap government-funded programs that began to explicitly reference the future, with the aim of equalizing Aboriginal versus national statistical measurements of health, education, and employment. Although these government programs may have introduced the concept of the future into the Balgo lexicon, futurity has a distinctive lineage in Aboriginal

Australian media scholarship (Ginsburg and Myers 2006). This book builds in particular upon the work of Michaels, who worked closely with the Warlpiri Media Association in the 1980s. He emphasized the importance of "cultural futures" that retain specificity and allow for shifting negotiations of contradiction, all while privileging "processes of reproduction over their products" (1994, 121).

The future that was engaged within Balgo films resonated less with bureaucratic programs and more with the recent rise of futurity as a central theme in Indigenous intellectual and political movements across the globe (Estes 2019; Medak-Saltzman 2017; Weiss 2018) and to an increasing extent within anthropology (Valentine and Hassoun 2019). Grace Dillon (Anishinaabe) articulates the intentionally plural conception of "Indigenous futurisms" as a way for Indigenous people to attempt to further understand and discard the impacts of colonization, recovering ancestral traditions within a world that is already postapocalyptic for many Native people (2012, 10). Indigenous futurisms assert what Mark Rifkin (2017) has described as "temporal sovereignty" through resisting the imposition of "settler time." Temporal displacement has fostered dispossession throughout the history of colonization (Donaldson 1996; Musharbash 2007), as well as within the formation of anthropological notions of difference itself (Fabian 1983). Rather than focusing on incommensurable aspects of temporality, I emphasize how conceptions of "the future" have emerged in Balgo through the corporeality of media that communicate within and beyond the limits of language (MacDougall 2006).

Indigenous futurisms confront implications of primarily framing Aboriginal Australians as the "world's oldest living societies," dating back to at least 65,000 years ago.[17] Fred Myers articulates this temporal issue at the heart of settler imaginings of Aboriginal people:

> With a view to the imposing, apparently unchanging landscape, the nostalgic may reflect sadly on the intervention of history in a timeless world. But these reactions would be mistaken. For all its trappings of worldliness and hard knowledge of history's inexorable laws, such a dichotomous "before and after" view reflects a rather shallow grasp of society as human action. Focusing on outward form alone makes it impossible to see the past in the present. Hunting-and-gathering bands, it is true, no

> longer exist for observation. Yet their substance, if not their material form, remains here: as part of the structure with which the present encounters the future. (1986, 11-12)

The temporal terminal narrative of colonial contact renders annihilation as inevitable, with tangible impacts on the terms and limits of sovereignty.

While Native Title land rights depend on demonstrating "uninterrupted" traditional cultural practices, Indigenous/state relations also hinge on the ability of Aboriginal people to imagine and amplify diverse future visions. In this book I follow the envisioning process of media productions by those most associated with distant pasts. The very media tools used to temporally trap Indigenous Australians within stereotyped representations are now being inverted and wielded to reimagine what Aboriginal people, publics, and policymakers believe is possible, desirable, and inevitable for communities such as Balgo and Yagga Yagga. Through media-making, Mark and others in communities are simultaneously envisioning and enacting their futures within postapocalyptic present realities.

When lost in the scorching heat and sands of an unknown desert, kartiya (strangers) often become susceptible to mirages: optical illusions of water in the distance caused by heat-bent light and exacerbated by desperation.[18] Yet Mark's vision was no mirage. A key distinction between vision and mirage lays in whether or not someone understands where they are. Mark could detail by moonlight what lies along the horizon throughout his Country. When he did get lost, he quickly reoriented himself. As improbable as his plans for Yagga Yagga might appear, it would be a mistake to dismiss them as fantasy. As a younger man, Mark successfully led the unlikely establishment of Yagga Yagga before there was even a graded road to it. He guided its ascension, witnessed its demise, and developed a practical theory for what to do differently next time. Mangkayi's calling was more than the aching pain of nostalgia. What he lacked in youth he made up for through hard-won lessons from heartbreaking setbacks that both scarred and emboldened him.

The future that Mark discussed was specific and placed—where his current and yet-to-be family could live beyond the reach of governmental intervention in Yagga Yagga. Sometimes he mused more amorphously about the future. In film shoots, when Mark used the phrase "in the future," it usually began or concluded a thought, and was accompanied by a pregnant pause as he seemed to focus inwardly and then toward Mangkayi along the horizon. Adriana Petryna's (2022) development of "horizon work" is illuminating here, as it captures the importance of navigating shifting expectations and frameworks of possibility while avoiding the paralysis of doomism. She translates this term into the verb *horizoning* as a way to conceptualize "thinking about and responding to complex futures" (5). Such imaginative processes are as powerful as they are fragile. Mark's horizoning work lived within zones and economies of abandonment, as he attempted to gaze beyond such constraints so that other future paths for his family might become possible (Biehl 2013; Povinelli 2011). His dreams were as temporal as they were spatial, southward toward Yagga Yagga and Mangkayi.

Although Mark and others often drew upon the language of futurity during film shoots, the future within daily Balgo life was usually engaged through metaphors of movement. Mark's nephew David "Shorty" Young would often describe the future as "down the track," capturing the extent to which future-making was an act of temporal place-making, collective travel toward homelands and horizons. While moving down the track implies moving forward, it resists notions of linear progress and points toward cyclical aspects of time. Tracks are not flattened highways or asphalt, but parallel grooves connecting communities, families, and Country. While rough on vehicles, they are gentle on walkers, who can travel side by side along their twin lines. Like Songlines, such tracks are defined not by completions or arrivals but by traveling along them—recurring returns that are renewed through engaging relations and places.

I came to know Mark late in his life, during only one of the many chapters he lived across decades. It was not until years after meeting him that I would begin to understand the heights of his triumphs and the depths of his grief. His lowest point occurred not long before I met him, though I did not know any of this yet. If I did, I would have understood that this was not just a story of catalyzing Yagga Yagga's rebirth, but also of a longing for a past that might have been, and a future for his family that still might be. Not hope exactly, but something adjacent to it, or perhaps, as I have discussed elsewhere, a sort of generative hope in the postapocalyptic present (Lempert 2018a), a reassembling of something fractured though unbroken, along the edges of a dawning horizon.

I center Mark's narrative for multiple reasons. His extensive experiences draw from and speak to a range of Aboriginal relations with the settler state that normally remain disconnected. He was born before his family made settler contact, went through Law, walked into and grew up in a Pallottine mission, lived through the rise of Aboriginal communities like Balgo, shucked pearl shells along the Indian Ocean in Broome, worked on regional cattle stations, returned to Balgo to be married, traveled across the continent to fight for land rights, led the opening of Yagga Yagga and witnessed its decline, and became a nationally recognized film director working to return with his family to their Country.

Mark's expansive life was coalesced within and translated through these films, and working with him over the years represents the longest, deepest, and most creatively engaged relationship during my fieldwork. His journey of cinematic awakenings confronts the paradoxical ways that media-making can seem all at once futile and gilded, while at the same time revolutionary and transformative. In this book, I trace Mark's life and films across time and space to reveal the ethnographic textures of Aboriginal cinema, from intimate moments of creativity to national festivals at the nexus of global Indigenous mediascapes and political movements. Last but not least, I share his story because he asked me to.

Mark often alluded to the idea that the time span for Mangkayi's calling might be considerable, and was for the benefit of future generations—that more than anything he was making films "to keep the story alive." As much as Mangkayi was his ancestral homeland, it was also his "children's Country," a notion that seemed to provide a wellspring of energy (Muecke and Roe 2020). I often kept this in mind when considering what Mark meant exactly by the future, by returning, and by the real. As he would make clearer over the years I knew him, returning to live in Country down the track could be realized regardless of when it happened or who in his family ultimately arrived.

In his home and surrounded by family, Mark passed away on June 9, 2020. There is more to say about this than can be contained within words. Stating this here at the book's beginning runs the danger of giving the false impression that Mark's dreams and awakenings have failed to come to fruition. This is not the case. The horizon that he envisioned remains, and his family continues to gaze upon it and to move toward it and within it. They continue to go back, and Mark still guides them home through memory, spirit, and cinema. From here up until the conclusion, I aim for him to remain as alive in the story as he was while it unfolded—as alive as he still remains within his films, and within his Country.

Slowly, Slowly

Shortly before we left his porch to drive back to the volunteer housing on the other side of Balgo, Mark took a slow drag and gestured the filter toward his mouth, reflecting, "Most people talk from here." Placing his left index finger next to his temple and then his heart, he continued, "I talk from here and here. I think from those places, and it comes out of my mouth. That's why we need to keep going, making more films, and that's why we need to take our time. We need to go slowly. Yeah, that's right, slowly, slowly." This phrase, "slowly, slowly"—translated as "purrka, purrka" in Kukatja—was commonly used in Balgo, especially while driving through Country. It was not about going *slow,* but rather, not rushing, so as to remain present.

While "slowly, slowly" was often a commentary on the frantic pace that typifies many outsider projects, high praise for a film was distilled within the word *palya*. Usually translated simply as "good," palya is not about something turning out well so much as things having been done the right *way.*[19] It was more often signed than spoken, with an index finger raised upward, tracing the sky from just behind to just in front of one's head. There is a vast spectrum of meanings for *palya,* expressed in the micro-details of gestural expression, from a tepid pointing up then fading forward, to an enthusiastic sharp index twist in concert with a slight lowering of the signer's head with a subtle smile. The meaning of *palya* points to more than a focus on process; it speaks to a broader approach about appropriate engagement through collective creation.

Due to its quick pace and the mass distribution of its products, filmmaking tends to focus on final outcomes and the efficient capturing of as much relevant footage as possible during compressed production schedules. This intensity informed Mark's initial impression of cinema in 2013. However, over the course of subsequent films and years his view shifted markedly. With each project came more time to allow it to unfold, to go *slowly, slowly,* to follow a palya process.

Rather than *film, video,* or *media,* I chose *cinema* to feature in the title and framing of this book. This might seem counterintuitive, since unlike *film, cinema* is not a word often used in Aboriginal community media. Yet the multiple meanings of *cinema* as product, process, and place speak to the concurrent qualities of these creative projects. Furthermore, I draw upon the rarified association of cinema with "high" Western production values as a way of challenging implicit assumptions of community Aboriginal media as somehow lesser. Rather than "lower" production values, these media hold a different set of values, which emphasize process and relationality.

This book itself is not distinct from the media projects I collaborated on. It too is woven into the social fabrics of these films. Mark often impressed this fact upon me. While sitting with our mutual friend Warwick Nieass, Mark once turned to me and asked, "Are you still planning to turn this into a book?" I nodded, then after a pause added, "Yes, unless maybe you feel differently about it now." He gestured his index finger to express palya and said, "No, it's important to have videos *and* books. Some people want to watch it on TV. Some people need to see the words. Especially the politicians."

Mirroring the film process, this book is animated by a life cycle that has progressed through similar steps, from initial idea, to the finished version, to this very moment of your reading. Like a completed film, it has been heavily edited before being finally rendered immutable within material and electronic circulatory systems. It similarly had constraints around time and funding, as well as expectations regarding production values and imagined audiences. As with film footage, ethnographic field notes consist of a sea of small moments whose meanings emerge most often in retrospect and through interrelationship. Working on dozens of films throughout this fieldwork process, I have been made acutely aware of the contrast between the final cut and the seemingly endless choices that would have resulted in different films, or in this case, different books. As authors and filmmakers do, I made innumerable decisions in editing and arrangement, with narrative cuts, montages, and time slippages between key connecting moments throughout.

In other words, this book is structured much like a film. This fact should cast no more doubt on an ethnography than the filmmaking process should on a documentary. I highlight this to be transparent about the choices that structure this book, and why I made them—to reduce, even if modestly, the distance between the film processes I describe and the creation of this text. If (and it is a real if) this book is ultimately held as palya, it will be because of its kinship with people and projects, as child and relation to those with the time and space to think from the head and the heart, to do things the proper way, to go *slowly, slowly.*

Overview

Dreaming Down the Track is based on thirty-one months of ethnographic fieldwork between 2006 and 2023, including twenty months of continuous primary fieldwork between 2014 and 2016. Throughout, I was embedded within Indigenous production teams and collaborated on thirty-two films with two Indigenous-owned, Indigenous-run media organizations: Pilbara and Kimberley Aboriginal Media (PAKAM) and Goolarri Media Enterprises (Goolarri). These two outlets employ contrasting media models while being located within the same building complex in the broader creative hub of Broome, a notably multi-ethnic town along the Kimberley coast. Each film project presented insights into the creative process of media-making amid various challenges. In this book, I follow a subset of these projects in and around Balgo.

Through a series of awakenings, Mark moved from cinematic ambivalence to advocacy, coming to view filmmaking as a powerful process for actualizing sovereign community futures on Country. His media journey paints a portrait of the exciting possibilities and sobering limitations of Indigenous envisioning within settler states, while demystifying paradoxes of Aboriginal visibility in the midst of ongoing policies of annihilation. His awakenings over this period were expansive, weaving together memories of Yagga Yagga, analyses of Balgo, and Mangkayi's continued calling. This book is structured through the arc of Mark's filmmaking journey and each chapter is anchored in an awakening grounded within specific films.

Chapter 1 introduces key people and places through the cinematic social life of the first film project in Balgo for both Mark and me. Although titled *Kurrarlkatjanu: The Last Generation* (2013), this was neither the first film nor about the last generation.[20] Described as "throwing me in the deep end" by *Kurrarlkatjanu*'s producer, PAKAM manager Neil Turner, I recount my first impressions of arriving in Balgo in an old troopy, working on a community film, and meeting Mark. I situate key ethnographic scenes that structure my fieldwork process. Such moments establish the gradual shift of my initial positionality as a kartiya to other relationships. Through the relatively short film process of a few weeks, this chapter introduces my relationship with Mark, the social life cycles of Balgo filmmaking, and the power dynamics on bush shoots. While initially tentative toward film, this project catalyzed Mark's first cinematic awakening as a literal and metaphorical vehicle to visit Country with his family.

Chapter 2 returns to Balgo one year later for the film shoot of *Tjawa Tjawa* (2014), part of the well-funded and high-profile Songlines on Screen film series. This weeklong bush trip represents the creative and social climax of the three-year life cycle of this project, as a convoy of vehicles travel through Mark's Country south of Balgo. *Tjawa Tjawa* is Mark's directorial debut, and for the first time he is in charge of a film's story, movement, and vision. I describe his awakening to cinema as a path toward reinvigorating his role as a community leader and storyteller. I trace irreconcilable differences that are revealed and relieved through comedy throughout this film shoot, some of which make their way into the film itself. Building upon the work of Michelle Raheja, I articulate the process of "laughing with the camera" as a way of navigating various tensions through "Black comedy." I discuss the dangers of becoming literally and metaphorically "bogged," and the value of becoming collectively unstuck. I describe how capitalist frameworks of productivity versus "laziness" can become projected onto the filming process, distorting lived rhythms of labor and creativity. Throughout, I integrate discussions of dignity, failure, and redemption through key moments in other film shoots in and around Balgo.

Chapter 3 chronicles the postproduction stages of *Tjawa Tjawa*. The chapter travels with film drafts between Balgo, the regional remote media hub of Broome, and festivals across Australia. While film editing is usually a technical process largely hidden behind closed doors, I describe the many lively "fix 'em up" collective editing and mid-process screenings that shape *Tjawa Tjawa* and other films. These events do not simply provide feedback for the editor to consider; they also depict a deeper and distributed social film editing process that includes Mark and other key community members. Instead of the typical distinction between postproduction and circulation, I illustrate how the shift from social editing to festival screenings is more accurately understood as a gradual expansion of the film's sphere of relations, in which the memories and discussions it sparks are at least as important as the media itself. The postproduction process represents an awakening for Mark that reveals cinema itself as a powerful tool for spreading messages widely. Such projects provide a context for him to not only travel home but also to festivals across Australia, speaking alongside and beyond the film toward his broader goals of returning to Country with his family.

Chapter 4 traces the creative explosion of envisioning-focused filmmaking in Balgo in the wake of *Tjawa Tjawa*'s completion. During this period, Mark intentionally steps back from the limelight and establishes himself as a supportive guide for other projects. These films proceed through the logic and sequence of kinship relations in Balgo, with the projects forming what I describe as a broader film family. I analyze how projects enact palya production values through the interrelated and locally resonant conceptions of creative *fires,* material *tires,* and bureaucratic *paper.* I describe how communities are structured by the government to fail, in ways that can be understood through the tensions between these three elements. This flourishing of Balgo filmmaking represents an awakening for Mark, as he comes to consider cinema not only as a process enabling movement through Country and the communicating of ideas, but also as a means for collective envisioning in and beyond Balgo.

In chapter 5, I consider what endures beyond the life cycle of a film, which I discuss through the concept of after-images, drawing metaphorically on this sensory phenomenon. I explore multiple after-images, from finished films that echo into emerging projects, to shifting views on showing images of the deceased, to the broader role of cinema in transforming Aboriginal community futures. Having now completed several films in his Country—and with the threat of community closures hanging in the air—Mark's political and media awakenings converge through the social life of the film *Mangkayi Calling*. This project integrates Mark's life history and plans for moving back to Yagga Yagga. It also carries explicit and implicit messages that he conveys to Balgo youth and Australian politicians. Following the emergent process of this project, I illustrate the ways in which cinematic envisionings are as constitutive as they are representational, with imagined futures coming into being through media practices of collective creation. Mark's awakening in this period is in coming to view cinema as a portal to conjure and transmit his messages from Country across time and space. He is possessed by clarity and purpose throughout this intensive period, culminating in our recording of his life history amidst the remains of the Old Balgo Mission where he spent his youth.

The social life of *Mangkayi Calling* illuminates the irreconcilabilities of envisioning a future on Country within and beyond the constraints of settler state relations. Chapter 6 expands insights from this and other films to demystify what I describe as a broader "visibility paradox." This highlights the ostensibly irreconcilable contrast between the flourishing sphere of Indigenous Australian media and concurrent escalating policies of Aboriginal annihilation. As the only major settler colonial nation without treaty relations, I emphasize the critical importance of Australian general public sentiment regarding Indigenous issues, and the role of Aboriginal media in shaping this. The visibility paradox is further grounded within responses in Balgo to "the list" of communities to close, as well as to the implementation of the Indigenous Advancement Strategy that deeply cut funding for Aboriginal community organizations during my fieldwork. For Mark, this onslaught seems to awaken within him the vision of cinema as a tool of political intervention at the highest levels, as he shifts from speaking primarily to Aboriginal youth to including direct messages to the Prime Minister and other politicians. I contextualize *Mangkayi Calling* within national Aboriginal political movements through my discussions with longtime activists at the Aboriginal Tent Embassies in Canberra and Redfern.

Drawing upon the visual metaphor of twilights, the conclusion brings together the intersecting processes of Mangkayi's calling, Mark's awakenings, and dreams of going back to Country along uneven tracks reaching toward shifting horizons. As Mark's health declines, he increasingly alludes to the idea that going back to Country may not include himself. He awakens to a clarity that "real" films are those that keep such stories alive for future generations. Dreaming down the track for Mark is now to envision the world of his grandchildren and the legacy that he can leave them. Here, I reflect upon sunrise and sunset as cinematic mirrors. It is only at the end that I come to understand that making these films was not only an arc of envisioning, but also one of redemption following a series of profound losses.

As the sun kisses the horizon, the spinifex grass casts spindly shadows across the pindan earth in front of Mark's house. As I lean against the rusty hood of the old PAKAM troopy, Shorty taps my shoulder after a long day of filming with Mark, who is now resting. "Let me show you what I'm talking about," he interjects, gesturing me to sit down on the ground next to him. Legs crossed, he meticulously flattens the ant paths in front of us with his palm. Carefully tracing a kinship chart with his index finger through the blood-red grains, he maps his family, periodically pointing out how the corrugated iron–clad homes in front of us correspond to it. He stops and smiles, then suddenly pushes his open hand down firmly through the center of the sand drawing, exclaiming, "It's all in HERE. It's in Country . . . family, Dreaming." Continuing, he extends four fingers toward his childhood home of Yagga Yagga to the left of the setting sun, just below the pink-hued orange sky. "The Dreaming. It isn't over. It's still happening. It's still down the track."

1

The First Film, *The Last Generation*

We're on the journey now.

—Warwick Nieass

This chapter is about neither Balgo's first film nor its last generation. It traces the cinematic social life of *Kurrarlkatjanu: The Last Generation,* a film that was shot, edited, and completed in June 2013. This was where I met Mark. It was also the first film that either of us worked on in Balgo. Here, I tell the story of this film. With a process spanning just two weeks, it provides a microcosm of the social life cycle of a Balgo film project. At the time, we did not know that the unfolding of this film would ultimately inspire several other media projects in Balgo, including *Tjawa Tjawa,* the film at the heart of this ethnography. While Mark was initially ambivalent about media-making, *Kurrarlkatjanu* catalyzed his first cinematic awakenings, and he came to see it as a literal and metaphorical vehicle for visiting Country with his family. During this trip I was taught palya values for conducting fieldwork and collaborating on films in Balgo. Participating in production meetings, shooting, editing, music recording, and transcription, I came to better understand the value of following the social life of such projects.

There are dangers in presenting ethnographic arrival narratives, including the mythologizing of a fieldsite as radically elsewhere and other. Mindful of this, I highlight moments that trouble expectations around initial and irreconcilable anthropologist encounters. Throughout, I aim to be transparent about the limits of my understanding and what it means for an outside participant to begin collaborating on

Aboriginal film projects. The following narrative approach provides the truest way I know to (1) introduce Mark and other central people, places, and organizations in this book; (2) contextualize my relationships with them; and (3) illustrate the interwoven social lives in my fieldwork and the films themselves.

Kurrarlkatjanu: The Last Generation

Knocking on PAKAM manager Neil Turner's office door, I hear his exuberant "come in!" I enter to find him leaning back in his swivel chair while on the land line, talking and laughing with one of the PAKAM remote community workers. "One second," he notes to the caller, looking up and exclaiming, "Good morning, Willi! Feel free to have a cup of tea and I'll be out in a minute." Responding with a silent thumbs-up, I swiftly close this door to trap in the cool air that is billowing into the main warehouse space, where it escapes through the fifteen-foot-high corrugated iron door and out into the rising heat of the Broome morning. I turn on the electric water kettle through the standard method of leaning a mug on the power switch, and prepare a cup of Earl Grey. A few minutes later, Neil nimbly bursts out of his office to enter the PAKAM radio hub in the next room. After adjusting various knobs and dials, he comes out and asks me all about my trip from Colorado to Broome as he prepares his own cup of tea. He kicks off his flip-flops as he glides toward two plastic chairs at the central table, with the Aboriginal flag painted on its plywood surface. There is a youthful vigor to Neil's movements that seems to defy his age. Wearing the seasonally appropriate Broome attire of shorts and a loose button-down shirt, his characteristically expressive eyebrows convey a gentle intensity of both listening and thinking.

After several minutes of catching up and inquiring about my plans—interspersed with a few impromptu phone calls from PAKAM workers—he smiles and asks, "You have a legal driver's license for Western Australia, is that right?" After confirming that my license would be valid throughout this trip, he continues: "So, I was thinking, if you want to really understand the social life of PAKAM media, what do you say, why don't we throw you in the deep end?" Without pausing, or understanding, I respond as PhD fieldworkers do and say "Yeah, sounds great."

I would soon learn that the "deep end" meant leaving a few days later on what he and others in Indigenous media organizations referred to as a "proper bush trip." I would travel to Balgo to work on a short film titled *Kurrarlkatjanu: The Last Generation,* which was funded through Pilbara and Kimberley Aboriginal Media (PAKAM) along with a small grant from National Indigenous Television (NITV), and in partnership with the Kapululangu Women's Law and Culture Centre (Kapululangu). I had no idea that this short trip would have a profound impact on the following decade of my life. After filling me in on key details, he told me to show up early Sunday morning to the house of a man named Warwick Nieass.

I vividly remember the first time I met Warwick. He was standing on top of an old vehicle, tying down nondescript duffel bags in the copper light of morning. It was only when he climbed down and came closer that I realized he was significantly older than his agile movements suggested. He dressed in a style that was quintessentially Broome, yet distinctly his own, with loose bohemian pants, a hemp seventies-style shirt, an artist's scarf, and a red bandanna. As he approached the already unlocked gate to greet me, his bright eyes crinkled behind wire-rimmed glasses as he smiled through a graying beard. "Good day, mate! You must be Willi. Come on in."

Sunday was a blur of frenetic energy: packing, unpacking, and repacking two four-wheel-drive Toyotas, interspersed with regular snack breaks of toasted cheese sandwiches and black tea. Throughout the day, I got to know Warwick as he explained the quirks of "Bushy," his 1970s troopy that he started by jamming an old yellow flathead screwdriver into the ignition and twisting it just so. Practicing driving in Broome's neighborhood backstreets, I learned that despite its alarmingly loose steering, Bushy could be coaxed toward the center of the road through a rhythmic left and right rocking of the wheel. Warwick found it hilarious that this was to be my first time driving a vehicle on the left side of the road, chuckling through comments such as "Mate, once you drive this to Balgo, you'll be able to drive anything, anywhere. Bushy's an old one, but I've checked her out and she'll get us there all right." As we finished packing, Warwick began to tell me about his own history of periodically living in Balgo over decades and of his role in the early development of painting in the community. I learned that he married a Kukatja woman whom he had a son with and that they had lived in Balgo and Yagga Yagga together. He also described his projects with a man named Mark Moora. The sun was setting by the time we triple-checked our knots, filled up the double tanks of diesel, picked up two passengers, and left Broome.

It was a long drive, away from the western Kimberley coast along the Indian Ocean, east across the verdant Fitzroy Valley, and then south onto the corrugated Tanami Road through the Great Sandy Desert toward Balgo. It was during this trip that I began to learn about the importance of silence and subtlety. Driving with two middle-aged men from Balgo, we would often go hours without speaking. I quickly realized that directions would neither be announced beforehand nor spoken, but gesturally whispered through the most subtle of finger pointing. Throughout, I sat next to William, a PAKAM media worker in Balgo at that time. Learning that my name was similar to his, he informed me that neither of us could use our first names there, as someone named William had recently passed away.[1] He suggested that I adopt the kinship category of "Tjangala," his own skin name. This would create a brother categorical relationship between us, and practically facilitate our working together.[2]

After two days of driving—including an overnight camp at one of Warwick's favorite spots by a creek—we arrived in Balgo in the late afternoon. It was difficult to find a place to park outside of the women's center, as there were several other Toyotas and dozens of people absorbed in various stages of packing-related activities. Zohl de Ishtar, the director of Kapululangu, came up to greet us. After I introduced myself, she smiled warmly and with tongue in cheek said, "Welcome to the circus."

As I would learn in the subsequent days, weeks, and years, the circus was not about Balgo or Kapululangu, but specifically referred to the large-scale bush trip involving a convoy of four-wheel-drive vehicles, visitors from around the globe, and community members. Kapululangu undertook multiple trips each year to take these paying kartiya to accompany the women Elders on Dreaming tracks in their home Country.[3] This particular trip followed a Seven Sisters Dreaming story and included the PAKAM crew to document it, which consisted of myself and two PAKAM workers.[4] This short documentary project would become the precursor to *Tjawa Tjawa*, a film that would be shot here one year later and feature many of the same individuals and locations. However, I did not know any of this yet, and there was much to do in the days leading up to the trip.

A Nameless Anthropologist

During one of my first days in Balgo, I was running errands with a few community members. While driving in Bushy, we chatted about the upcoming film. It came up that I was studying anthropology in graduate school, and one of them paused and remarked, "Ah, anthropology. I know what you want to hear about. There are a few people in the community that the anthropologists always talk to about the old days." When I noted that I was looking forward to working on film projects with anyone in Balgo, they seemed to find that interesting and perhaps a little unusual. This early interaction stuck with me, and I would often think back to it. Sometimes I would consider it in relation to Vine Deloria Jr.'s (1969) incisive and darkly comedic commentary in "Anthropologists and Other Friends," where he satirically expounds on the opportunism and single-mindedness of some anthropologists in Indigenous communities. There is much truth to be learned in comedy, which, as it turned out, even applied to navigating my own name.

Following William's advice, I introduced myself in Balgo as "Kumanjayi," which roughly translates to "nameless." This signaled that my own name could not be spoken due to the recent passing of a local man with that name. The comedy of my own misunderstanding of context did not go unnoticed around this topic. This was made particularly apparent during a trip to the community store to purchase supplies the following day, when a man came up and introduced himself. After I began my response with, "Hi, I'm Kumanjayi," he laughed and responded, "Yes, yes, Kumanjayi. There are lots of Kumanjayi, but who are *you*?" Trying to not speak this name, I thought about it and said, "I'm Tjangala," which also provoked a chuckle as he said, "Yes, me too. Plenty of Tjangala, but what is *your* name?" I explained that it was the same as someone who passed away, and he noted, "Ah, I understand now. You know, that's only important for some people, for others you can go by Willi, no worries. Hmm, but you might not know who the right families are. . . . What is your middle name?" This led me to go by David for a few days, until I found out that a man with that name had also recently passed away in a nearby community, with relatives living in Balgo. In one of my first conversations with Mark Moora before the trip, I asked him about this. He responded with "Let's see, your Country is Colorado. That's a good name, people like that place here, cowboy country." After that, I generally went by Colorado during this trip, though there was an enduring comedy of confusion about what my name in fact was, with different people alternately calling me Kumanjayi, Tjangala, David, Colorado, Willi, and a variety of creative combinations. Even years later, people still sometimes jokingly call me by these names.

The next two days were an intensive crash course in bush trip preparation. Troopys and trailers were packed, repacked, and packed again to maximize efficiency and access for the upcoming week. Food, swags, and equipment were laid out in their entirety as various leaders and volunteers discussed and Tetrised them in. The vehicles themselves were inspected several times: hoods opened, batteries charged, and oil dipsticks checked, with as many spare tires as could be obtained tied down on top. During this trip, I got to know the other two members of our small film crew well, Anne and Anna. Anne was a PAKAM worker from Bidyadanga, a small community along the ocean coast south of Broome. Anna was a whitefella (non-Aboriginal person) with years of experience as a PAKAM trainer. Both had worked on many small community projects, and often as a team. They found my name debacle particularly amusing, calling me Colorado in jest. I did not know it at the time, but I was incredibly fortunate to learn from these two women, who provided as thoughtful of a model for collaborative community filmmaking as I would ever encounter.

On the day before the convoy left, there was a meeting at Kapululangu for everyone going. Zohl and the lead volunteers overviewed various cultural protocols for the visitors, including the importance of not taking photos without explicit permission. They explained how we were following a Seven Sisters Dreaming track that would take us to several key cultural sites south of Balgo past the community of Yagga Yagga. Toward the end, Mark Moora spoke briefly. This being a women's trip, he was not the central storyteller, and he mostly emphasized the power of the women Elders' knowledge, including his sister Payi Payi. Though clearly a strong speaker, he seemed somewhat weary and leery. That evening, the only thing left was to wrap the rental cars in cut-out sections of tarp to protect them and to get as much sleep as we could for our early departure.

Toyota Dreaming

"No worries, we're on the journey now," Warwick said with a knowing smile as the troopy pulled out from Kapululangu. I had just asked him about whether we should try to finish tarping the side of one final car. His response came as we passed the precipice of Balgo's paved roads transitioning to corrugated tracks near the water tower, as we rhythmically bounced upon the dusty troop carrier benches facing sideways toward sliding windows. Gone were the numerous lists and logistical concerns, replaced with a collective surrender to the trip. Each person seemed to have a unique strategy for sitting in the back of a troopy on a bush trip. Some locked their legs onto a packed object. Some stabilized themselves with arms and elbows. Others seemed to surf the vibrations, holding themselves lightly, absorbing and moving with the

FIGURE 3. Troopy convoy during the *Tjawa Tjawa* shoot. Photograph by PAKAM crew; courtesy of Pilbara and Kimberley Aboriginal Media, copyright 2014.

shifting forces. I would quickly come to realize that I was a leg locker, though over time I locked less and less. As we stopped for a bathroom break, I learned that the most important thing to understand about sitting in the back of an older troopy was how to open the second back door, which was invariably in some stage of worsening malfunction. This involved pushing one's finger into the mechanism in such a way that it released. Opening the door quickly was crucial, as the PAKAM troopy left first and arrived last so that we could stop on the side of the road and film the convoy passing by.

A few hours into the trip, we arrived at Yagga Yagga for lunch and our first overnight stop. After a couple of failed attempts, I finally got the second back door to open. Hopping down, I looked around and realized just how big our convoy was—eleven troopys holding thirty-five women, a few men, and a film crew. Warwick and Mark often referred to such trips as "Toyota Dreaming," which humorously paired the Japanese vehicles with what is normally understood to be the serious business of following a Dreaming story. It was both a joke and their ethnographic observation, since the faded white troopy has become a

FIGURE 4. View out of a troopy window during the *Tjawa Tjawa* shoot.

primary symbol for moving through Country. Furthermore, community members often personified old vehicles, especially those that had traveled widely in their lifetime, like Bushy. For example, in discussing one particularly old Toyota, Mark's nephew Shorty remarked, "This fella has been to some good Country and is setting down to rest in Balgo. He's an old fella now, poor thing."

We set up camp at Yagga Yagga. Although I was technically on the film crew, during this first trip I helped out wherever I was most needed at the campsite. Besides, Anne and Anna were a complete and tight crew, and they had developed an intuitive rhythm from having worked together previously. When they asked for my assistance, it was more than anything a reflection of their inclusive kindness. Having only taken a few film production courses to provide foundational skills, my real training began during this trip, and would unfold over dozens of Kimberley projects in the coming years.

Kurrarlkatjanu was not really a film-oriented trip so much as a culture convoy with an attached film crew to document it, a fact that resonates with much Indigenous media around the globe, in which social relations and cultural activities are often more important than the media itself (Dowell 2013; Ginsburg 1994; Miyarrka Media 2019; Thorner 2010). This was apparent in meetings throughout the week. While during the future *Tjawa Tjawa* trip the cinema schedule was prioritized, in this journey it was usually acknowledged toward the end, with comments such as "Oh yes, and our trusty film crew will be around taking footage to document the trip!"

After waking up in Yagga Yagga and finishing the collective frenzy of preparing and cleaning up breakfast, we had our morning meeting. Here, it was announced that we would smoke a house, spend a little time in Yagga Yagga, and then head off to our next destination. While I understood the general reason for smoking a house—to spiritually cleanse it following a death—Warwick explained to me that this was a profound moment in other ways too, as Yagga Yagga had been deserted for years following a suicide. Our film crew captured the process, including a smoking ceremony for a baby to ensure its well-being.

Afterward we set up a quick film shoot for Payi Payi, her sister Linda, and her brother Mark. Here, they discussed the brief history of Yagga Yagga and the purpose of the smoking ceremony. It seemed in this moment that something had changed for Mark. After the smoking, his spirits appeared to be lifted. Smiling, he spoke briefly though proudly of Yagga Yagga and the importance of coming back to live here someday. I would come to find out that this moment was a crucial turning point for him after years of profound difficulties, including Yagga Yagga's closure.

I began to understand a little bit about the significance of this trip from Mark a few nights later, when he and I were sitting around a fire with others, chatting in small groups. I listened carefully to him as he told me about the areas we were moving through. It was clear how impressive of a storyteller he was, effortlessly pacing drama, suspense, and humor. The more I listened, the more intensely he spoke. This went on for over an hour. Then, as if suddenly realizing that something was not quite right, he stopped and said, "Tell me a story about you. I've been telling you about my mob, so I should know about your family, where you come from."

In that moment, I realized that I was perhaps overly concerned with not interjecting myself during fieldwork. I implicitly imagined this as decentering myself, but in the context of relationships it invited an imbalance amid the generous sharing by others. This only became obvious to me in hindsight. While I was focused on listening and contributing labor, as Mark pointed out, I had revealed little about myself. So, when he asked me to tell him something about my family, I was momentarily at a loss for words. The stories he shared with me were vulnerable, and while they had humor, each was tinged with historical tragedy. After a long moment, I told him about my grandmother's teenage experiences of being one of very few in her family to escape Nazi Germany and to finally arrive in New York City, where she met my grandfather and namesake Willi. He listened closely, and at the end sat quietly, before gravely noting, "Yuwai [Yeah], that's a hard, hard time." This shared moment was the beginning of our many-years-long relationship, in which I listened more than I spoke, but increasingly I also shared. This is the approach I also take in this book, resisting my own inclination to remove myself from the story. This ethnography is through me but not about me, and I have aimed to keep the narrative spotlight off of myself whenever possible.

Throughout the weeklong shoot for *Kurrarlkatjanu,* we visited several important sites that we would return to in future films, including *Tjawa Tjawa* and *Mangkayi Calling.* Our crew knew that this trip was meant to result in a tightly edited thirteen-minute film for NITV, though it went almost without saying at PAKAM that it would also be edited into a longer format for community use and broadcast on Indigenous Community Television (ICTV). Therefore, we shot liberally to capture not just the core story and scenes but also a multitude of everyday moments. Each night, as Anne and Anna logged and reviewed footage, it was clear that they were mentally preparing for the edit, which would have to be done quickly upon our return to Balgo.

In many of the films I collaborated on, there was a deliberate slowness in the postproduction process. For logistical reasons, this was not the case for *Kurrarlkatjanu*. Anne and Anna had only a few days to complete the final film edit before leaving for their next project. While they could have taken it with them, they were committed to editing it in Balgo where they could get ongoing feedback, regardless of schedule constraints. Astoundingly, they completed a rough cut in just over a day, which benefited from their preparation discussions over the previous days. They edited on a folding table in one of the small bedrooms in Kapululangu, near where they slept. Because of their proximity to the women Elders, they were able to receive regular feedback and guidance throughout this intensive process.

Meanwhile, I was tasked with organizing local musicians to record the film's soundtrack in the art center's music studio. In the coming years we would collectively reorganize this impressive studio that had fallen into disuse. However, in this tight timeline musicians simply gathered around a handheld Zoom audio recorder with attached microphones, recording songs while one person played an acoustic guitar. I spent much of these days driving people to and from Kapululangu to share their thoughts on the evolving film edit, as well as visiting families to confirm permissions and name spellings for the long list of credits. Late in the evening before our departure back to Broome, we showed the completed thirteen-minute film over dinner in the central space of Kapululangu. Mark watched intently, leaning forward and seemingly lost in thought. The next morning, the three of us left at dawn, chasing the rising sun back toward the Indian Ocean.

Kimberley Media Circuits

My fieldwork was based in the coastal pearling town of Broome, as well as remote communities (especially Balgo) in the Kimberley region, referred to locally as the Kimberley. As a hub of Aboriginal political action and creative innovation since the 1970s, the Kimberley is an especially rich place to understand the lineage and expansion of the Indigenous Australian mediascape.

The home of seventeen thousand out of the region's thirty-seven thousand people, Broome is small by most standards, though is three times the population of Kununurra, the second-largest Kimberley town. Broome is the primary visual touchstone of the Kimberley, featuring dramatic views and contrasting hues—brilliant cerulean skies that sun-soak verdant vegetation on blood-red cliffs amidst pastel beaches that feature some of the biggest tides on Earth. It is the most cinematic place I have ever seen, so it is perhaps no accident that it became the nexus for media in the region.

Broome is also the cosmopolitan locus of the Kimberley and one of the most ethnically diverse towns in Australia, promoted to tourists as a bastion of harmonious multiculturalism. The high levels of "mixed relations" (Ganter 2006) between Aboriginal, Asian, and European people are a result of exemptions from strict "White Australia" immigration policies. These exceptions were motivated by commercial concerns, as this immigration bolstered the town's pearl shell industry, which was so lucrative that it produced the vast majority of the world's supply in the early twentieth century (Bach 1962). This regional head start on ethnic diversity positioned it as a bellwether in Australia for understanding both the limits and potential future trends in Aboriginal/state relations. However, despite local land claim victories and *relatively* less segregation, this region—like the rest of Australia—remains marred by violent histories of intermarriage prohibition, stolen children, racial riots, and economic exploitation (Attwood 2005). These colonial legacies continue to manifest through governmental and corporate pressures to gain natural resource rights in and around Broome, which have been opposed, often successfully, by a coalition led by local Aboriginal groups.

My fieldwork included seven research trips to Australia since 2006 in the Kimberley, where I collaborated on dozens of media projects within the production teams of Pilbara and Kimberley Aboriginal Media Association (PAKAM) and Goolarri Media Enterprises (Goolarri). Both are Indigenous-owned and -run multimedia organizations that focus on Kimberley Indigenous video, radio, and music production, though

PAKAM is more oriented toward remote communities, while Goolarri's mission focuses on the coastal area around Broome. As described on their website, Goolarri also includes "non-Indigenous communications" and an emphasis on public events. Various aspects of their bureaucratic organization, such as bookkeeping, are interwoven.[5] They are bound together not only organizationally but also through shared space and proximity. Both are located within the three massive and connected corrugated warehouse sheds originally built to house the collections of Lord Alistair McAlpine, a man who was centrally responsible for turning the town into a tourist destination over the past several decades. Beyond their many areas of overlap, there are some differences between them. PAKAM's relatively egalitarian horizontal organization contrasts with Goolarri's more hierarchical and vertical structure, which is apparent in their offices, policies, and media.

In a general sense, PAKAM and Goolarri provide a local microcosm of broader differences between the two national Indigenous TV networks: ICTV, located in Alice Springs, and the Sydney-based NITV. PAKAM generally mirrors ICTV's emphasis on grassroots media in Aboriginal languages produced by and for remote communities, whereas Goolarri, like NITV, specializes in more broadly appealing videos with more mainstream production values. PAKAM is more flexibly

FIGURE 5. PAKAM and Goolarri sheds.

Figure 6. Goolarri offices.

organized than Goolarri, operating in a warehouse setting of less formalized meetings and with more frequent trips to communities. It serves as the organizational rebroadcasting hub for twelve community stations and eight town stations. Organized into departments with cubicles and state-of-the-art equipment, Goolarri specializes in documentaries on local history, public service/health programs, and shows about local Aboriginal knowledge, such as their popular *Catch and Cook* (2005) series on hunting and cooking. They feature a market-leading FM radio station along with two TV channels. They serve as a gateway for supplemental national Indigenous media content, as Goolarri radio is often picked up by the National Indigenous Radio Service. They also broadcast ICTV on their third local channel. In total, Broome has *four* free-to-air Indigenous channels. The roles and overall visibility of NITV and ICTV have resonances with Māori Television's two national channels. To paint with a broad brush and to put it into the framework of Barry Barclay (Ngāti Apa), the primary Māori TV channel, like NITV, "talks out" to broader audiences, and Te Reo, like ICTV, focuses on media in language and "talks in" to Indigenous audiences (Strickland 2013, 157).

There is bound to be occasional tension between two different media organizations in neighboring buildings. That said, my experience there continually reinforced the notion that PAKAM and Goolarri benefited overall from their complementary capabilities, networks, and

Figure 7. PAKAM shed looking in.

Figure 8. PAKAM shed looking out.

Figure 9. PAKAM radio hub.

infrastructures—including their differing perspectives on process and purpose. It was often this synergy and generative friction that helped to bring films such as *Tjawa Tjawa* to fruition.

The Art of the Double

Ethnography and cinema meet at an intersection of doubles. As French anthropologist and filmmaker Jean Rouch put it, "The cinema, the art of the double, is already the transition from the real world to the imaginary world, and ethnography . . . is a permanent crossing point from one conceptual universe to another; acrobatic gymnastics, where losing one's footing is the least of the risks" (2003, 20). Cinema is soaked through with doubles: images and sounds rearranged and recast across time and space. It relies on stunt doubles, overdubs, reshoots, and the layering of sonic doubles (Fisher 2016). Rouch connects this with the ethnographer's art as well, and the many ways in which it requires the imaginative gymnastics of communicating between communities and audiences who are often disconnected.

The relationship between fieldwork and film harkens back to the dawn of anthropological engagements with cinema. While Margaret Mead and Gregory Bateson agreed that film could capture aspects of culture that writing could not, they disagreed about its greatest potential as either a tool for data collection or an artistic mode of analysis. Over the decades this debate has been revealed not only as a false dichotomy but also as limiting the collaborative potential of media in ethnography. Rouch understood this as far back as the 1950s, noting that "knowledge is not a stolen secret later to be consumed in Western temples of learning, but rather it is to be arrived at through an unending quest in which ethnographic subjects and the ethnographer engage with one another on a path that some of us are now calling 'shared anthropology'" (qtd. in Henley 2010, 316). This book aspires to share this sensibility.

The ethnographer is also blessed with and plagued by doubles. I do not mean this in a commiserating sense, but rather to convey the double-sided coin that the process entails. As Dominic Boyer (2008) cautions, it is important to not let this doubling negate the potential of ethnography to generate important knowledge. Often attributed to Marcus Aurelius, the sentiment that "whatever's in the way is the way" is as applicable to ethnography as it is to life. The paradoxical doublings within fieldwork are not the bug but the feature, since ethnographers "attempt to understand another life world using the self—as much of it as possible—as the instrument of knowing" (Ortner 1995, 173). Ethnographers are confronted with the problems of disentangling the observer and the observed. They are compelled to see both sides of the mirror, or at least to try. Those are the moments that reveal the ruptures and textures of understanding. In the following section I illustrate a crucial aspect of doubling in my own fieldwork, which led to my following the social lives of cinema over years. This process emerged to become my ethical, methodological, and analytical framework. Like the films I worked on, this was not the outcome of a carefully orchestrated plan, and it unfolded in a way that could not have happened otherwise.

Beginnings

Throughout my primary fieldwork I documented media practices through daily participation within production teams, observed meetings, interviewed media workers and community leaders, and followed films to national festivals to contextualize their broader circulation and reception. I participated in three extended remote media projects, including two convoy trips into the Great Sandy Desert with film crews and dozens of Elders. I followed these films to the Sydney Film Festival and two National Remote Indigenous Media Festivals, where I assisted with film programming and festival setup, and spent time volunteering with NITV and ICTV. To receive regular feedback—mirroring the mid-process screenings in the films I worked on—I presented my ideas regularly in Australia through radio interviews, public talks, and professional conference papers. Talks often took place just across the street from PAKAM and Goolarri, at the Nulungu Research Institute at the Broome campus of the University of Notre Dame Australia (Nulungu).

Some of the most pivotal experiences occurred before my primary fieldwork began, through the seedlings of the trips leading up to it. The Yiddish phrase "The way it begins is the way it ends" captures a fundamental dynamic in and beyond the fieldwork process. When things do not end well in relationships, generally speaking, those involved can look back and realize that there were many forewarnings from the beginning that were ignored. Relationships and projects that go well are also unsurprising when retrospectively reflecting upon early interactions.

A telling quality for relationships that do not end well relates to the amount of control that each side attempts to exert. The formalization and constraints of ethnographic research can pose challenges to releasing control. There are various pressures to develop a topic of disciplinary interest, find a fieldsite to engage it, and then hit the ground running as soon as feasibly possible. My experience in fieldwork took a circuitous route, on paths I could not have predicted. Largely through good fortune, I had mentors and advisers who guided me toward a research process with the aim of exerting as little control as possible, while developing projects in partnership.

I did not originally intend to engage in a project on remote community media, but rather with PAKAM and Goolarri in the uniquely heterogeneous town of Broome. In 2006, I was studying for a semester in Australia and had become a fan of several songwriters that I came to realize were all from this small town in the Kimberley. I first contacted Goolarri in 2006 to ask if I could work on a student project with them. My email to the Goolarri COO, Kira, was met with a concise, single-sentence response, suggesting simply that I come in to talk about it and that we would see. Draining my bank account, I flew from the east coast of Australia and met with Kira. In our first discussion, I started to realize just how important having aligned interests was, as well as the benefits of a foundational media skill set. Kira asked what I wanted to do and I responded that while I was interested in local bands, I would be happy to do whatever was most useful. They had a need for more radio shows on their station and recorded interviews with musicians to fulfill grant obligations, and having had previous radio experience, that is what I did. While there, I was saturated with the vibrant multimedia world that PAKAM and Goolarri fostered from their collective sheds. The project felt more like volunteer work than fieldwork, which in effect it was.

When initiating my PhD research years later through the University of Colorado Boulder, I was guided by my PhD adviser, Jennifer Shannon, and her ethnography of the National Museum of the American Indian titled *Our Lives,* whose multi-sited and project-based collaborative process I mirrored. I visited Broome in June 2012 after emailing PAKAM and Goolarri to ask if they might be interested in working on a larger collaboration together. Again, I received a short, cryptic, and positive response suggesting I visit to talk about it in person. And again, I arrived with interest and few concrete research questions. In 2006 this had been unwitting, the result of an excess of enthusiasm and a lack of experience. In 2012, arriving without a specific research agenda was an intentional practice for initiating an appropriate relationship. My goal for this six-week trip was to answer three questions, in the following order:

1. Would you like to work on a project together in the first place?
2. If so, what would be the most productive things for me to do?
3. How can this form the foundation for a relevant ethnographic project?

While most ethnographic research asks these questions, I came to realize that it is their *order* that is most crucial to a meaningfully collaborative practice, and by having the third question follow the second, a project can more closely align practical daily utility with the heart of the research itself. Projects can become superficially collaborative when the second question follows the third. In that sequence, it is more likely that priorities will remain in tension.

After emphasizing that there was absolutely no need for us to do a project at all unless there was specific interest, I received the response, more quickly than expected, of "Let's do it, assuming we all agree on it." I spent the next six weeks attempting to answer the second question by talking with a variety of stakeholders within and beyond these organizations. Over time, it became clear that for Goolarri this would involve working on media projects in and around Broome, and for PAKAM it would consist of spending my time supporting media workers in remote communities. This foundational pilot trip was crucial in setting the stage for a mutually beneficial project.

I spent the following year integrating what I learned in question two to answer question three, as I attempted to formulate a relevant ethnographic project. I returned in 2013 to discuss my proposal with them. I distributed it throughout PAKAM and Goolarri, and we revised it together until there was agreement that it was the right project and process. I then spent several weeks working on a PAKAM community film, *Kurrarlkatjanu,* to understand how to further design a project that integrated well within the realities of their media work. Before returning home, I engaged Aboriginal scholars at Nulungu in Broome and the Australian National University in Canberra to get their impression of the project within the scope of Indigenous studies in Australia. I specifically sought out scholars who were known for being skeptical of white anthropologists, and of American researchers, so that I could receive critical feedback about my project.

As fruitful as it turned out to be, it was not academic interest that led me to follow the social life of cinema. This was the emergent outcome of building this project upon the foundation of what was useful for the organizations, which ultimately led me to follow film projects as they unfolded. I returned for twenty months spanning 2014–16 and collaborated on dozens of films with PAKAM and Goolarri. My involvement was based upon my ability to contribute to particular projects depending on the shifting needs of the organizations.

With the process firmly in place, I began to draw upon the long-standing interest of anthropologists in following the social lives of objects, issues, stories, and people across time and space (Cruikshank 1998; Marcus 1995). This framework integrates scholarship on material culture, which traces the social life of objects through their life cycles of creation, circulation, and use (Appadurai 1986; Drazin and Küchler 2015). I was inspired by the idea that following the social life of things makes "salient what might otherwise remain obscure" (Kopytoff 1986, 67). Webb Keane (2003) builds upon the biographical model, paying attention not only to human perspectives but also to the materiality constituting and surrounding media (Larkin 2008). While it might at first seem unexpected to apply a materiality framework to media, William Mazzarella (2004, 359) argues that media are ethnographically "powerful because they do not have to rely primarily on speculative abstraction" in that they produce a tangible process and product. Furthermore, he emphasizes the importance of "mediation" itself as a foundational quality of social life, "where value is often produced and contested, more or less self-consciously, in the name of culture," facilitating local theorizing on global phenomena (345).

Much as a biography illuminates each aspect of a person's life, tracing the social life of cinema deepens understandings of who, what, and why these media represent. Rather than highlighting the exciting moments of production or analyzing its final cut, this process imagines these as components of a project's larger life cycle. Just as important are the seemingly banal bureaucratic activities in preproduction and the various editing sessions in postproduction; these less-charismatic stages often reveal crucial insights. This holistic approach also informs how I include myself in the narrative.

The extent to which anthropologists should write themselves into ethnographies has been thoughtfully debated for decades. At the extremes, erasing oneself can give the false impression of authorial omnipotence, while centering oneself can descend into navel-gazing. Adding further dimensions of complexity are questions on *how* anthropologists include themselves. To what extent should they focus on their activities and involvement, or their subject position and self-reflexivity? There are of course no simple or singular answers to these questions. One can become lost as easily in objectivity as in the mirror.

Relationship-oriented approaches reframe questions and implications of how to include oneself. A powerful model is provided in

Miyarrka Media's *Phone & Spear: A Yuṯa Anthropology* (2019), in which a collective of seven writers, including Yolngu Elder Paul Gurrumuruwuy and anthropologist Jennifer Deger, reimagines the ethnographic text with a common creative goal. This requires not only understanding and observation but also mutual sharing and reciprocity. As Ruth Behar suggests, worthwhile ethnographies require vulnerability and openness (1996, 177). There is no formula for a relationship or how to integrate oneself into an ethnography. And yet, the quality of a relationship quickly becomes apparent to those within and near it.

While many ethnographers thoughtfully use the terms *interlocutors, participants,* and *research subjects,* none of these rang quite true during my fieldwork, as they seemed overly distanced and technical. Hortense Powdermaker's (1966) juxtaposition of *stranger* with *friend* is incisive, as all friendships begin with a meeting of strangers. *Collaborators* and *friends* more accurately capture how I came to understand many of the relationships I had in the field. Notably, in Balgo the category describing outsiders and most whitefellas is *kartiya,* which is itself translated as "stranger." I was referred to as a kartiya for my initial months in Balgo, while I was getting to know people. However, as much as *collaborator* and *friend* describe elements of these relationships, they also do not seem quite right. Anthropologists engage with a focus rarely found in most other relationships of similar duration. Therefore, these connections tend to have an unusual mix of more- and less-distanced qualities, all at once the friendly stranger and strange friend.

For all of its resonance, *friend* carries some troubling implications in fieldwork. It is associated with nonprofessional relationships that usually lack significant power imbalances. As a national term with more flexibility around familiarity and power, the ubiquitous Australian colloquialism of *mate* is perhaps more appropriate. It has no analog in the United States, as it can be used to describe nearly any generally positive relationship. It is equally at home between business people closing deals, surfers sharing stories, children playing together, and family members spanning generations. Unlike *friend, mate* regularly traverses relationships that have multifaceted power dynamics even as it resists being interpreted as condescending. While *mate* was historically gendered male, as with the Aboriginal English term *bella* (fella), it is now often used as a gender-neutral term. To me, what seems most faithful, or least problematic, is to consider those I worked with as "field mates," grounding mate within the context of fieldwork.

Another set of dynamics—student and teacher—exerted a gravity within my research. Before fieldwork I had taken a couple of film production courses with the aim of not being a weak link on projects. I would have taken more if I could have. In retrospect, however, there were some upsides to not having extensive media expertise. Vulnerability is essential in the research process for leveling power dynamics. While I was sometimes positioned by PAKAM and Goolarri into a teacher role when working with community members who were making films for the first time, I was just as often situated as a student to media professionals. My modest amount of previous media training had the inadvertent effect of providing spaces for my teachers to share the unspoken common sense around how media should be made in this context. Such knowledge is often only explained to beginners.

On a slow afternoon in the stormy wet season, I was chatting with Neil Turner as we watched torrential waves of rain splatter through the open shed door at PAKAM. While discussing the role of ethical representation in community media, I commented that it seemed that the process of filmmaking increased clarity about what could and could not be shared, and that transparency was less fraught in those projects. Neil sat quietly for moment, thinking, then suddenly he laughed, responding, "Yeah, sure, but don't worry, it's still plenty fraught." He was right, of course, though perhaps these processes are at least more transparently fraught. I have no illusions that this ethnography somehow escapes the many dangers of representation that are bound up in the doubles and mirrors within cinema and fieldwork, as well as my embodied positionality and privileges as an American Jewish man from Ohio. My commitment to you is to be as transparent in every way I can, to frankly describe what I do not understand, and to appropriately frame any insights as gained through the generosity of field mates.

This research is modeled upon recent compelling ethnographies that are based on close collaborations with Indigenous Australian media projects. In addition to Miyarrka Media's *Phone & Spear* (2019), I am inspired by Jennifer Deger's *Shimmering Screens* (2006), Melinda Hinkson's *See How We Roll* (2021), Daniel Fisher's *The Voice and Its Doubles* (2016), and Jennifer Biddle's *Remote Avant-Garde* (2016), as well as scholarship from North and South America (Aufderheide 1995; Bessire 2017; Dowell 2013; Ginsburg 2011; Halkin 2008; Hennessy 2009; Shannon 2014; Wortham 2013). I have found guidance not only within their scholarly works but also though various personal interactions over the years. Their magnanimous collegiality is inspiring, and yet perhaps unsurprising in light of the qualities required to meaningfully engage in such collaborations.

Throughout my fieldwork, the "project" was the structuring form of interaction and the unit of analysis. This described most of the things that people creatively collaborated on. This book itself is a project about projects. Though there were other activities, such as radio *shows* and training *sessions,* films were nearly always referred to as projects with stages. Through projects, we worked together toward common goals. While I regularly reminded field mates about my ethnographic research, after the first few months it seemed that they viewed me as a media volunteer who was additionally, and less significantly, writing about the experience. While I took notes every evening and sometimes during the day, there were moments when I forgot that I was an ethnographer. Rarely did my ethnographic project feel like the central or most important thing I was doing.

Although I worked with the organizations of PAKAM and Goolarri, my presence was only made meaningful in relation to specific projects with specific people. And while roles at the outlets were relatively fluid in transitions between projects, they tended to remain set and stable during them. Unlike most film projects, roles here seldom seemed to confer social status outside of that particular project. Rather than confronting glass ceilings, crew were generally encouraged to rise into more-senior roles based on their interests. Roles were framed as contributions to a project rather than signals of broader status. There was no one who was above stacking chairs, or more than one good idea away from becoming a director.

Tjawa Tjawa

In the year following *Kurrarlkatjanu,* PAKAM was one of ten organizations to receive funding for the inaugural Songlines on Screen program funded by NITV and Screen Australia, the nation's peak film body. This included an unprecedented investment of over one million dollars into remote Aboriginal-produced films, which are usually made on far more modest budgets. Each project received approximately $130,000. As an example of the disproportionate importance of Broome on the national Indigenous mediascape, three of the ten Songlines on Screen grants were received by media outlets based there, including PAKAM, Goolarri, and Wawili Pitjas, a small, independent Aboriginal film company.

Tjawa Tjawa traced a Dreaming story following women from Ieramagudu—the area near the present-day coastal town of Roebourne—as they traveled underground to and from Tjawa Tjawa and other areas south of what is now Balgo. It was a natural follow-up project to the Songline film *Kurrarlkatjanu,* and in some ways served as its doubling. *Tjawa Tjawa* was about a trip with a similar number of people and vehicles traveling to an overlapping area of Country south of Balgo. The convoy trip lasted roughly the same amount of time and traveled during a similar season one year later. Yet, unlike *Kurrarlkatjanu,* it was not an add-on to another trip but a full-fledged and film-focused desert convoy. Previously, Mark was included but remained tentative. Now he held the mantle of director and central storyteller.

As an NITV-branded landmark series, there was a sense in this and other Songlines on Screen films that their success would be pivotal in determining future major investments into the Aboriginal mediascape. Therefore, great care and oversight was involved throughout the process. In contrast to the effective and beloved "run and gun" process of *Kurrarlkatjanu* and many other PAKAM films, as part of the Songlines on Screen grant to PAKAM, *Tjawa Tjawa*'s preproduction was highly structured and involved various meetings at PAKAM and between stakeholder organizations.

Rather than the in-house budget process, such larger and externally funded projects were bound up within the ever-dreaded "A to Zed" (A–Z) budget, a byzantine Excel-based form that could confuse even the most experienced managers. There seemed to be a relatively binary grant distinction, according to which small projects operated under a relatively informal budgetary model, while larger projects—above the threshold of roughly $10,000—required A–Z budgets. This was especially true for NITV, which was constrained by the bureaucratic procedures of SBS, its parent company. Unlike the lean crews of one to three

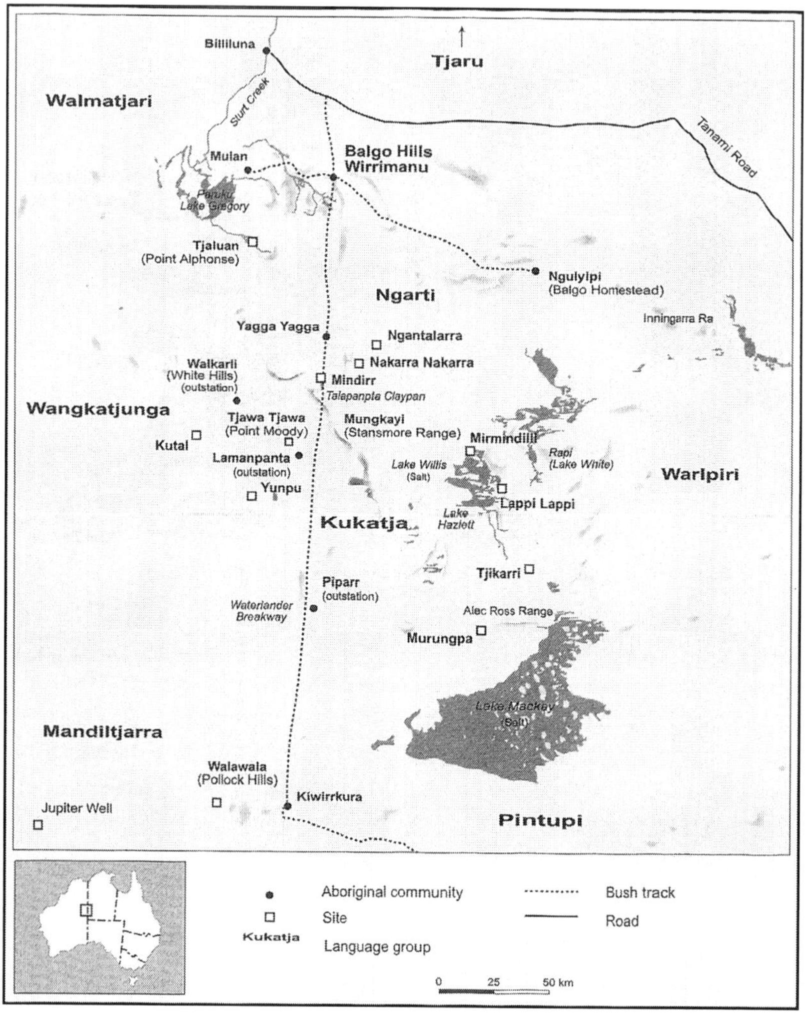

FIGURE 10. Map of Balgo, including the area and sites featured in *Tjawa Tjawa*. Map courtesy of Sylvie Poirier, 2005.

that typified most PAKAM films, *Tjawa Tjawa* had a relatively large crew with specialized roles, including Mark as director and Neil as producer. It also included a director of photography, sound recordist, camera operators, media mentor, and cook, as well as production assistants such as me. Neil was able to negotiate the bureaucratic morass of paperwork required to make such projects possible, fine-tuning the balance between satisfying technical requirements and fostering as much flexibility as the process allowed. Although smaller films demonstrate the intimacies of Aboriginal community media processes, such an extensive project provides the time and space to illustrate the various interwoven stages within its social life.

Tjawa Tjawa was the most expansive film project I participated on. With a life cycle spanning three years, this short documentary circulated widely throughout the Indigenous Australian mediascape. Between 2014 and 2016, I traced the cinematic life of *Tjawa Tjawa,* including film treatments, budgets, and bureaucratic negotiations between Balgo, PAKAM, NITV, and Screen Australia, as well as the logistics leading up to the shoot around food, crew, and drivers, as well as which locations could or could not be filmed. I assisted in a variety of roles throughout the production, and in postproduction I was involved in editing and transcribing, making the twelve-hour drive back to Balgo five times throughout the film's translation, mid-process feedback, and screenings.

I also accompanied *Tjawa Tjawa* to the ICTV film screenings at the National Remote Indigenous Media Festival in Lajamanu—an Aboriginal community in the Northern Territory—and to the 2015 Sydney Film Festival. It would go on to screen at a variety of international festivals, including the imagineNATIVE Film & Media Arts Festival in Toronto and the Margaret Mead Film Festival in New York City. While the social life of *Tjawa Tjawa* began before its conception, it has also outlived its own production, sparking a variety of other projects.

2

Laughing with the Camera

One of the best ways to understand a people is to know what makes them laugh.

—Vine Deloria Jr., *Custer Died for Your Sins*

"This is the real story, mate. We should be making this film," Joe Pickering quips as we sit down in the spotty shade of a thin tree to evade the baking afternoon sun. A Fijian veteran of the film industry and the media mentor for the *Tjawa Tjawa* crew, Joe has as much of an eye for humor as he does for cinema. "It's a comedy," he continues, subtly nodding toward the unfolding scene. In an effort to back up, a trailer on one of the troopys has become wedged in a large patch of dried spinifex grass. Surrounding the trapped trailer hitch, several whitefellas begin swinging shovels and picks into the spinifex to no avail. The Aboriginal community member we are sitting with shakes his head in a half-smile, noting in a hushed tone, "This is how people die out here. You are always just a couple of mistakes away from disaster. It's the panic after the mistake that is worse than the mistake itself. Luckily, we're here." Twenty minutes and as many animated discussions later, they are overexerted and take a break to reconsider their approach. At that moment, the man next to us stands up and sticks a long crowbar deep into the compressed grass underneath the hitch. After giving it a final look of consideration, he frees the trailer with a single strong push. As everyone laughs at the absurdity of the moment, Joe looks over at me and repeats through chuckles, "It's a comedy, mate."

Comedy is a realm of social life that encodes and compresses volumes (Apte 1983). As Vine Deloria Jr. (Standing Rock Lakota) argues in *Custer Died for Your Sins*,

> One of the best ways to understand a people is to know what makes them laugh. Laughter encompasses the limits of the soul. In humor life is redefined and accepted. Irony and satire provide much keener insights into a group's collective psyche and values than do years of research. It has always been a great disappointment to Indian people that the humorous side of Indian life has not been mentioned by professed experts on Indian Affairs. . . . People have little sympathy with stolid groups. (1969, 39)

As Deloria explains, understanding humor is particularly important in Indigenous-focused research, and its engagement—or lack thereof—has serious implications. In their overview of humor and laughter in anthropology, John Carty and Yasmine Musharbash echo this sentiment, describing how the ethnographic potential of comedy provides a largely untapped means for revealing the fault lines of power, particularly regarding "the fraught relationships between Indigenous people and 'whitefellas' " (2008, 213). Despite its ubiquity, humor remains an uncommon ethnographic topic.[1]

Along with Aboriginal land, the broad and ongoing processes of settler colonialism have dispossessed popular perceptions of Indigenous humanity. This dehumanization includes the silencing of not only Aboriginal futures but also one of the most fundamental aspects of life: comedy. A humorless people are also a futureless one. As Lauren Berlant puts it, an imposed "humorlessness wedges an encounter in order to control it, creating a buttress of immobility and impasse . . . to produce the fear that protects power" (2018, 157). In a mass-media landscape of dystopian representations of Aboriginal communities, foregrounding humor and comedy can itself be a transformative political act, as these are "not only important dimensions of social life to be better understood, but important perspectives on the understandings we already take for granted" (Carty and Musharbash 2008, 209).

This dynamic of humorlessness is crucial in settler/Indigenous relations across the globe. In Native North America, comedy groups like the 1491s and breakthrough TV hits like *Reservation Dogs* draw upon comedy to push back against stereotypes of stoicism. Donna Goldstein (2003) illustrates how laughter that is seemingly "out of place" in Brazilian favelas and other marginalized places can provide insights into a community's daily life, as well as how they come to be understood as humorless. Too often, humor in Aboriginal communities is perceived as out of place in the national imaginary, though this could not be further from the truth. As those who have lived in Aboriginal communities well know, in spite of and amid profound problems of ongoing colonialism, like most communities, they are filled with laughter.

Irreconciling Comedy

What is comedy, such that it lies at the heart of what Joe described as the "real" film? It is helpful to distinguish between laughter, joking, humor, and comedy (Apte 1988; Beeman 1999; Driessen 2015; Zijderveld 1983). For clarity, I will reference *laughter* as the embodied and sonic act, *joking* as communication intended to be funny, *humor* as a shared sensibility about what is funny, and *comedy* as situations that are perceived as funny whether intentional or not. Counterintuitively, while laughter may be associated with humor and comedy, this is rarely its cause (Provine 2001). Laughter most commonly arises when people experience heightened states of pressure, danger, and misunderstanding—qualities that are part and parcel of convoy trips.

Here, I focus on how irreconcilability animates the dynamics of comedy and laughter in shooting *Tjawa Tjawa* and other Balgo films. As Lawrence Gross (Anishinaabe) explains, there is a scholarly consensus that humor hinges on incongruity, which creates "a juxtaposition between two items that normally would not be associated with each other, the proximity of which causes surprise," and often delight (2007, 69). While laughter regularly erupts as a catharsis after being confronted with incongruity, comedy and humor run deeper, infused with cultural expectations around respect and dignity. Comedy typically plays upon brief and passing incongruities. However, in an intercultural setting such as the *Tjawa Tjawa* shoot, it often emerges amid irreconcilabilities, exposing though not resolving them. In these moments, power dynamics are temporarily revealed and relieved.

I draw upon Michelle Raheja's (Seneca) (2010) articulation of "laughing at the camera," which analyzes how Nanook and other iconic ethnographic film subjects wielded humor to both acknowledge and critique the anthropological gaze. I extend Raheja's work through what I describe as "laughing *with* the camera." This expands her conceptualization in the context of Indigenous production teams holding cameras and narrative control. The shift from laughing *at* to laughing *with* repositions the filmmakers as the curators of irreconcilability and its fractures, with the camera serving as a proxy for audiences, who are welcomed in on the joke (Gross 2007, 69).

Tjawa Tjawa's intensive film shoot represented its creative and social climax. Here, I follow Joe's impromptu suggestion regarding the importance of comedy in understanding its process. I articulate power dynamics and irreconcilable differences that ruptured through comedy during this shoot, some of which made their way into the film itself. Centering comedy within the production process helps to reveal how the footage came into being via a variety of collaborators and stakeholders. In moments ranging from levity to mortal danger, I interrogate power dynamics in Aboriginal/whitefella relations through analyses of comedy and laughter on- and off-screen.

Having grown up in the (relatively) nearby Tanami Downs Station, Kim Mahood has spent much of her life in communities near Balgo. She is a rare whitefella writer who has at least as much credibility and relevance within communities as she does outside of them. Community members, managers, and visitors alike regularly brought up her work in Balgo as a useful and funny way of understanding kartiya. Mahood articulates a vivid and nuanced social dynamic:

> The hothouse environment of remote Aboriginal communities brings out the worst and the best in the kartiya who work in them. During my time in Balgo and Mulan, I've seen irrational hatreds, petty power struggles, physical and verbal assaults, incompetence, sabotage, and abuses of power. I've also seen people achieve remarkable outcomes under extraordinarily challenging conditions, and I've made lifelong friendships based on bonds forged under pressure, when the raw material of personality and character is exposed. (2016, 201)

While comedy does not seem to be a primary aim in her writing, the absurdity of these scenarios renders it inescapable in engaging these relations.

My goal is not to stoke flattened narratives of the "bad kartiya" but rather to unpack what is at stake in these power dynamics—the irreconcilabilities that comedy lays bare. These moments include unexpected laughter when the *Tjawa Tjawa* crew accidentally crashed a drone into sacred sites, disagreements on where people should sleep, and a debate on which colors Elders should use in their acrylic paintings. I unpack how comedic movements reveal frameworks of productivity versus "laziness," and how they can become projected onto the filming process and community life more broadly. I highlight a single moment in the finished film that makes a wide variety of audiences laugh, yet for different reasons. Such moments of comedy coexist with the deadly serious, including the dangers of becoming literally and metaphorically "bogged," and the value of collectively becoming unstuck. These close calls often dance with dignity, failure, and redemption in unexpected ways.

In considering Joe's discussion of the "real" film, this chapter illustrates that for many crew members, the real film was the story of the shoot itself. *Tjawa Tjawa* was Mark's directorial debut and the first time he was in charge of a film's story, movement, and vision. His awakening in this process was in coming to understand cinema as a path toward reinvigorating his role as a community leader and storyteller.

You Had to Be There

It is uniquely difficult to engage humor after the fact. Indeed, many failed recountings of funny moments end with a half-hearted "You had to be there." This challenge is exacerbated in academic writing, which tends to work in opposition to the improvisational and playful register of humor. However, because of its corporeal (MacDougall 2006) qualities, film is well suited to recording and presenting comedy. Funny books exist, yet funny films abound. In situations where you had to be there, the audience is present, at least in a basic audiovisual sense. While I emphasize the role of humor in the *process* of filmmaking, comedy also imprinted itself into the footage and finished films.

At a screening, laughter is the most explicit real-time audience feedback. Unlike more subtle emotional reactions, laughter is a lively, audible response that generates a moment of mutual recognition. It reveals that a viewer has likely understood at least some social context surrounding the humor. While micro-distinctions of understanding are crucial for how humor operates in everyday social interactions, when producing media for mass distribution a frequent goal is to foster shared understanding whenever possible. Broad audience comprehension was especially emphasized for projects slated for national broadcasting, such as *Tjawa Tjawa*.

There was one particular moment in the film that evoked similar amounts of laughter at each of the widely varying screenings I attended across Australia. In a short scene, Mark recounted the part of the *Tjawa Tjawa* Dreaming story in which women were deciding which men to sleep with, after traveling hundreds of miles from the coast into the desert in search of husbands. Mark acts out their bickering in the present-tense first person, exclaiming in subtitled Kukatja:

> "That one's for me!"
> "This one's mine!"
> "I want him!"
> "I'll have this one!"
> "Let's all three share one man!"

It was not surprising that this evoked similar reactions in Balgo community screenings, or even at the 2015 National Remote Indigenous Media Festival in the nearby desert community of Lajamanu. Yet it also received a similar response at the Sydney Film Festival in a room of many urban white attendees. This scene was funny for diverse audiences because it drew on a broadly relatable social taboo around publicly discussing sex lives. The scene utilized editing techniques to amplify its humor, cutting quickly between different close-up framings of Mark as he embodied the characters in the story.

A moment in our short film *Marumpu Wangka: Kukatja Hand Talk* (2015)—featuring hand signs by Balgo women Elders, and discussed further in chapter 4—received similarly consistent laughter from various audiences. This film presented a short visual dictionary on Kukatja hand signs that received unexpected circulation and interest, largely due to moments of joviality. During a scene, Manaya, one of the women Elders, mimicked someone asking for money within the mimed experience of winning at cards. As with the moment in *Tjawa Tjawa*, this was funny because it drew on cross-cultural touchstones of charm and social boundaries.

In both of these scenes, although each audience laughed, Balgo community members laughed for more complicated reasons. The *Tjawa Tjawa* scene evoked local laughter about sharing a man, because while polygyny is traditional, sex in such a public setting is certainly not. Manaya's gestures were funny in Balgo because they reference the regular card game that moves around to different houses, referred to locally as "the casino," and because a large pot would soon be returned to community members through continued playing, as well as sharing it afterward. Despite the more contextual understanding of these moments in Balgo, they worked well on film because their embodied comedy communicated quickly at multiple levels. Both clips invoked laughter to bridge the tension between serious and lighthearted topics to reach broader audiences: women teasing each other about sexual partners in relation to a Songline story that involved death and Law, and a grandmother acting out the movements of a card shark in the midst of a visual dictionary on revitalizing Kukatja language. In essence, community members laugh because of particularities, while outsiders laugh because of universalities. Despite such differences, both laughed with, rather than at.

A key element here was the deliberate ways that both Mark and Manaya laughed in these moments while looking directly into the camera. With control of the narrative and process, they laughed along with the camera, a proxy for and portal to the audience. This deceptively simple act of laughing along with the viewers communicates multitudes. It tells the audience that the moment is funny, provides a cue to laugh, and (for some) compels them to consider deeper reasons why the moment is comedic. And by being embedded—ostensibly out of place—within the serious topics of Dreaming stories and visual dictionaries, it also implicitly illustrates that humor is commonplace and valued in Aboriginal communities. By laughing with the camera in such moments, Mark and Manaya drew upon the disarming invitation of humor to enrapture audiences who might otherwise be put off due to prejudice or disinterest. This contrasts with dominant media narratives of Aboriginal communities as one-dimensional sites of suffering, rendering such depictions as irreconcilable for audiences. Humor on bush trips was often based on the sharp contrast between serious Aboriginal film themes—including traditional Law, Dreaming, and Songlines—and the absurdities of the convoy filmmaking process.

Such comedic scenes were neither scripted nor planned. They emerged from processes of filmmaking that went *slowly, slowly* and allowed for irreconcilable comedic moments to rupture and breathe. There were many that surprised our film crew, myself included. Our first major aerial shoot involved flying a drone past a hill named Yampart, which in the Songline story was a Tjakamarra (skin-name kinship category) who was chasing two women (smaller nearby hills). It was especially windy that day, and after several attempts the drone crashed near the top of the hill. After a bit of discussion, the crew decided that I should climb up and get it, since I was a "whitefella from far away" and was less likely to be negatively affected by this interaction with a sacred site. This in itself was joked about, though we were all concerned about what Mark would think. When we arrived back at camp later that afternoon we told Mark, and to our relief his immediate response was to give a long and hearty laugh, remarking that we "must have given that fella quite a shock, ha!" Throughout the rest of this windy trip, the drone crash-landed at other sites, which Mark found to be increasingly hilarious each time. Indeed, the "drone became a character as well as an allegory" during which the "ancient play of wind and water and sun still interferes" (Bessire 2017, 126). As Mark conveyed, these unexpected mishaps reiterated that these sacred sites are alive, interacting with Tjukurrpa beings and drones alike, commanding respectful intention rather than rigid doctrine.

Sometimes comedy translated into the footage and film. In one crucial scene, the crew was attempting to figure out how to shoot a moment when the women sat down to urinate, creating an important water hole. In the light of the evening sun, crew members joked around as we realized that what would work best cinematically was to film the shadows of squatting crew members, with water sounds to be added in postproduction. This involved what Tess Lea and Elizabeth Povinelli (2018) describe as "improvisational realism," in which spontaneity is fostered to produce scenes with emotional resonance.

Although climbing sacred sites was usually forbidden, and depicting urination could be seen as inappropriate, context was paramount for understanding why and when. Essential to whether or not violating such rules was funny or offensive seemed to be largely determined by attitude and intent. Our crashing into sacred sites was funny precisely because we were trying so hard not to, all the while working on a film about the Songline that was directed by Mark. However, not all social rule breaking was comedic, and not everything that was funny was downstream of well-intentioned plans gone awry. A contrasting genre of humor on these trips derived from tension within power relationships between whitefellas and community members.

Black Comedy and White Labor out Bush

In this section I illustrate black comedy, encompassing both literal and figurative meanings. This dark humor about and with kartiya speaks to layers of Balgo power relations in and beyond the social lives of media. As Aileen Moreton-Robinson (2015) argues through her conception of "the white possessive," this dynamic points to an insidious process in which kartiya are often attempting (consciously or not) to claim possession and control over Aboriginal life, politics, and representation.

"Kartiya Are Like Toyotas" is perhaps the best-known academic article within Balgo and Aboriginal communities more broadly. Penned by Mahood (2012) and based on her extensive experience, it takes seriously the comedy of how outsider whitefellas cycle through managerial positions in communities until they break down, much like Toyotas. Discussions of her article occurred frequently in Balgo, including the following example:

> "Have you read Kim Mahood's kartiya article? If not, you just have to."
> "Oh yes. I just love it. She really gets it. And it's funny!"
> "Right, it's funny because it's true."
> "Exactly."

Mahood's article *is* funny, and not at the expense of serious content. She describes the dysfunctional structure of the continuous cycling through of kartiya "mercenaries, missionaries, and misfits" in Aboriginal community positions (2012, 2).[2] Much of its humor comes from describing secular missionaries who arrive wanting to fix things. Community members often noted that such kartiya "think they know everything and can save us." An older man in Balgo jokingly distilled his experiences with new whitefella managers: "It's the same damn horse, just a different rider." After a long day of conflict between volunteers, one whitefella filmmaker noted in exasperation that "Every visitor is on their own journey in Balgo, which is rarely about Balgo."

In addition to kartiya workers living in community, Mahood describes the many non-Indigenous organizations that briefly pass through and engage Balgo for their projects, initiating an often comedic dance around negotiating access, resource and knowledge sharing, and who will accompany trips. Emblematic of this dynamic was the search for the ostensibly extinct night parrot, which in recent years had been spotted in the Great Sandy Desert. Mahood's tale was referenced and expanded upon in late-night chats in Balgo, and it was jokingly noted that the ideal outcome of a night parrot trip was to hear it though not see it, which would require another bush trip back to Country.

However, quests for endangered animals were not always animated by levity. On one of my last trips to Balgo, Mark noted that he had too much back pain for more film trips. Just after sunrise a few days before I left, I heard a beckoning honk at the gate of the volunteer quarters where I was staying. Opening the screen door to see who it was, Mark was already standing in front of a packed-up troopy with an improbable number of new, brightly colored swags tied to its roof. Mark explained, "I just wanted to say goodbye before you go. They are looking for bilbies [small marsupials], so I'm going with them." After I asked about his back, he sighed, responding, "Yuwai, but it's my Country. I have to go."

Of Labor and Laughter

As the debacle of the stuck trailer illustrates, black comedy regularly emerged in situations where whitefellas were frantically attempting to solve problems that community members would seem to be obviously more experienced at solving. There was often a perplexed amusement by community members about the choices and comments of some whitefellas. For example, during one of the first nights on the *Tjawa Tjawa* trip, Mark had just settled into his camp. He had unrolled his blankets around a fire along with a few family members and was starting to cook lamb chops on a wire mesh over some hot coals, while also boiling water with a small "billy" pot consisting of an empty powdered milk container that he moved with an orange-peel handle. While preparing his tea, a whitefella came up and exclaimed, "Mark! You can't sleep here near your mother-in-law. It's not proper Aboriginal way!" Slowly shaking his head, Mark seemed to think about explaining this before stopping himself, laughing as he responded, "Ha, I think I know the proper Aboriginal way!" This seemed to end the discussion, with Mark avoiding the need to describe complex kinship nuances, or engage in an unpleasant disagreement, while also not validating the comment.

Throughout the trip, Payi Payi and other women Elders were painting a large canvas meant to collectively document the journey through a different creative form. Near the middle of the week, I was sitting with them in early evening's fading heat, retrieving paint and occasionally mixing colors as directed. After staring at a flower she had just outlined, Payi Payi asked me, "Can you get me the blue paint?" I went to the art supplies and found the small container, at which point an art center volunteer realized her plan to use blue paint, quickly responding, "Oh no, they can't use blue, only natural colors." I went back to Payi Payi to make sure that I had heard her right. She affirmed, "Yep, the blue one, for the flowers." When I relayed this to the volunteer, an increasingly improbable debate ensued. Essentially, the volunteer argued that Payi Payi had already decided that the artists would only use natural colors such as orange, red, and brown. At first, Payi Payi's opinion in the matter did not seem to carry much weight in the moment, even after another volunteer pointed out that none of the acrylic paints were "natural" anyways. This led to a half-hour discussion between some of the whitefellas about whether Payi Payi truly wanted to use blue paint, while she patiently waited. After the discussion reached an irreconcilable impasse, Payi Payi simply chuckled and stated, "I'll paint 'em blue." There was no arguing with that. I still do not fully understand why there was pushback against the blue paint, though it presumably related to the painting's value on the art market (it had been pre-sold) in relation to perceptions of ochre-associated tones. In the grand scheme of things, this was only a passing moment in a multiday collaborative painting that the women described as a deeply meaningful creative process in Country.

FIGURE 11. Women painting during the *Tjawa Tjawa* shoot.

Humor does not always suffice as an effective diplomatic strategy. This was especially apparent in perceptions of labor equity. A small though vocal minority of trip volunteers complained that they were doing a disproportionate amount of work as "white slaves." This contingent made comments such as "Well, the problem is that Aboriginal people have been given sit-down money for so many years that they have come to expect whitefellas to do everything."[3] Sit-down money—a derisive inversion of sitting on Country—referenced the fortnightly payments that many in communities receive from Centrelink, a governmental welfare services agency. Yet, from the point of view of many community members on the trip, it was the whitefellas' insistence on working at irrational times in illogical ways that was challenging to reconcile.

For example, on a sweltering afternoon during the *Tjawa Tjawa* shoot, I was sitting in the sandy shade of the food trailer next to Payi Payi. She was watching two whitefella volunteers on the crew disputing where the fire should be started for dinner. Laughing quietly, she leaned over to me and observed, "Whitefellas growling in the sun. Too hot!"[4] The whitefella labor rhythm of working nine to five in one of the most scorching and UV-intensive places on Earth was antithetical to thousands of years of Aboriginal experience in living in this region. Mark would often reference this in relation to his years of working on cattle stations with Aboriginal crews. Despite many efforts by managers to convince them to move the cattle during the day, they preferred to travel under starlight, as Mark and his family regularly did in his youth. As Elizabeth Povinelli (1993) argues in *Labor's Lot,* there is an inherent conflict between Aboriginal and whitefella work scheduling, and with rare exceptions, whitefella labor structures have dominated not only during bush trips but also in community employment opportunities through the imposition of "settler time" (Rifkin 2017).

Balgo community members often discussed such conflict. During bush trips there was an undercurrent of commentary about what was going on, whispered and gestured by community members and crew in convoy group meetings. This included murmurs such as "Whitefella talk too much" and "It's already ten, the morning is over, we might as well sleep until it cools down." In larger projects such as *Tjawa Tjawa* with dozens of people, this dynamic resembled Vicki Mayer's (2011) description of the solidarity of film crew positioned "below the line" of lead film roles. In Indigenous shoots, however, the cultural dimensions of hierarchies exacerbated power dynamics, through which comedy provided both critique and catharsis.

Dignity

Ultimately, whether laughter is funny or degrading comes down to its relationship with dignity. Like humor, dignity is essential and ever-present in understanding the dynamics of labor relations in Aboriginal film shoots. Defined as "the state or quality of being worthy of honor or respect," it is perhaps unsurprising that the primary example provided in the *New Oxford American Dictionary* is "the dignity of labor." Dignity is not respect itself, but rather its precursor and context. Therefore, irreconcilabilities around dignity tended to be humorless and unspoken due to its relationship with respect (or its lack thereof).[5] This is often as profound as it is subtle. For example, it is generally considered impolite or worse to directly respond "no" to a request in

Balgo, though the extent of this pressure varies depending on kinship relations. This is navigated by shared understandings of how to shape language and behavior to avoid placing others in awkward positions of public refusal. To behave otherwise would be undignified.

This dynamic led to various misunderstandings that informed labor perceptions. For example, volunteers often asked community members if they could complete a specific task later that afternoon or the following day. The response was usually "Palya, no worries." If the community member did not show up, this bolstered a preconceived narrative about Aboriginal unreliability. The volunteer in this case was committing a basic social error, placing someone in a position in which they could not decline the request with dignity. For example, the question could have been phrased along the lines of "Are you busy at such and such a time tomorrow?," which gives the responder the opportunity to respond affirmatively or ambiguously. There were fundamental misunderstandings of acquiescent responses. Palya was not simply an agreement, but pointed (figuratively and literally through its gestural expression) to an affirmation of the good and proper way, which did not necessarily mean "yes." Furthermore, in Balgo, casual agreements about future meetings tend to be understood as tentative, and it is considered baffling for someone to be upset if another person does not show up (Kendon 1988). Interpreting this as a personal slight is considered foolish, as it is normally assumed that something more important presented itself.

When I was tasked with facilitating a few projects toward the end of my fieldwork, our crew drew upon months of guidance by Mark and other Elders to immediately stop a project if anyone even slightly implied that they might not be happy about the process, especially if someone stated "Nyamu" (No more). Responding with the question of whether the shoot could continue later is a standard media practice in such moments, yet this would have placed that person in the undignified position of having to directly refuse. In each case, after we stopped and began packing up, that individual decided that they wanted to continue, which we then did. While it surprised me every time, it seems to me now that Balgo community members were used to being pressured by outsiders and were thoughtfully testing the boundaries of their own ability to control situations. Community members seemed to invoke the principle that projects that are difficult to stop probably should stop, while projects that are easy to stop should probably continue. In following the social life of media for dozens of films, I was in the unusual position of being able to see how they unfolded. It is important to reiterate that my perspective, approach, and positionality were based upon a substantial amount of privilege as a white foreigner with research funding. I was burdened with few short- and medium-term pressures to deliver productions or other outcomes. In other words, I had the great privilege of conducting ethnography.

With the benefit of hindsight, it seems that I and other whitefellas were regularly, and quite rightly, tested. While collaborating with PAKAM and Goolarri in Broome, there were several times—especially early on—in which people seemed to want to find out through daily pranking and joking if I was "too stuffy." Most of the people I worked with had the stated impression that Americans tend to take themselves too seriously. This was distilled in their impression of responding "HOW DARE YOU!" in a comedic American accent. People tested this stereotype by seeing if I would be offended by various antics, often making jokes like "Careful, he's American. They will sue you, hah!"

As time went on and we got to know each other, I became included in multiple "goof reels," which were montages of favorite bloopers and pranks from throughout the year to be shown at the annual Goolarri and PAKAM Christmas pool party. These gags included hidden camera footage of people surprising each other, made all the more entertaining after security cameras were installed. Perhaps the most memorable goof reel clip involved a parody that everyone participated in through the style of Goolarri's Kimberley Girl, a series of workshops around personal development for young Aboriginal women. Re-creating the finale catwalk event with everyone in makeup and comically fitting dresses, we shot a runway scene with cameras that slowed down every single micro-movement of our exaggerated catwalking. This gag drew explicitly on British-inflected Australian comedic TV traditions.

Because I am a fairly introverted person, this pushed the limits of my comfort zone. The fact that I felt (and must have seemed) hesitant about participating in a public spectacle, yet did it anyway, perhaps only made the event funnier, as my scenes received extra screen time and laughs during the goof reel. Making oneself vulnerable at times is essential in an emotionally equitable ethnographic process. While Ruth Behar (1996) notes that vulnerability in fieldwork can break your heart, vulnerability applies as much to comedy as it does to tragedy. Since I was an ethnographer asking others to be vulnerable, stretching my own comfort zone, within reason, seemed like the least I could do.

Deadly Humor and Bush Mechanics

Comedy has an intimate relationship with risk, especially in Australia, where maintaining a sense of humor in the face of mortal danger is basically a national pastime. Rural Australians are well known for comedically blasé attitudes toward the variety of lethal creatures that saturate the continent. Referencing this genre of humor was common in each of our trips, with crew members regularly quoting Paul Hogan's "That's not a knife! Now *that's* a knife!" from *Crocodile Dundee* (1986) or Steve Irwin's many antics (though only during my first trip in 2006, before his tragic death later that year). It was routine to joke about the prospect of dying through comments such as "That salty [saltwater crocodile] just wants a bit of a snack, just a leg I reckon, barely a scratch!" One morning when I was picking up the art center's mail at the Balgo air strip, I noticed a small snake with red marks on it. When I asked a community member next to me, "Is that a death adder?" he responded, "Yeah, mate, hah, I wouldn't wake her up unless you are bored with living." In Balgo, comedy was frequently a deadly serious affair. "Deadly" is itself an Aboriginal English slang term that roughly translates to "great," with edgy and comedic undertones. Laughter is not necessarily oppositional to suffering; sometimes it depends upon a looming threat.

In Balgo, laughter can just as easily stem from joking as from close calls with disaster. As humorist Erma Bombeck put it, "There is a thin line that separates laughter and pain, comedy and tragedy, humor and hurt" (2013). Comedy in the midst of danger operates partly through what Anthony Redmond describes as "short circuits," innovative metaphors that transfer "meaning across domains, which, while holding onto the original referent of a symbol, simultaneously creates a new relation that extends the original meaning" (2008, 255). This was especially common during larger and extended bush trips, which positioned the film crew as a cohesive social group.

There is also black comedy around fighting. The first time I saw kids watching fights on their phones and laughing, I was confused about what exactly was funny. When physical fights occurred in Balgo, they were no laughing matter. However, fights are imagined differently when they are elsewhere and elsewhen. This is partly explained through the system of "payback." Often mistranslated along the lines of violent "revenge," payback is more accurately described as a process of expeditious peace making. The system of payback has been essential for people in the region around Balgo for millennia; as there is little room for error in an unforgiving environment, desire for revenge could have catastrophic consequences for entire groups. Payback fosters the resolving of disputes without lingering negative feelings. Before the imposition of whitefella law, a person might be speared during payback, though this was a precisely inflicted injury, after which the wounded individual would be cared for by their spearer, toward the goal of total resolution. Misunderstandings about payback have led to its criminalization, replaced by whitefella laws that lock people in jail away from their Country, a practice widely considered by community members to be torturous by comparison to the immediate physicality of payback (Finnane 2001).

This context helps to explain laughter when watching videos of physical fights in Balgo. While fights are serious in the moment, there was traditionally little resentment afterward, altering the narrative of fighting from the initiation of a long-term feud to its resolution. The systemic disruption of the payback system has, like many other consequences of settler colonialism, fomented much unnecessary contention within communities. Accordingly, fights that foster feuds seem to become differently funny through a "perilous laughter," which Yasmine Musharbash (2008b) describes in her fieldwork in Yuendumu. She cautions against the tendency to wholly accept Freudian-lineage theories that laughter simply relieves anxiety or cloaks aggression, and provides examples in which it weakens and wounds. There has recently been an increase in mainstream understandings of the importance of payback justice, with some modest attempts at integrating it within the Australian legal system.[6]

Bogged

Despite the desert's many deadly creatures, becoming stranded was by far its greatest mortal danger. The only factor that ever compelled us to turn back on our dozens of bush shoots was the threat of running out of tires. There was a persistent background fear of getting stranded, or as community members put it, bogged.[7] This was certainly the case in *Tjawa Tjawa*. Toward the end of the weeklong shoot, most of the vehicles and participants had returned home, leaving only two troopys carrying Mark, Neil, Larry Gundora, and the film crew as we continued on to Lake Mackay to film the final crucial shots. Driving parallel to a ridge, we searched for the lake. Two hours and three tires later, our situation quickly turned dire. Our water and fuel were running low, and we had far to go. Furthermore, we knew only roughly where we were due to a tall ridge we were driving alongside.

With only one spare tire between the two troopys, we needed to adjust course quickly and get over the ridge to gain perspective and find a less treacherous path. Making a right turn perpendicular to the forty-foot-tall incline, we drove directly up, only to find that we did not nearly make it. Backing up, we made several more attempts, getting closer though falling short of the summit. We decided that loud music would help. Cranking up our favorite song by the Australian band Sheppard, we backed up even further and gunned it, barely and dramatically reaching the top. Over the next day, our precarious situation led us to a variety of memorable moments, including camping next to a small lake as a male camel in heat howled at us from the edge of camp, and driving into the community of Kiwirrkurra on a bare wheel rim, where we bought supplies and two patched tires to get to Lake Mackay. While such moments were anxiety-ridden at the time, we collectively remembered them fondly as funny. Over the next several months, the PAKAM crew and I joked about these many close calls on a daily basis, which led to inside jokes that became regular staples of banter.

The ever-present danger of getting stranded in the desert has inspired an entire subgenre of Aboriginal video production. This was made most famous in the landmark series *Bush Mechanics* (1998), directed by David Batty through Warlpiri Media, located in the community of Yuendumu. It highlighted the creative techniques that people use to keep from becoming bogged, such as placing a dead battery next to a fire to give it an extra charge, and cutting a car roof off with a hatchet to create a makeshift trailer. We regularly employed such techniques in our trips, once, for example, making jumper cables out of instrument cords by scraping away the rubberized exterior to reveal the copper core. In another instance, after a variety of local fixes to Browny—an old PAKAM troopy that was left in Balgo to "retire"[8]—we had to start it by physically rubbing two frayed wires together in lieu of keys, essentially hot-wiring it each time. However, for every near disaster or close call, there were other instances in which things did not work out smoothly, and we actually did become bogged. I came to learn that such failure, like danger, had unexpected relationships with both humor and dignity.

Redemptive Failure

"Yep . . . looks that way," I reply, confirming that the tire iron is the wrong size to change the flat. "Well," Mark finally says, "might as well light a signal fire and make lunch." Checking our surroundings and the breeze, he walks downwind several car paces and ignites a wide line of spinifex grass with his lighter. In the opposite direction, our small group collects firewood and soon we have enough to cook the kangaroo tails we brought for the overnight trip. Meanwhile, back in Balgo, Mark's son Eric is watching the horizon in our direction for any sign of trouble. As soon as he sees our single large fire—in contrast to a series in a line—he fills up his vehicle with fuel, tires, and a couple of passengers and embarks to rescue us. After burying the tails between layers of coals, a red Toyota appears beneath a cloud of desert dust in the distance as if on cue. Eric and his companions arrive in time for lunch, and after using his tire iron to change the flat we share the tails and make our way back to Balgo. I drop Mark and Larry off at their houses and, to my surprise, each invites me inside for the first time. What feels like profound failure on my part suddenly seems otherwise.

It has been a few weeks since getting stranded with Mark, and I am driving the PAKAM troopy with Shorty, an art center worker, and Jimmy Tchooga on an overnight trip for the film *Jimmy Tchooga: Painting Two Snakes* (2015). This is a short documentary about Jimmy's life history and how he became a prominent painter. We just finish inside his old home—amid what he calls "the homestead"—a few hours outside of Balgo. He describes life there before it was closed down due to the governmental defunding of outstations. Jimmy directs us toward the local river where he will paint on camera. As we approach the dried-up riverbed that only runs in the wet season, we look for a manageable way to drive down into it. We think we have one and Jimmy tells me where to go. Driving over the precipice, I hesitate for the slightest moment. It is enough. This critical mistake leads to our front tires sinking just fast enough to catch the middle of the troopy. It does not sound good and when we get out to have a look, it does not inspire confidence. Laughing, Jimmy exclaims, "Bogged, eh? Hah, well might as well start painting." The art center worker sits down with Jimmy to film him painting the river, as Shorty and I attempt every technique we can think of to free the troopy.

A long hour later, it is clear that we are not going to succeed. We are bogged. Shorty begins lighting several fires to signal to Jimmy's son in Balgo to come help us. The comedy has faded. We do not have Jimmy's medication and are not prepared to camp overnight. Furthermore, this area is a women's site, and it is forbidden for men to camp here. Making matters worse, as the wind shifts we are now combating the very fires we lit, as they close in on the troopy. As nightfall approaches I am deeply worried, and I attempt to hide it with limited success. "That's them, just on the horizon that way," Shorty remarks in an even tone. Squinting at the horizon, I do not see anything, though I have no doubt that he is right. Fifteen minutes later, I see it too, and before long they arrive with a tow line. After a bit of digging and pulling, we are free, driving through the signal fires back toward Balgo.[9]

As in the trip with Mark and Larry, I felt acute responsibility for this failure, and again, I was surprised that Jimmy invited me into his house for the first time on the morning after our return. There, he showed me photos of his late father's artwork. Jimmy shifted from fairly interested to exuberant about the film, excitedly sharing ideas about his vision for it. At the time, I was perplexed by these moments. From my point of view, I had made mistakes that had potentially put people in danger. Yet such situations proved to be some of the most important in my relationships during fieldwork, and in retrospect some of the funniest. I still cannot fully reconcile aspects of these moments, which remain enigmatic to me.

In reflecting upon these failures over time, I think that their redeeming qualities had something to do with the way they revealed priorities. In these instances of failure, the film we were working on became instantly deprioritized. Perhaps seeing me so concerned, yet relatively helpless, dispelled the implicit power relationship of myself as a whitefella. After these situations, people would often joke with me, saying "Hah, you were so worried about us, I think you thought it was our last day! As I told you, people are looking out for us, mate."

As perilous as it seemed in the moment to me, it was not dangerous from Mark's or Jimmy's perspectives. Contingencies were already planned for, with their sons' eyes scanning the horizon for any trace of a signal fire. What seemed to me like disaster was for them a minor glitch that simply provided time to cook and relax. These situations felt embarrassing as I mulled over what I could have done to prevent them. Yet sharing them is crucial here, as they opened doors into relationships and helped me to comprehend just how little I understood.

Failure, of course, is not always constructive or redemptive, even when things turn out okay in the end. To take one stark example, in the middle of the *Tjawa Tjawa* shoot the crew realized that we did not have enough water in the trailer to complete the trip. We were running out of the most important substance in a desert. This concern was dramatically foregrounded by a series of bush fires that had been lit surrounding our camp, contrasting dramatically with the sunset. At that moment, Neil approached me with his experienced and buoyant optimism and asked, "Say, how would you like to go on a bit of a water adventure?" As with his previous year's question about being thrown in the deep end, I heartily agreed without understanding, as PhD fieldworkers do. After hearing the details, I climbed into the driver's seat of the troopy with water trailer in tow, sitting next to Eric with one of his cousins in the back.

Three hours away from the Yagga Yagga water pump and with only one tire to spare between the troopy and the trailer, we head off into darkness, guided by Eric's subtle index finger gestures. I feel palpable pressure, as dozens of people on the film shoot, including Elders, are reliant on our successful return. These are difficult tracks to follow, and I carefully navigate the troopy and trailer tires along the uneven terrain. One wrong move would result in cascading consequences. I try to banish the stakes from my thoughts, staring only at the dimly lit and hypnotizing track.

It is with great relief that we first glimpse the white Yagga Yagga water tank in the distance, illuminated by moonlight. Driving past the old community store and the decommissioned power station, I back the trailer up to the water tank, which I know from previous visits is a verdant oasis of color due to the condensation of precious moisture on its surface, and the tap's slow drip. Lacking a hose, we begin the long process of filling the thousand-liter tank up with over one hundred big buckets of water, alternating three positions of filling, carrying, and pouring. As with the rest of this seven-hour ordeal, we carry this out in silence, sharing knowing looks and periodic wordless laughter at the scenario (Gross 2007).

An hour later it is filled, and after a brief scare of getting stuck in the mud next to the tank, we are off again. Along the return trip, there are several times that I am sure that Eric is asleep—leaning against the door with his eyes seemingly closed—only to notice his hand rise to indicate the correct trail at just the right moment. Arriving back a few hours before sunrise, there is broad relief that our trip has succeeded. Unfortunately, the combined stresses of the evening have taken a toll, and several people decide to return home this morning, days before the trip's scheduled conclusion.

In hindsight, redemptive failures tended to occur more often during small, intimate shoots, in contrast to convoy trips like *Tjawa Tjawa*. During small shoots with a single troopy a crew is especially vulnerable, as there are no backup vehicles. This precarity amplifies the emotional vulnerability of everyone involved. It becomes essential that all can rely on one another, not only for the film to go well but also for the group's safety, and even their survival.

Awakening and Arriving

On the *Kurrarlkatjanu* trip, Mark was a storyteller and navigator. However, he was not deeply involved in the film process, and the shoot traveled to familiar places with established pathways that Kapululangu regularly visited. In contrast, *Tjawa Tjawa* positioned Mark as the film's director and leader, requiring him to travel to places that he had not been to in many years. It was during the moments of becoming temporarily disoriented that Mark seemed to find his footing for filmmaking. While few would describe Mark as a comedian, he had a keen sense of humor that he employed with ease to relax the anxious and disarm the strident.

During *Tjawa Tjawa,* the crew's most common joke was about taking shortcuts. Leading the convoy of Toyotas, Mark would often say, "Actually, I reckon we can take a shortcut *that* way, no worries at all." Invariably, none of these shortcuts went exactly as planned. "We'll just take a shortcut the Dreamtime, ha ha," an Aboriginal crew member joked, filling the troopy with laughter once again, as Mark's lead vehicle came to a near stop and began slowly turning off into a new direction. With each setback, Mark, unfazed, pointed again to the horizon and declared, "Not far now, not far," which in Kukatja meant that we were going the right way, not that we were necessarily getting close. That information was embedded in the corresponding hand sign of pointing in that direction toward the ground three times. By saying "Not far now," Mark was simultaneously using this phrase to precisely express the situation to the Aboriginal crew, while remaining acutely aware that the shortcut had taken on a comedic tone for whitefellas who were just coming to understand that this did not mean what they had assumed. In one instance he publicly proclaimed, "Not far now, maybe one, two, or six hours away, hah."

Such moments did not represent getting "lost" or going the "wrong way," but rather were integral to the process of remembering Country by moving through it. Although trips often took longer than anticipated in our schedule, with each debate about where to go next, Mark, Larry, Payi Payi, and others from this Country connected with their childhood memories along with Dreaming stories. The women regularly broke out into spatially embedded songs as the convoy made its way. The choice of vehicle to lead each trip was crucial, as was where each individual sat. Driving or sitting in the front of the first troopy not only represented a dignified way of demonstrating Mark's status as director but also provided minimal interference in his rediscovery process. Often, when beginning an alternative route, Mark's and Larry's memories would be triggered by a place, leading us to, for example, a centuries-old grinding stone.[10] At the same time, there was significant and explicit pressure on Mark to know which way he was going, which he later told me motivated him to act confident even in situations where he was still figuring out the best way to go. As Mark explained, he was sure about the right way to walk; the issue was that this did not always translate into passable tracks for vehicles.

Through this process, *Tjawa Tjawa* became for Mark more than just a trip to Country with his family. This shoot seemed to awaken in him an interest in the film process itself and what it could offer on multiple levels. His position as director renewed the central leadership role that he had occupied before Yagga Yagga closed. The role positioned Mark as visionary and storyteller along a Songline that he was re-remembering by moving through it. In doing so, this also reinvigorated the calling of his Country of Mangkayi to explore, share, and return to.

Revisiting Deloria's observation that "people have little sympathy with stolid groups" (1969, 39), the political importance of being humanized through comedy is difficult to overstate. While it should be obvious that Aboriginal communities, like all others, are replete with laughter and humor, the humorlessness of national Aboriginal imaginaries has meaningful policy consequences.

To conclude on an appropriately comedic note, during my fieldwork a landmark Australian Broadcasting Corporation's sketch comedy series was released, titled *Black Comedy* (2014). With a cast including some of the most prominent Aboriginal comedians performing *Saturday Night Live*–style skits, this was a rare mainstream and well-funded show centering Aboriginal humor. Many of the jokes were made at the expense of white Australians and the history of colonization and missionization. It satirically inverted the dominant stereotypes used to depict Aboriginal people. Tracing its lineage from the *Basically Black* (1973) series[11]—a revolutionary sketch show with incisive and provocative skits including Aboriginal people in whiteface—*Black Comedy* was not afraid to tackle politically charged topics. These included Indigenous sexual identity, white appropriation of Aboriginal culture, and even an anticolonial parody of *Star Trek* titled *Star Blaks.*

Unsurprisingly, the show was controversial with general audiences. In the mainstream Australian mediascape, *Black Comedy* represented a radical departure through its amplification of Aboriginal humor. Echoing its comedic lineage, it confronted irreconcilabilities of Indigenous life within the Australian settler state through caricatures that illuminated these realities. However, at PAKAM and Goolarri it was a hit, and punch lines from favorite sketches entered into daily banter, interwoven with reenacted close calls from *Tjawa Tjawa* and other bush trips past. It provided one more set of jokes to add to a rich comedic repertoire.

The ubiquity of humor within the social lives of these projects provided creative inertia and emotional sustenance throughout their filming. The following chapter focuses on postproduction, and video editing in particular. Typically, this film stage contrasts with the exuberance of shoots, shifting from social crews to isolated editing. Yet for *Tjawa Tjawa* and other Balgo films entering postproduction, the social process had only just begun.

3

Social Editing and Screening

Editing is the art of making something out of nothing.

—Mark Cochrane

As Mark Moora carefully opens the door to the small Radio Goolarri building in the late morning, he and I immediately see Sandy Dann in action through a glass wall. Shuffling through CDs while announcing the break, Sandy raises the volume slider for her first song just in time for the end of her sentence. As Tina Turner's "What's Love Got to Do with It?" begins, the red "on air" light switches off. I lightly tap on her door, which is followed by her signature cheerful response of "Come on in!" Smiling, she gestures us toward the two guest seats facing her as she continues to adjust dials, all while asking us about our morning. She then explains to Mark the topics she wants to ask him about, before fading out of the song and introducing him. It would be easy to miss noticing her reduced vision in light of her flowing dance of mechanical precision that does not impede her seemingly singular focus on her guests. Building upon her previous phone chats with Mark—as well as her vocal charm and incisive memory—in a matter of minutes she has him regaling her with stories about his wide-ranging life experiences. At the end of the interview, Sandy takes a joyful sigh and says, "I'm glad that this particular program is going out all across Australia through the National Indigenous Radio Service. It's important that we hear from actual people in our communities all around, from the source. Bless you, Mark." Simultaneously cutting to commercial, fading knobs, and feeling for her next CD, she thanks Mark and insists that he come back to continue their conversation on a show later in the week. He gladly agrees.

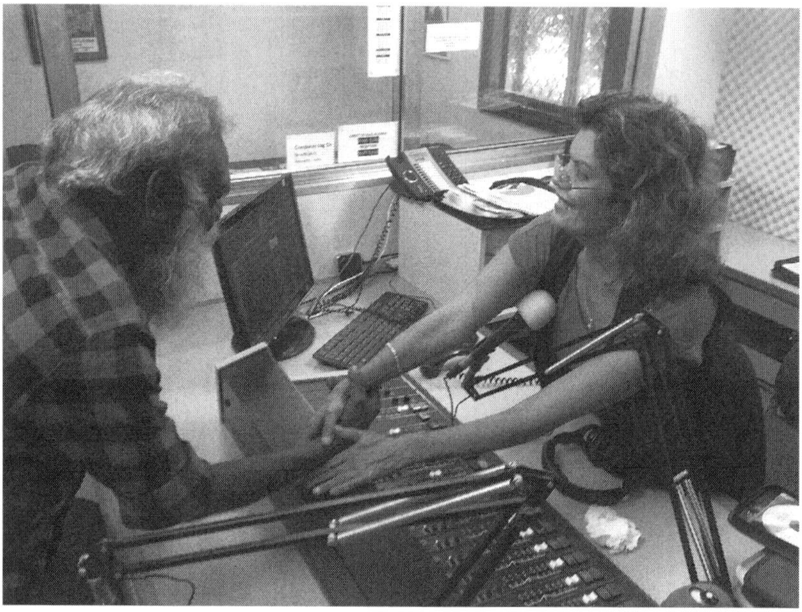

FIGURE 12. Mark Moora and Sandy Dann after their interview at Radio Goolarri.

Typically, the filmmaking process is divided into stages anchored around the film shoot, which is otherwise known as the "production" stage. The "preproduction" stage includes everything preceding the shoot, including grants, storyboarding, logistic planning, and other preparations. The film work following the intensive shoot is distilled as "postproduction," which emphasizes editing though includes other concurrent processes. When the "final cut" of a film is completed, the process shifts toward the "circulation" stage of its screening at festivals, cinemas, and/or on television.

However, the Balgo films I worked on lacked this typical distinction between postproduction and circulation. Rather, there was a conversation around arranged footage that gradually expanded outward over time: from the filmmakers to the video editor, to film participants, to the community, to the region, to remote media networks, and then to national and international networks. These expanding circles of circulation began the moment the *Tjawa Tjawa* shoot ended, and vacillated between sociable and lonesome processes through which the film came into being. The gradual increase of the film's social exposure was partly due to labor practicalities and the distance between Balgo and PAKAM's hub in Broome. It was defined by palya creative processes in Balgo and the political urgencies of the moment. During each expansion, there was a sense that the film was not an end unto itself, but a means, or vehicle, for engaging crucial issues in Balgo and other Aboriginal communities. The on-air discussion between Mark and Sandy epitomized this expansive process, as a moment that was about, yet beyond, *Tjawa Tjawa*. Through the imaginative medium of radio, their discussion was delicately subtle, all the while broadcasting to every listener across the nation tuned in to the National Indigenous Radio Service.[1]

In this chapter I trace the expanding circles of engagement that blend the postproduction and circulation stages of *Tjawa Tjawa*. I begin by discussing the processes that directly followed the film shoot, including translation and the vacillation between solitary video editing and collective social editing, often described as "fix 'em up." I then describe how mid-process screenings gradually proceeded toward *Tjawa Tjawa*'s premiere in a Balgo film festival. *Tjawa Tjawa*'s circulatory circle then expanded across the region through the National Remote Indigenous Media Festival in the regional community of Lajamanu, which balanced screenings with active training and workshops that actively articulated Aboriginal production values. Finally, I describe the extension of *Tjawa Tjawa* onto global stages, including international film festivals in Sydney, Toronto, and New York, as well as into online streaming and broadcasting through National Indigenous Television (NITV) and Indigenous Community Television (ICTV).

"Fix 'em up"

Postproduction includes activities such as translation, mid-process screenings, and additional "pick up" shots—though it is most closely associated with film editing. But what is that exactly? Anita Chang frames it temporally, noting that "Editing is organizing time. Footage that was shot in the past is brought into the present, to be seen in the future" (2022, 128). This speaks to Gilles Deleuze's (1989) conception of cinema as a time-image that is more about the manipulation of temporality than movement. Editors construct films on a "timeline," which involves not only the rearrangement of footage but also the cut scenes (usually a vast majority) that are torn out of it entirely. And yet, for all of its fourth-dimensional orchestration—or perhaps because of it—editing tends to be rendered invisible for audiences. The technical manipulation of images and sounds rarely rise to conscious awareness, even in the compressed temporal frenzy of a montage.

I aim to reveal the importance of such often-hidden postproduction practices in the Aboriginal projects I collaborated on. Especially noteworthy was the alternating and stark contrast between lonely and collective aspects. I emphasize community mid-process screenings not simply as moments for the editor to receive feedback, but as *fix 'em up* sessions of social editing that were as important and agentive as the computer editor's decisions. The construction and reconstruction of time within these edits flowed back and forth between forms of editing, unfolding largely beyond timelines and outside of electronic rectangles. In short, social editing *was* video editing, and involved multiple levels of translation.

Translations

After the *Tjawa Tjawa* film shoot concluded, I returned with the PAKAM crew from Balgo to Broome along with three Kukatja translators. Supported by the relatively generous budget of the project, an entire week of dedicated translation was scheduled in Broome. Although Mark and other film narrators had recorded in both Kukatja *and* English, the consensus goal was for the final cut to be fully in subtitled Kukatja, with the English versions serving as helpful context for translators and editors. The final cut was to be 13.5 minutes long, and the only way to edit the story appropriately was to translate several hours of Kukatja footage so that the narrative could be constructed within the broader story context.

Even with five full days and three translators, this process was intensive. Each morning, PAKAM manager Neil Turner and other crew members picked up the translators, either at their relatives' houses or from dorms across the street at the University of Notre Dame Broome. For a few hours in the morning and a few more after lunch, PAKAM was buzzing with the work of translation in three different rooms, where a crew member worked alongside each translator. To complete the extensive translation work in a week, each line was handwritten in notebooks in lieu of the longer process of embedding text into the digital footage within the editing program. Due to the labor of translation, making films in Aboriginal languages regularly doubles postproduction work. That said, virtually all involved in those films argued that this was more than worth the effort. Mark often emphasized the imperative of featuring Kukatja within films, stating, “You know, that’s what the main thing is, looking after our language. We’re alright as long as we’ve still got languages. Yuwai.”

At the end of this lively week, I drove the translators home to Balgo. Back in Broome, the next step consisted of embedding these initial translations into the subtitles for all of the footage within the editing timeline. Therefore, it was crucial that the initial notebook translation had recorded the exact start and end time stamps for each phrase. This tedious process contrasted with the previous week’s gregarious translation. It was difficult and even isolating at times. However, it was essential in preparing the project so that an editor could begin arranging key scenes together for the “rough,” or initial, cut of the film.

Since the translators returned to Balgo after that first week, having a producer who broadly understood the film’s language was crucial. Neil not only had virtually unmatched experience in producing Aboriginal media projects, but he also held broad understandings of the overarching Pama-Nyungan family of Western Desert languages. He had facilitated some of the very first Aboriginal video projects while living in the Pitjantjatjara community of Ernabella (now Pukatja) in South Australia in the early 1980s. Through these experiences he became fluent in Pitjantjatjara. While distinct from Kimberley coastal languages near Broome, Pitjantjatjara shares many elements with Kukatja. As the son of a linguist, Neil had a long-standing interest in the deeper aspects of Aboriginal languages and the nuances of translation. As he noted on multiple occasions, “In another life I reckon I might have been a linguist, or even an anthropologist.”

His linguistic knowledge was especially important in moments when translators had to navigate what was culturally dignified for them to say. For example, in one section of the film’s story, the ancestral men and women were burned to ashes, creating the dry white salt lake of Wilikinkarra (Lake Mackay). The transcript noted that the women then came back to life by sprinkling themselves with the men's urine. However, Neil noticed that the word spoken in the film did not seem to match what had been translated. When he called Mark to ask him about this, I could hear laughter through the phone as he explained to Neil, "Hah, women can't tell you what that is!" As it turned out, they had translated "semen" as "urine," since it was undignified for them to relay this in such a setting.

Susan Gal describes translation as a family of semiotic processes that "purport to change the form, the social place, or the meaning of a text, object, person, or practice while simultaneously seeming to keep something about it the same" (2015, 226). The challenge of what she distills as "sameness-in-difference" imparts much of the sentiment that Wilhelm von Humboldt identified in back in 1796:

> All translation seems to me simply an attempt to solve an impossible task. Every translator is doomed to be done in by one of two stumbling blocks: he will either stay too close to the original, at the cost of taste and the language of his nation, or he will adhere too closely to the characteristics peculiar to his nation, at the cost of the original. The medium between the two is not only difficult, but downright impossible. (quoted in Wilss 1982, 35)

Most of the discussions on translation had to do with this fine balance between precision and comprehension. Mark Cochrane—the primary video editor—and Neil held overlapping though disparate commitments on the spectrum between precision and comprehension trade-offs. In short, Neil translated like a linguist and Mark like a video editor. Wanting to get it right, Neil focused on making sure that translations were as close to what was said in Kukatja as possible. Mark, an accomplished and creative video editor, was more inclined toward adapting approximations that audiences might better understand amid quickly paced visual storytelling. As he would often say about video editing, "Film is not about a perfect translation. It's about the story."

In addition to the tension between precision and comprehension, there were sometimes debates on the nature of orthographic accuracy itself. This was less of an issue in *Tjawa Tjawa,* with its large budget employing multiple translators, but for leaner films this was a more common point of gentle contention. Disagreements on the correct spelling of words were founded upon deeper philosophical debates regarding the primacy of missionary dictionaries versus current community members' expertise and consensus. Such exchanges quickly delved into the murky waters of definitive spellings in the context of long-standing oral languages. Knowing this, opinions on related matters tended to be held lightly.

The Lone Editor

"Ah, you're still here too," Mark Cochrane observes, barely glancing up from his screen as I enter the editing room in the corner of the PAKAM shed. The windowless walls betray no hint of the hour. The desktop, keyboard, and external hard drive are illuminated by a faintly humming florescent light. It is six in the evening and everyone else has been gone for an hour. As a whitefella video editor who worked for years in Sydney advertising firms, long hours of editing are old hat for Mark. "Have a look at this. Fresh eyes would help," he manages, gesturing me toward the backless rolling chair next to him. He is working on a fire effect in Final Cut 7 for a crucial scene in *Tjawa Tjawa*. In this moment, the traveling women and their new lovers are being dramatically burned—resulting in the white ashen appearance of Lake Mackay—before the women come back to life to travel onward. Mark is assembling several versions involving multiple layers of fire overlaid onto the footage of the lake. I point out my favorite, the simplest one with fire at only the bottom of the screen. Without moving his gaze, he chuckles, noting,

> Yeah, I figured. That was the first one I did, hours ago. I've been trying to do something more elaborate, but as usual, the first instinct is the right one. No worries, just a couple more hours to go. I like working here at night, when it's quiet and no one is around. It's fun. Editing is the art of making something out of nothing. But it also gets lonely. Editing is a lonely job.

The process of building a rough cut far from Balgo often involved long hours of solitary labor, unlike the social editing that was to follow.

Not unlike anthropologists curating written field notes to write an ethnography, for filmmakers it is a professional truism that editing choices are among the most consequential. Editing includes reviewing the footage, cutting relevant clips, and arranging them into a coherent narrative, as well as adding transitions, effects, and visual and audio overlays. Despite the monumental importance of this process, it is usually rendered invisible to audiences. Most editors who have been confronted with ample footage have faced moments in which the sheer number of choices became momentarily paralyzing. Mark Cochrane often elaborated on the innumerable decisions an editor faces when constructing a narrative. When he mused that editing was "the art of making something out of nothing," he was not disparaging footage as nothing, but rather the opposite, speaking to its ability to contain multitudes. To put it another way, "Film is about something, whereas reality is not" (Vaughan 1974, 80).

While a skillful editor (or ethnographer) can make a final structure and form seem inevitable, the reality is quite the opposite. The invisibility of video editing and ethnographic writing is what makes their concealment and revelation so illuminating. Behind Oz's curtain is a temporal magician doing their best: pulling levers, projecting images, and summoning apparitions to project as faithful of a reality as they can manage. As much as PAKAM and *Tjawa Tjawa* embodied collaboration, editing often requires a period of focused attention by a single individual who can hold all of the elements in a relational balance within their mind, at least as a starting point.

Providing a portrait in contrast to the bustling work of translation, Mark labored on the *Tjawa Tjawa* edit for days on end in PAKAM's back corner room, regularly staying past 8 p.m. Yet, as Goolarri's head of television, he was not originally meant to edit this film. After *Tjawa Tjawa*'s production and translation, everyone on that trip was understandably exhausted. One crew member attempted a basic assemble (placing scenes in very approximate sequence), though NITV's deadline loomed and that person had other projects calling as well. In an effort to inject renewed energy after an intensive production process, Neil recruited Mark by simply walking behind their contiguous sheds, through Goolarri's sliding glass door, and asking if he could "jump onto the project." Sharing labor between PAKAM and Goolarri was relatively common. For example, shortly before the *Tjawa Tjawa* shoot, Goolarri's sound recordist, Arthur, joined the crew. After weeks of full-time editing in consultation with Neil and other crew members, Mark presented a rough cut of the film to be shared in Balgo.

While becoming the editor in this impromptu way was atypical, the broader dynamic of a whitefella editor spending long hours assembling a rough cut was a fairly common occurrence. At Goolarri, Mark was one of very few whitefellas on staff. He and another whitefella, Nigel, were the most active editors during this time. Both could often be found working much of the day within video-editing timelines. As with Mark in *Tjawa Tjawa,* Nigel was the primary editor of *Naji* (2014), Goolarri's Songlines on Screen project during this same period.

Just before I left Broome to spend months in Balgo shortly after the *Tjawa Tjawa* shoot, Neil and I were sitting in his office, reviewing the details for my impending trip. After we double-checked the troopy and all of the equipment, I was ready to go. He sent me off with a spirited goodbye in front of the monumental iron shed door. As I was making a three-point turn to leave, he added, "Oh yes, one more thing: It's great of course if you can jump-start and support projects, but remember, black hands on camera!" I had heard Neil say this several times before, and as he previously explained, he meant that it was important that Aboriginal crew members do the actual camera and production work whenever possible. Although he was approaching this boundary of engagement in a lighthearted way, his comment spoke to PAKAM's clear perspective on collaboration in Aboriginal media.

He and other media managers emphasized Aboriginal camerawork more than video editing, partly due to the latter's often solitary quality. As Mark Cochrane noted, within the social life of a film, digital video editing was often quite isolating and was among the least-popular film roles for Aboriginal crew and community members. This preference was pronounced in Balgo, where staring at a computer alone for long hours was generally considered to be whitefella behavior. In contrast, film trips and shoots were imbued with social complexity. Furthermore, who held the camera—an act seen by all in the film shoot and in production photos—conveyed much about who held the ultimate creative power in a project. However, even when there was a lone whitefella editor in a back room, their rough cut was not the end but simply the beginning of a dynamic social-editing process.

Social Editing

Nearly every media project I worked on included multiple mid-process screenings. These were not retrospective stamps of approval. Rather, they initiated complex discussions on how to reimagine various aspects of the film, with the rough cut serving only as a starting point. "Alright, let's fix 'em up," was often the first comment uttered at the start of a Balgo social-editing session. I consider *fix 'em up* as a local analytic encompassing an implicit theory regarding the purpose and process of editing itself. It metaphorically imagined the rough cut as a troopy that required repairs. Along with other regularly used aphorisms and metaphors of mobility, it implied the importance of the cinematic process as a vehicle to be adjusted and tweaked along the way, toward the collective purpose of the journey.

There is a long history of mid-process screenings in anthropological filmmaking. Some of the earliest were conceptualized and practiced by French anthropologist and filmmaker Jean Rouch. He framed such sessions as an audiovisual countergift, which served as "a catalyst for the development of mutual understanding" (Henley 2010, 316). This sensibility also applied to the screenings in Balgo. They took place in various circumstances, from small dark rooms to makeshift cinemas under the stars, and from as few as two people to dozens, whose distance spanned from a short walk to a day's drive. Due to my flexible schedule, I was often tasked by PAKAM with facilitating mid-process screenings in Balgo, including multiple for *Tjawa Tjawa*. While time consuming, these screening trips were essential. At one level, they provided feedback for Mark Cochrane's edit back in Broome; however, they were much more than stakeholder thoughts. They represented a different, yet no less crucial editing process.

When digital video editing took place in the same community in which it was filmed, *fix 'em up* screenings were even more embedded within the initial editing process. This was true in *Kurrarlkatjanu* as well as another film I assisted on titled *Dunba* (2015). The latter was a thirteen-minute NITV documentary that followed the life story of Dunba

Nunju—an Elder and healer from the community of Beagle Bay who PAKAM director Henry Augustine had long planned to make a film about. We shot it over an extended weekend, as Henry and I traveled with Dunba up the coast of the Dampier Peninsula to his favorite fishing spots. The shoot highlighted the Sacred Heart Church in Beagle Bay, made famous by its pearl shell–adorned altar that he had helped to construct. I assisted with the technical aspects of the filmmaking process as Henry shot and directed it. I helped to set up the camera and sound equipment, confirming that everything was running smoothly so that they could focus on the story. In postproduction, Henry similarly asked me to assist on the technical components of digital video editing.

From most understandings of film labor, I would have been considered the editor. However, in this project Henry was the more important and consequential editor. After stripping away the surface meanings of film titles, the editor, like the director, is best described as the person making the key decisions to enact a clear and focused

FIGURE 13. Henry Augustine filming Dunba Nunju at Dunba's favorite fishing spot.

vision. Much like an orchestra conductor who guides the music without directly playing it, Henry would often joke, “You are my fingers on the computer,” or even “You *are* my computer, ha ha.” I was a social interface through which he would construct the film. It was Henry's vision that we were working toward. While it was certainly a collaborative process, he more than anyone was most crucial in both the initial rough cut and the social editing *fix 'em up* processes.

For several days after our shoot, I slept in a canvas swag in the PAKAM media trailer in Beagle Bay, importing and roughly organizing the footage. Although Henry was busy with various community and family obligations, he made frequent visits. During these, he described the film's structure from granular details to its broadest purpose as we watched the current draft. Viewing them within the editing suite, we discussed both the video output in the top right of the screen as well as the composition of audio and visual clips within the timeline.

Henry did not concern himself with every technical detail of video production. However, as a longtime media maker he had a comprehensive vision, especially since this was a project he and Dunba had planned for several years. Knowing I would be the fingers on the keyboard, they had thoughtfully communicated this vision throughout the shoot itself. In this way, their social editing was embedded within each of our shoots. When something important happened, Henry was careful to let me know exactly why and in what way. This contradicts best practices in most filmmaking industries of selecting someone uninvolved in the shoot to bring “fresh eyes.” Conversely, palya values are at times better served when editors have been engaged throughout the social life of a film. This experience is often crucial for understanding cultural nuances and establishing the relationships necessary for social editing.

For example, at a key point in the shoot, Henry encouraged Dunba to repeat off-camera comments about the complexity of forgiveness. As I stood there with them, the gravity of this intimate scene was so clear that Henry did not even mention it to me, though he commented “Yeah, that's the moment” during one *fix 'em up* discussion. Such emotional imprints were, in effect, analog versions of the digital markers that film editors use to tag their first impressions of the scenes most essential to a story. Henry also explicitly described what was important to emphasize during shoots and editing. For example, he often reiterated that although Dunba might be shy on camera, we should aim to capture his affable nature and "show him laughing and smiling, because that's how Dunba is in normal life." Therefore, we included virtually every instance of him expressing joy from our footage. Many moments of background levity would likely have been cut by an editor with fresh eyes in the context of serious themes, yet they added complexity and character truth that Henry understood.

Another common issue of translation related to whether or not to subtitle an Aboriginal person who was speaking in English. On the one hand, it is a seemingly reasonable and accessibility-minded request for a broadcaster to subtitle any speaker that audiences would not easily understand. However, in the case of Aboriginal Elders the act of subtitling their English was viewed by some community and crew members as disrespectful or even insulting. Before we drove up to Beagle Bay, Neil had the foresight to discuss this issue with Henry and me. Dunba was known to be quite shy and soft-spoken. Based upon Henry's past footage of him, Neil was concerned that NITV might request subtitles, since this project was intended for a national audience. Both Neil and Henry wanted to avoid this, noting that this could implicitly denigrate the speaking ability of Dunba, a masterful storyteller. To avoid this, throughout the shoot we were focused on making sure that the audio was recorded as clearly and loudly as possible. At the end of the editing process, we were pleased that this was effective, as NITV agreed that the film would not require subtitles. Other film processes similarly anticipated issues of subtitling Elders in English.[2]

Overall, Henry was less interested in technical details like transition fades and audio correction than in higher-order elements. For example, he often made comments such as "That section goes on too long here, giving the wrong impression," "That transition is a bit off of the message we want to send," or "This part is a bit too depressing; mix it up with some of the happier moments to show who Dunba really is." When something was not quite right, he would point and say "Rub that part out." This was a common phrase in various *fix 'em up* editing sessions. It was usually accompanied by a gesture that mimed how one physically erases part of a sand drawing, a ubiquitous representational practice in desert communities. After making a variety of constructive comments, Henry would often confidently assert that the film would work out in the end, with encouragements including "No worries, mate. There's no rush. We'll just keep at it: slowly, slowly." The film process became integrated within his daily PAKAM radio show, which he conducted in the same trailer room where I slept and worked on the edit, and during which we often chatted on air about the process. As he emphasized to the community in these shows, it was important that we took our time and got it right.

After a week of editing, Henry followed a viewing with a gradually expanding wide grin, noting, "I reckon it's pretty good. Let's show Dunba." Later that day, the three of us sat down in the PAKAM trailer and watched it in full-screen mode. Pleased with the draft, and with his characteristically understated depth, Dunba smiled and said, "Yeah. Good one." Then, after thinking for a minute in silence, he started to tell us what watching the film made him remember. As I came to learn, a key sign of a palya response in social editing came down to the connections that it sparked beyond the film itself. When social editing was

FIGURE 14. Henry Augustine and Dunba Nunju watching the rough cut of *Dunba*.

done appropriately, it became a vehicle for the memories of its makers. Often the screenings toward the end of the editing process were more about the act of engagement than making further technical changes.

Social editing in larger projects often catalyzed discussions around current community issues. In his work with Ayoreo communities in collaborative film projects, Lucas Bessire describes the way in which "nightly screenings incite village-wide debates that influence subsequent filmic decisions and accumulate through further screenings. What arises is a unique collective meta-commentary about existence, practice, causality, and event" (2017, 121). As with intimate social editing, the most important outcome in bigger groups included, yet often expanded beyond, technical editing decisions.

This was the case in *Tjawa Tjawa,* which involved the most complex and extended *fix 'em up* process I participated in. Following the primary shoot, I returned to Balgo five times (2014–15) with various crew members to work on different elements of postproduction, with the first trip being to return the translators home. In each subsequent visit, I engaged with mid-process screenings while also collaborating on projects inspired in the wake of *Tjawa Tjawa.*

In December 2014, I traveled to Balgo with a rough cut of *Tjawa Tjawa* that Mark Cochrane and Neil felt was coherent enough to begin workshopping. I arrived with several USB drives containing the *Tjawa Tjawa* edit, in addition to copies of all of the other recent Balgo film projects. Since Mark Moora was the director and primary storyteller, it was crucial that he watch it before expanding the screening circle. Sitting down with him in the PAKAM radio station, I dragged the file onto the computer, double-clicked it, and pressed play. Mark's meticulous silence was interrupted only by sparse laughter. When we reached the end, he simply said, "Let's watch 'em again." After viewing it two more times, Mark sat back and with a smile noted, "That's a true story. Yeah, palya. Let's go show my sisters."

We made our way to Kapululangu at their preferred visiting time, just after lunch. Zohl, its executive director, and all of the Elders huddled around the TV amidst an air of excitement. As beds and chairs scraped toward their viewing locations, I connected my laptop to the TV. Now settled, Mark and the five senior Elders were seated in front with a few family members and caretakers behind them on the edges of beds around the room. We watched it three times in quick succession. Unlike the previous screenings with Mark, the audience interacted with the film throughout. When the women began singing on-screen, their off-screen selves joined in. Mark and the women Elders, led by his sister Payi Payi, made comments throughout such as "That's true! It's right. Palya." They also pointed to the direction of the specific places from their current geographic location and orientation, noting, "That's good Country." As with *Dunba,* the aim of the screening was deeper than making sure that the women were simply happy with the film draft, and I took detailed notes on their many levels of feedback, including the subtlety embedded within hand sign gestures. This first broad social-editing session was also important for reiterating and confirming film permission agreements. Over the next several days, Mark and other community members provided a variety of *fix 'em up* corrections and adjustments, which I carefully added to my list to convey to Mark Cochrane.

The most animated discussions centered around who had the authority to tell this Songline story and to which audiences. These debates

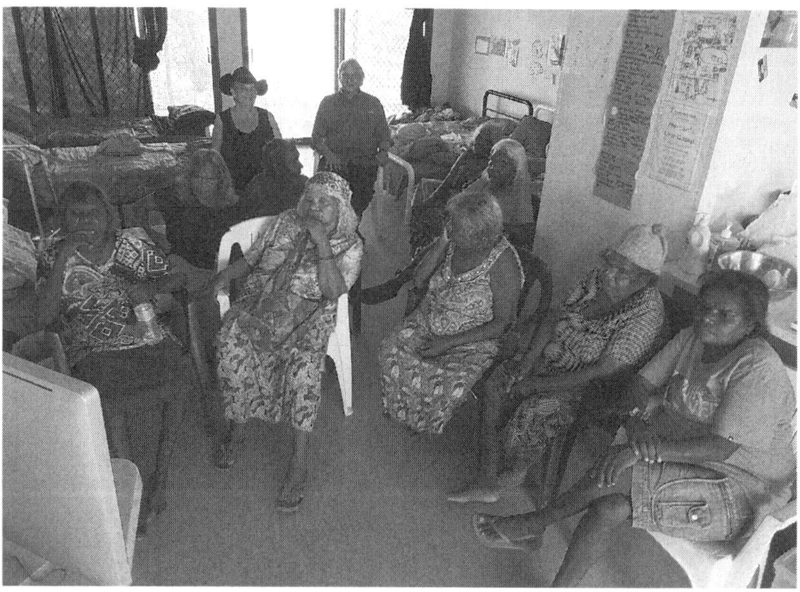

FIGURE 15. Screening *Tjawa Tjawa* at the women's center in Balgo.

had less to do with the particularities of the film edit and more with whether it was appropriate for Mark to narrate the story of *Tjawa Tjawa* in this context at all. Crucially, Bob Dingle—an Elder of Mark's—had ultimately declined to participate in both *Tjawa Tjawa* and its precursor, *Kurrarlkatjanu: The Last Generation.* While it remains unclear to me whether Bob had ever planned on participating, or was cautiously navigating the process of avoiding a direct "no," by all accounts his concerns were clear. He was worried about the potential repercussions of disclosing sacred knowledge and being critiqued by other Elders in the region who might decide to cause him harm by "singing him."[3]

An influential community member in Balgo also brought up the question of whether the story should be shared so widely. She agreed with Bob that it was possibly dangerous. When I asked Mark and the Elder women what they thought about this, they responded, "It's alright. We'll speak to them and they will understand." Over the following days, these issues seemed to somehow become resolved. As Mark often noted about this topic more broadly, "Some people are a bit worried about getting sung, but I told them don't worry, I'll make everyone understand, and if they have a problem they can talk to me." In shouldering the responsibility for the film, Mark was able to keep the project moving forward while quelling enduring concerns.

Expanding Circles of Circulation

Usually, after editing in solitude, the final cut is revealed to the world in a festival. And yet, this standard cinema process also did not apply to the films I collaborated on. For example, in *Tjawa Tjawa* there was instead a remarkably gradual broadening of audience conversations, as it moved from the initial to the final draft, which gradually expanded across time and space from Balgo to international media stages. This process moved slowly and surely, from Mark watching it closely, to its first showing at the women's center, and then to various other social screenings. The premiere of the final cut in Balgo was not so much an unveiling as it was the continuation of an ongoing discussion.

In this section I trace the expanding circles of *Tjawa Tjawa*'s circulation from the Balgo premiere through regional, national, and international mediascapes. I highlight its screening at the National Remote

Indigenous Media Festival (NRIMF) in the relatively nearby community of Lajamanu. *Tjawa Tjawa*'s organic movement outward from Balgo was not simply geographic, but also relational as it spread throughout overlapping kinship and media networks.

Tjawa Tjawa's World Premiere in Balgo

When Mark Moora returned to Sandy's show later that same week, the foundation of their first interview changed the quality of their discussion from that of a radio chat to something both more intimate and political. They discussed *Tjawa Tjawa* briefly, though for both of them this was simply a springboard for engaging larger issues, including the specter of defunding Western Australian communities. As Mark told her toward the end of this expansive chat, "That's why I'm making films. It's good to make movies to help people understand what we know. It might get them to help us. You never know in the future. I hope somebody helps us." As Sandy closed the show, she thanked Mark and said, "You're not just a guest now. You've become a friend. Thank you for sharing your stories. These are the kinds of things that will keep our communities going during difficult times. Bless you."

Not only did discussions about *Tjawa Tjawa* spark the kind of broader conversations Mark and Sandy shared, but so too did the screenings of the final cut, especially in Balgo. I attended dozens of its screenings in various settings in Balgo. While some were large, many included just a few individuals. As with the first screening to Dunba, these smaller sessions tended to remind viewers of people, places, and times past, often leading to long conversations afterward. The difference between social editing and final cut screenings was subtle and of degree rather than kind, instigating broad discussions beyond the film itself. While social editing emphasized community feedback for the in-process film, screenings of the final cut amplified collective reflections on family, Country, and politics often lasting hours. The screenings had a discursive quality due to the social context fostered in such interactive co-viewings (Spitulnik 2002). Amid the ongoing weight of colonial dispossession in Balgo, the screenings visualized "emergent subjects in a place where world-ending violence is a taken-for-granted historical event" (Bessire 2017, 121). There was no need to explain such stakes of representation in Balgo. As Grace Dillon puts it,

"The Native Apocalypse, if contemplated seriously, has already taken place" (2012, 8).

I often assisted media makers and art center workers in organizing larger community viewings. After one such screening of *Tjawa Tjawa*, a close relative of Mark's came up to me and said,

> I loved that film because when you watch it you feel the land. We have to balance kartiya and Tjukurrpa to be strong. That's the only way to a bright future. We need the old people. They know how to live and what is right and wrong. There is a big black hole that some young people have. Old people never suicide or anything like that, because they talk to the land. When you talk to the land, it talks to you. It's a good film, a true film.

To explain a Balgo film festival, it is critical to first understand community legacies of suicide and other acts of profound self-harm. Suicide had reached multiple crisis points throughout the previous decade. In Balgo in 2009 the suicide rate was one hundred times higher than the state average and arguably the worst globally per capita (Hope 2012, 38). Mainstream psychological approaches provide profoundly incomplete frameworks for understanding the rise in Aboriginal suicide, as they are embedded within ongoing legacies of colonization that inflict immense harm to families, communities, and Country (Tatz 2001; Trudgen 2000). Media- and music-making have long been locally identified as preventative measures. This insight led to the successful funding of an expansion at Warlayirti Artists to include the media-creation and music-recording spaces that exist today adjacent to the culture center space. In the years following these additions there was an explosion of media- and music-making, supported by grant-funded whitefella facilitators.

Community members overwhelmingly agreed to focus these initial media around vehicles, imagined broadly as the Motika (Motor car) Project. In the spirit of the popular Warlpiri *Bush Mechanics* show—which demonstrated various creative and comedic vehicle repairs on Country—this led to a series of video and music recordings about adventures in vehicles around the region that included comedies, music videos, and a horror short. It also involved videos warning local youth about the dangers of huffing petrol, a practice that had caused rampant brain damage to young community members in previous years. Suicide rates did decrease during and beyond these projects, a correlation often emphasized by community members. However, as one art manager noted, "Of course the funding ran out quickly with little possibility for continued support." While art centers make money, community media housed within art centers tend to rely on inconsistent external funding.[4]

Public film screenings in Balgo often coincided with broader community events. Such was the case for Balgo's golden jubilee celebration, where I assisted in organizing the screening of several locally made films in the art center, including the world premiere of *Tjawa Tjawa*'s final cut. During this fifty-year anniversary event, Mark's role in Balgo's history was celebrated by the Diocese of Broome, and he was featured on the cover of their regional magazine. We made a series of flyers for this premiere film festival, yet the only one necessary to get the word out was the initial one that we posted on the front door of the community store. After tacking it on in the morning, by the afternoon nearly everyone knew about it. While most in Balgo had already viewed *Tjawa Tjawa* through various social-editing sessions—as well as through USBs that had been circulated—there was palpable excitement for the first official community screening. The event attracted over sixty people, with dozens of kids playing just outside. After introducing the film through a portable loudspeaker in the culture center, Mark talked about the importance of keeping Balgo from being closed, as well as going back to Country in communities like Yagga Yagga. Throughout the screening itself, a buzz of quiet discussion filled the room as viewers pointed to places and people, making connections to family members and important locations. Most stayed to view dozens of other locally produced videos over the next couple of hours, which catalyzed more memories. Other Balgo film festivals took form more organically, including a series of drive-in screenings in 2016.

Arriving a half hour before sunset, I help a local youth worker to set up the drive-in. Unrolling the trusty salmon-colored extension cord across the basketball courts, we unfold two plastic tables twenty meters from the screen, itself a four-by-seven-meter section of plywood on the back of the court, painted bright primer white. As the sun sinks, we set up a

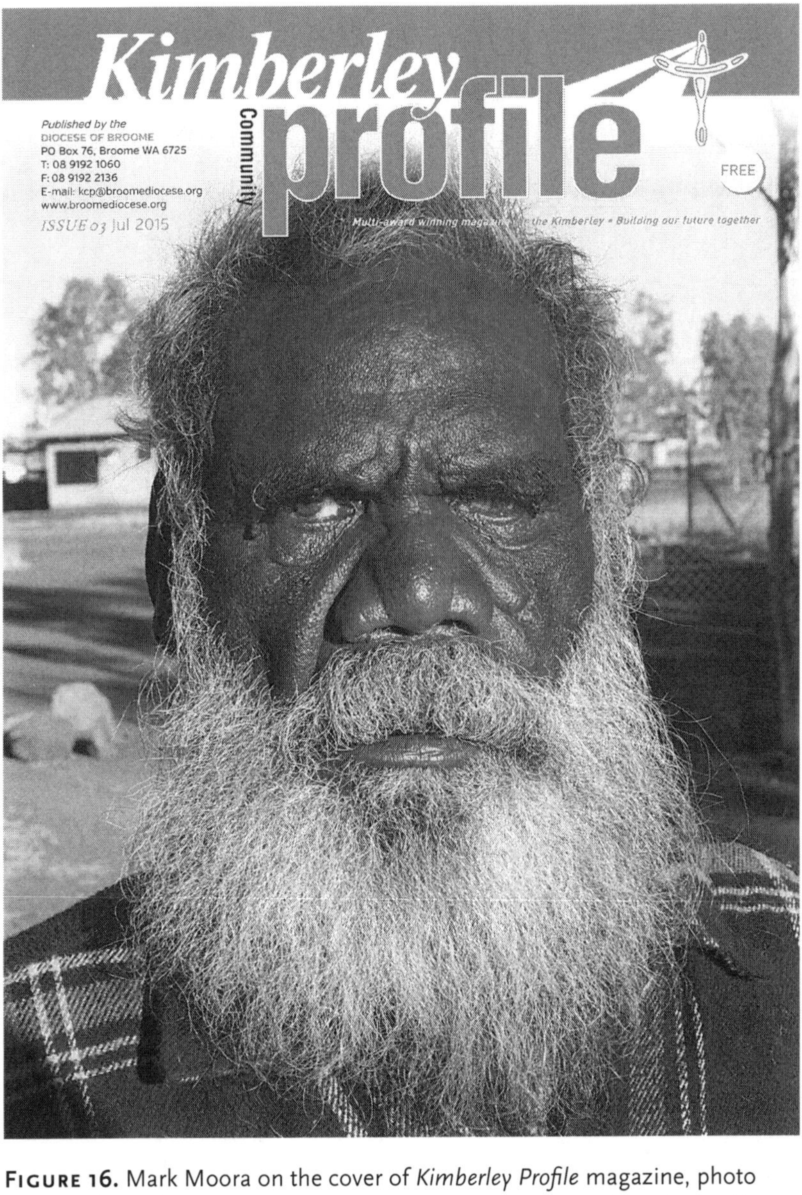

FIGURE 16. Mark Moora on the cover of *Kimberley Profile* magazine, photo taken at the Balgo golden jubilee. Photograph courtesy of *Kimberley Profile* magazine, Diocese of Broome. Used with permission of the Moora family.

microwave to make popcorn next to a cooler full of fruit and drinks. The kids arrive first. Sitting in front of the screen at dusk, they take turns trading USB sticks with the youth worker, playing photo slideshows they have meticulously set to music. As the sky pitches to black, vehicles form half rings around the screen and more and more community members gather to watch. This night is especially crowded, as we are showing not only *Tjawa Tjawa* and other Balgo films but also a recently released documentary titled *Putuparri and the Rainmakers* (2015), about going back to Country. It was filmed north of Balgo over several years, and audience members vividly describe their connections to the film throughout. Mark watches it with rapt attention, often pointing during key moments and saying "That's true" or "Yuwai." As it ends, he notes, "Yeah, I knew all of those fellas. A lot of rainmakers back then."

Tjawa Tjawa so resonated within Mark that he talked about it for weeks. Like its protagonist, he noted that he too was in a race against time to reestablish his homeland community while he was alive. As the film took him to festivals across Australia, he would emphasize this message increasingly within and beyond those trips over the following years.

FIGURE 17. Community members watching films at the Balgo drive-in.

The National Remote Indigenous Media Festival

Just as the transition from *fix 'em up* screenings to Balgo's *Tjawa Tjawa*'s premiere represented a slowly and steadily expanding circle of circulation, this also characterized its first national film festival screening. Taking place in Lajamanu—a Northern Territory community (only) a day's drive northeast from Balgo—the 2015 NRIMF incorporated several invaluable elements. Since I had attended the previous year, it was already clear to me that this was much more than a film festival, and included a host of interactive workshops, meetings, and meals. Remote media workers often highlighted the intangible social benefits of the festival. There was an indefinable atmosphere of support that permeated this networking of colleagues, bolstering its larger organizational infrastructure.

The Indigenous Remote Communications Association (IRCA) ran the weeklong NRIMF in partnership with ICTV. As the peak body for remote Indigenous Australian media, IRCA organized the events throughout the day, while ICTV sponsored extensive nightly screenings of Indigenous community films from across the continent and presented media awards at the end of the week.[5] *Tjawa Tjawa* and other

FIGURE 18. PAKAM crew at the 2014 NRIMF. Photograph by PAKAM crew; courtesy of Pilbara and Kimberley Aboriginal Media, copyright 2014.

films from the Songlines on Screen series were shown together during a special evening program. The discussions during and following the series focused on the relation of those present with the people and places in the films. The audience laughed at inside jokes and hushed to silence during pivotal moments. In an event where most people were from Aboriginal communities, the specific discussions on relationality and Country were similar to its premiere in Balgo.

Mirroring the three meanings of cinema, the NRIMF was simultaneously a product, a place, and a process. It was a product in that it provided a clear demonstration of a vertically integrated remote Aboriginal mediascape, with keynote speakers, training sessions, and a film festival including awards reaffirming organizations, filmmakers, and communities. It was placed and contextualized within Lajamanu, with Warlpiri Elders opening and guiding the festival in language throughout the week. This included taking festival participants to nearby important places on Country, which further enmeshed the week within Warlpiri relational networks. Crucially, as with the films I worked on in Balgo, the festival was ultimately more about process than product, emphasizing "the social relationship and kinship ties produced through Aboriginal media" over screenings or awards (Dowell 2013, 107). It was more than an event; it served as a media pilgrimage whereby each Remote Indigenous Media Organization (RIMO) organized, traveled to, and collectively engaged in dense experiences there and on the way.

PAKAM was known for having the most video output of any RIMO in recent years, though more important seemed to be the fact that their crew especially enjoyed the festival. Amid PAKAM's conspicuous laughter, it seemed to be common sense at the NRIMF that productivity and levity were fundamentally intertwined. This is not to suggest an idealized vision of PAKAM. Individuals there, as elsewhere, struggled with the realities of life that were often inescapable in relation to settler society. However, from the music-filled troopy trips that rumbled over corrugated roads to the joke-filled and firelit evenings in swags, there was an organizational culture of lifting and supporting one another. As Yasmine Musharbash (2008a) describes in her ethnography of daily life in the Warlpiri community of Yuendumu, sleeping near one another was foundational to the intimacy that allowed for such joviality, including light teasing about who snored and how loudly.

While I already had a sense that Neil was an exceptional RIMO manager, I only fully came to understand this at the NRIMF, where he was widely respected by all of the managers and directors of national Indigenous media bodies. They often enlisted him as a diplomat in the sector, even placing him in national peak body board positions during periods of dispute. IRCA manager Daniel Featherstone described Neil as his "mentor and model," while ICTV manager Rita Cattoni would often bring Neil up during their staff discussions, making comments such as "Let's try to imagine what Neil would say about this." In light of his experience, contributions, and reputation, it was no surprise that he received the Mr. McKenzie Lifetime Achievement Award at the NRIMF. Neil was the first whitefella to win this award, which recognized an individual's long-term contribution to remote Indigenous television. This was a particularly meaningful award for Neil, as he had worked with the award's namesake, Simon Tjiyangu McKenzie, decades earlier in Ernabella. Afterward, several people noted that it "was about time" that he won a lifetime achievement award. I highlight Neil here not simply because we worked together but because he was a model of thoughtful collaboration, as was repeatedly noted by his crew, remote community members, and throughout the Aboriginal mediascape.[6]

Overall, the NRIMF experiences not only enriched media understandings for RIMOs like PAKAM, but just as importantly, reaffirmed and forged bonds within their team and across the continent. While listening to speakers and presenting awards were core activities at the festival, it was the workshops that seemed to be most animated with vitality, as participants learned by making media together in Lajamanu. Here I turn to one of these, which embodied the power of the NRIMF workshop in collective creation. This workshop in particular provided the clearest articulation of Aboriginal production values that I encountered during my fieldwork.

Workshopping Production Values

Production values are socialized, aesthetic, and moral sensibilities set within particular worldviews. Yet when someone declares that a film has "good production values," it is rare that this is followed by the question, "*Which* values?" Unlike other value-based discourses, production values in dominant media worlds are seemingly self-evident and already known. Production values point toward what Neil often described as "flash production," a constellation of visual and audio norms around framing, movement, editing, narrative structure, color grading, sound dynamics, and pacing.

Even when fundamentally disagreeing about a film, Western film critics rarely have conflicting views on what production values reference. To this point, in "White Forms, Aboriginal Content," Mudrooroo (1995) critiques the judgment of Aboriginal creative work according to white standards and has called for novel critical frameworks to understand Aboriginal production values (Ginsburg 1995). Here I highlight how Aboriginal media makers denaturalize assumed values of production while centering others. Such distinctions reveal "regimes of value," which Arjun Appadurai (1994, 83) describes as the uneven construction of valuing cultural objects in specific contexts. Palya production values are not simply about cinematic aesthetics; more importantly, they center the production process itself as the pathway for doing things in the good and proper way.

Throughout dozens of film projects, a system of production values emerged. This was made most explicit during a three-day NRIMF workshop I participated in, led by Pauline Clague (Yaegl) and Cornel Ozies (Djugun), whose own backgrounds demonstrated the Aboriginal mediascape's interconnections. For years, Pauline had served as the commissioning editor for NITV, where she developed the Our Stories, Our Way, Everyday program that funded dozens of RIMO documentaries, including *Dunba* (2015). More recently she was instrumental in initiating and running the Winda Film Festival, developed in partnership with the imagineNATIVE Film + Media Arts Festival in Toronto.

Cornel grew up in Broome and began his media career working at Goolarri, where he was trained as a video editor. As he noted in this workshop, "I got tired of sitting in a dark room looking at other people's footage. I wanted to get out there and make my own." He worked on the locally produced SBS TV miniseries *The Circuit* (2007), which followed the story of the circuit court in the Kimberley. He described gaining the confidence to push himself after being mentored by cinematographer Joe Pickering, the same media mentor from *Tjawa Tjawa*. Like many who started at Goolarri, Cornel was guided in how to navigate the broader Australian mediascape. He attended the prestigious Australian Film Television and Radio School and worked on a variety of film and TV projects. He went on to become the director of photography for Wawili Pitjas, the family media production company run by his mother Mitch Torres. Wawili Pitjas was the third Broome-based organization to receive one of the ten grants to produce a Songlines on Screen film. Cornel was deeply involved in that film, titled *Footprints* (2014).

Pauline began the workshop with a broader discussion of voice, noting: "In the end, voice is what matters most. What is important is for you to find your voice, your own personality. The more money you get and the more people are involved in it, the more that others will tell you what your voice is. You need to know what you want to say so that you can hold onto that throughout the process." As Daniel Fisher argues, voice "does more than simply echo an Indigenous agency; it also gathers to itself powerful, at times incommensurable agencies and interests" (2016, 250). Pauline emphasized having one's own voice as essential. She noted that while accomplishing a big-budget project could be great, it was usually easier to retain one's voice in smaller-budget films.

This workshop extended beyond the tenets taught in a typical Introductory to Documentary course. It articulated how Aboriginal media makers could draw on Western production values while simultaneously subverting how these values reinforce unequal power relations. Beginning with Bill Nichols's canonical framework (1991), our first lesson was to go through his typology of six modes of documentary film, including poetic, observational, reflective, expository, participatory, and performative. Pauline explained how each style had historically represented Aboriginal people, noting that "You can tell which government is in power based on documentary styles of the time." For example, she illustrated how expository ("voice of god") projects were dominant under Liberal (right-wing) governments, largely because they let narrators declare what is true about subjects. While she presented each mode as having advantages and dangers, she encouraged participatory projects, noting that "it would be good for our mob to do that, because they are from their communities."

Cornel discussed practical filmmaking strategies by showing how they have been historically used to disempower Aboriginal people. He began by stating that "we are used to seeing how others have shot us. Having watched all of those programs, we sometimes can even replicate what they have done to us. Be aware of that and change it in your own films." For example, he described the classic rule of thirds, a fundamental principle that photographers and cinematographers use to frame images. He explained how this rule can structure the power dynamic between the filmmaker, subject, and audience. He showed examples in which experts are framed in the middle as well as how subjects can be framed sympathetically with their eye at the intersecting top third looking across the open space in a frame.

He provided several examples of how Aboriginal people are regularly shot from above, looking down at them on the ground, and visually communicating inferiority. "You want to be aware of these things and power up that person using frame and perspective," he noted. In addition to the angle and framing of subjects, he discussed how color-grading tools in video-editing programs are optimized for light skin, especially in commonly used "three-way color correctors." This was a topic that Goolarri video editors often emphasized, noting strategies for mindfully color-grading films featuring Aboriginal people, as well as the history of physical film and skin tone.[7]

In reflecting on this workshop, I came to realize that many of these values were embedded within *Tjawa Tjawa*. The late director of photography Clint Dixon (who worked for years with Cornel, a family member of his) went to great lengths to make sure that Mark was positioned and lit just right. When sitting, Mark was consciously framed using the rule of thirds with the camera close to the ground. During the most crucial sections, including the film's intro and conclusion, Mark was standing up and placed in the center, communicating expertise. Throughout, the camera was not raised above his eye line, and we would often use sun filters and reflectors to make sure that he was not washed out by the contrast of bright backgrounds, which would have been difficult to correct in postproduction color grading.

Cornel also described why he decided to violate basic rule-of-thirds framing during some of the interviews for *Footprints,* showing faces pointed away from the open space, which subconsciously communicated an unsettling feeling to the audience. He noted that visual rules are typically based on making audiences feel comfortable, but that there are certain topics that should make them uncomfortable, especially around Indigenous politics. Gesturing the hand sign for "begin rolling"

FIGURE 19. PAKAM film crew setting up for a *Tjawa Tjawa* shoot. Photograph by PAKAM crew; courtesy of Pilbara and Kimberley Aboriginal Media, copyright 2014.

FIGURE 20. Mark Moora being filmed at ground level during a *Tjawa Tjawa* shoot. Photograph by PAKAM crew; courtesy of Pilbara and Kimberley Aboriginal Media, copyright 2014.

FIGURE 21. Mark Moora carefully lit in a cropped film still of *Tjawa Tjawa*. Photograph by PAKAM crew; courtesy of Pilbara and Kimberley Aboriginal Media, copyright 2014.

(drawing a circle in the air vertically and perpendicular to the body), Cornel emphasized the value of using signs during film shoots, which communicate without adding unwanted audio to the footage.

This workshop of sixteen people, including a few whitefellas such as myself, was as practical as it was conceptual. It included classroom instruction in the mornings and active practice in the afternoons with iPads shared between partners. Each of the eight pairs shot and edited a short film about the local library and art center, including *Painting Bush Potato* (2015), which I collaborated on with Mark Pindan in subtitled Warlpiri. Shooting and watching eight films on the same subject allowed us to collectively share footage and photos, as well as see just how differently people imagine the same places.

Pauline and Cornel skillfully distilled many crucial aspects of filmmaking, including community control of footage, how release forms are explained, and other responsibilities that extend beyond legalistic frameworks. While they discussed films shoots, they gestured toward a broader value system of production around a dignified and appropriate—or palya—process. Resonating with Audra Simpson's (2014) assertion of "ethnographic refusal," Cornel emphasized the importance of *not* including footage that a community comes to decide has a limited appropriate audience.[8] Synthesizing the broader themes, Pauline concluded by noting that the effect of film varies widely and that we should be careful not to assume that it is always empowering. To that point, Cornel reiterated the importance of not letting whitefella outsiders come in to tell stories without community involvement or control. Both ultimately affirmed the power of filmmaking, especially when the production values and voices of Aboriginal media makers remained central.

On the Global Stage

From *Tjawa Tjawa*'s social editing in Balgo, to the community film premiere, to its ICTV festival screening in Lajamanu, the circles of its circulation grew organically outward and through relational networks. However, its movement onto the urban stages of international film festivals was markedly less incremental, much akin to the abrupt shift to a corrugated road after a long stretch of highway.

Red Carpet Festivals

The Sydney Film Festival contrasted with previous screenings in multiple ways. I attended this festival in June 2015 with Mark and Neil, as well as several members of Goolarri who were screening their film *Naji*. Featured at this most prestigious film festival in Australia, the Songlines on Screen special event was an important part of NITV's initiative to build mainstream legitimacy and reputation around Indigenous community filmmaking. After waiting in long lines that snaked past red carpets and celebrity photo backdrops, we finally found our way into the sold-out theater of over three hundred audience members, made up mostly of whitefellas from Sydney. The screenings were introduced by Rachel Perkins (Arrente and Kalkadoon), the award-winning filmmaker and daughter of Indigenous civil rights leader Charlie Perkins. Notably, she directed *Brand New Day* (2010), the big-budget adaptation of the Broome musical *Bran Nue Dae,* involving many Aboriginal media makers in Broome.

Of all of the filmmakers in the Songlines on Screen program, Mark had been selected to say a few words before the films began. Standing in front of the bustling audience, he straightened his back and lifted his shoulders high with one arm holding the other behind his back, proclaiming, "I'm from Balgo. I made this film to show people all over the world a message. This is our story, and story is very important for us." He briefly summarized the film's narrative, noting that it would take a long time to truly explain it. Afterward, he sat down in one of the cinema's plush red velvet seats as the Songlines on Screen series played.

The after-party down the street was a wine and cheese affair. Walking past a who's who of faces ripped from the Australian silver screen, I found Mark on a couch organizing paper copies he had recently printed, which summarized his mission for Yagga Yagga and going back to Country. As he straightened the edges of the pile he said, "These people might want to help our community. Some of them have money and want to learn more. You never know." Money often came up as the key resource that urban whitefellas could offer. As Mark saw it, he had no need for bureaucratic programs, just the funding to enact his vision

FIGURE 22. Mark Moora speaking at the 2015 Sydney Film Festival.

for going back to Country. He often described this within his broader thoughts on the increasingly central role of money in Balgo:

> I used to work for free smoke, and now I've gotta pay for it. We're in the money world. Money, money, money. We're gonna lead them the right way to a better future. But for a better future, where's the money? It's about freedom. We came in, did hard work, and made nothing. I'm telling you this while I'm here now. While I'm still here alive.

Tjawa Tjawa would go on to screen at prestigious festivals around the world, including imagineNATIVE in Toronto and the Margaret Mead in New York City. Jodie Bell and Kimberley West—the producer and director of Goolarri's *Naji*, respectively—traveled to North America and represented *Tjawa Tjawa* overseas at these festivals, publicly introducing it and reading statements by Mark and Neil. While Mark was encouraged to attend these, he remained steadfast in not wanting to risk passing away far from his Country.

In the months and years to come, Mark would often mention the Sydney festival. On the one hand, he noted that he would have liked more time to speak. Unlike *Tjawa Tjawa*'s previous screenings, every moment had been tightly timed, leaving less than a minute for him to address the crowd. He also talked about how difficult it was to have meaningful conversations about community closures and going back to Country at the festival. At the same time, more than anything, he seemed to think back on it fondly: "The Sydney Festival, it was really good. I still can't believe it. I still can't get over it. People came together and met. It was a good experience in Sydney. Yeah, we need more coming together in Australia. That is very important." He described the festival limitations as stemming mostly from his being in the wrong place, though he noted that media technology provided pathways forward. "I'm gonna put myself on the internet so people can contact me. They can come and talk to me about what is happening here, not asking me in the city. That is wrong for me."

Broadcasting Back to Balgo

Tjawa Tjawa's final circulatory stage after many expanding circles of circulation was a return to its origin. Shortly after its international film festival screenings, the NITV-branded series was broadcast nationally on their network. Although I only had anecdotal access to national TV audience perspectives, I did watch it when it aired with some of my whitefella friends outside of the Indigenous media sector. As we watched the film in silence, it occurred to me that this was the first screening that had lacked commentary and laughter. While it seemed that the quietude was meant to be respectful within Western norms of media consumption, I was struck by the stark contrast of viewing *Tjawa Tjawa* quietly on a small screen, devoid of social context or the cueing of audience stories. In theory, NITV's broadcast represented its peak level of circulation—potentially reaching anyone across the country who owned a television—though its actual numbers were a fraction of that. For those who did watch it, I could not help but wonder: what would they see and hear?

For several subsequent months, it was broadcast exclusively on NITV and streamed on its website. Following this period, it began to be additionally broadcast on ICTV in remote communities. It remains indefinitely available on their streaming site, ICTV Play, where it was promoted on social media by PAKAM and others. This final move into ICTV's circulatory circle of remote communities closed the loop and completed the cycle. It was not a mystery how it would be received, as months later there we were again, watching it on the women's center's TV amidst the laughter and commotion of stories that danced along with the film.

4

Fires, Tires, and Paper

Roll 'em.

—David "Shorty" Young

I awake to the scraping of plastic across concrete. After reaching around for my glasses in a leather hiking shoe, I squint to see Mark rolling up his blankets and canvas in the early twilight. It is 5 a.m. and we are at the free-throw line of the basketball court in Halls Creek, the closest small town to Balgo. I've slept lightly, knowing that Mark wants to leave right when the petrol station opens to avoid becoming involved in family business all day. After carefully putting in my contacts under the light of my phone on the troopy hood, I roll up the dusty army green canvas swag and we silently pack up. After filling the twin tanks with diesel, Mark flatly notes, "I just have one stop this morning. We need to pick up an old fella." He directs me through a neighborhood just off the main road. As we pull up to our destination, Mark squints at the house next to us. "That's the one. I'll be right back." He returns a few minutes later followed by an Elder who spryly hops into the back with only his dog. Mark is unusually deferential, asking him if he wants a smoke and if everything is alright in the back. As we turn from the highway onto the corrugated Tanami Road for the three-hour drive back to Balgo, I realize that this is Bob Dingle.

Bob Dingle was initially meant to direct *Tjawa Tjawa*. Before that he was meant to lead *Kurrarlkatjanu: The Last Generation*. It was originally titled *The Last Man Standing*, as Bob was often described in Balgo. Leading up to the shooting of both of these films, he decided to not participate for a variety of reasons, including fears of reprisal from other groups, not feeling well enough for the trip, and his travel schedule. Mark led these film shoots specifically because Bob, his Elder from their Country, elected not to.

Over the following months, I saw Bob each morning in front of the Balgo shop, accompanied by his dog and a gentle smile. We often sat together amid the bustle. Sometimes Bob would make a comment about his Country and ask if I had been to certain places on previous trips over the past two years. I let him know that many people in Balgo were working on various film projects and that he was more than welcome to start one too. Knowing his previous hesitancy about films, I mentioned this out of respect and assumed that he would not be interested. I was wrong. A couple of months later, we were sitting in the morning as usual. While petting his faithful companion, Bob pointed south and said plainly, "We'll go tomorrow at 7 a.m. just for

FIGURE 23. Balgo shop from the point of view of the radio station.

the morning. We'll drive down that way toward my Country and then come back." Surprised, I nodded and responded, "I'll fill up the troopy and get supplies this afternoon."

It is just after sunrise when I arrive with Shorty to pick up Bob at his bottom camp house. As in Halls Creek, he climbs in with his dog and gives a single smiling nod when he is settled. We drive south as the sun creeps over the horizon to our left. Shorty cautions me to drive extra slowly, not wanting the ride to be bumpy for Bob or to take any risks with flats, as we have only a single spare that has been patched several times. A couple of hours later, guided by Shorty's hand sign directions, we arrive at a prominent overlook. While he chats with Bob about what he might want to say on film, we set up two cameras and a radio mic.

Once everyone seems settled, Shorty says—and gives the circular gesture for—"Roll 'em." Seeing the red light on the camera, he begins asking Bob questions. They speak in Kukatja, while Bob's dog walks around him, curiously sniffing the cameras and then lying at his feet. Ten minutes later, Bob smiles after finishing an answer and turns to look at his Country in the distance. After a long moment, he states "Nyamu" and we stop. After sharing tin meat and white-bread sandwiches, we pack up and cautiously drive back to Balgo, arriving by midday.

The next morning, Shorty, Allison (his wife and PAKAM partner), and I sat cross-legged on their front porch, carefully translating the video on a laptop. As we worked line by line through the recording, the cool of the smooth concrete gave way to the desert's rising heat. In the short shoot, Bob had broadly traced his life. He talked about his childhood, going through Law ceremonies, arriving at the Old Balgo Mission, and then helping to build the new Wirrimanu community (Balgo). Gesturing toward his Country in the distance, Bob's final comments spoke of what it meant to him to be called "the last man standing":

> My name is Tjapanangka. My name is Bob Dingle, that's my name. Yeah, Robert. I'm here at Warwuya Hill, yeah. My Country is straight up there. Other side of Mangkayi, of Emily Springs. Well, we might go there one day with two vehicles, yeah. We can go see that place, not far. Yeah, this man who is taking the picture, you got to see this place. All my family passed away. My brothers passed away. Cousins, uncles, all gone, everybody. I'm the only one standing, only me. Yowie [Sorry], I'm by myself, no brother, just myself. No mother, no uncle, finished. My uncle [Payi Payi's husband] passed away. Old lady Payi Payi [Mark's sister] grew me up. I stayed with my uncle and they both grew me up. And old lady Linda [Mark's half sister]. I didn't lose them, they're still alive, I'm still holding them with me. Yeah, nyamu.

After many years of declining to participate on film projects, why did Bob decide to initiate this particular trip? In light of this most improbable of shoots, what is the delicate balance that animates a palya media process?

During the months following the completion of *Tjawa Tjawa,* I stayed in Balgo as a media volunteer for PAKAM and the art center, Warlayirti Artists (Warlayirti). In the wake of *Tjawa Tjawa,* there was an explosion of interest in making video and music projects. During this period, Mark self-consciously stepped back from the limelight and established himself as a supportive guide for others' projects. This flurry of community media-making proceeded not in the order of suggestion but through the logic of kinship relations in Balgo, with the projects forming what I have come to think of as a literal and figurative film family. The flourishing of Balgo filmmaking represented an awakening for Mark. He came to consider media not only as a process of moving through Country and communicating widely, but also as a means for collective and intergenerational creation.

A Palya Trinity

I focus here on one deceptively simple question: What makes a Balgo film project palya? Describing a project as palya is quite distinct from saying that it turned out well. A palya film is good in the sense that it was done the right way, emphasizing what Faye Ginsburg describes as "embedded aesthetics," where "the quality of work is judged by its capacity to embody, sustain, and even revive or create certain social relations" (1994, 368). Throughout my fieldwork, I noticed that many films were considered successes by communities, media organizations, national broadcasters, or audiences, but only a rare few were beloved by all of them while also embodying palya for community members.

Drawing on some of the videos and music recordings from this creative period in Balgo, I illustrate palya production values through the interrelationship of a trinity of locally resonant themes: creative *fires,* material *tires,* and bureaucratic *paper.* These tropes emerged slowly while I was participating in and reflecting upon dozens of films. I describe how *paper* often exacerbated irreconcilabilities that exerted control over *tires* and threatened to extinguish *fires.* I explore the literal and metaphorical elements of each, including the continual lighting of bush fires on film shoots, the politics around acquiring tires and repairing flats, and ubiquitous challenges stemming from bureaucratic whitefella paperwork. At a broader level, the tension between these three elements illuminates how communities are structured by the government in ways that foster conflict. They also provide a framework for navigating respectful roles of outsider collaborators within palya projects.

Creative Fires

Marumpu Wangka—which translates as "hand talk" in English—was an unexpected outcome of several months of hanging out with women Elders at the Kapululangu women's center following *Tjawa Tjawa*. Having known these Elders for years, we would regularly spend long afternoons sitting around joking and chatting, often discussing the complex system of hand signs. While I was learning basic Kukatja in my earlier trips, the women had often showed me signs as a learning device. Over time, this had developed into a lively gestural banter between us that expanded from dozens to eventually hundreds of signs, and included Zohl de Ishtar, the center's executive director. While hand signs are used throughout the community, the women Elders seemed to have a special love for them. This was in part because, as some of the oldest community members, they fondly associated signs with their youth, before they came into the Old Balgo Mission (de Ishtar 2005). The Elders, I, and Zohl quickly arrived at the idea of trying to film some of the signs, and we began organizing and translating them.

Mark would often visit Kapululangu with me to spend time with his sister Payi Payi and the other women. When he learned that we might make a film about the hand signs, he immediately offered to help expand and refine the list. He was passionate about the project's focus on language. As he told a group of youth in Balgo, "Language is very, very important. Language is culture, and nobody can change that. You've got to keep it. It's part of your blood, part of your tribe. That's why we put films in proper Kukatja." Even though he likely had the most extensive knowledge of hand signs in Balgo, he insisted that he only assist in the background, reflecting that he had been in the spotlight too much with *Tjawa Tjawa* and that it was important that other people had a chance to make projects for a while. When I would periodically ask him if he was thinking about films, he would pause contemplatively and then respond, "Slowly, slowly. Other people have films they want to do too. That's good."

I wipe the thin layer of ochre dust off of my phone as I climb into the troopy at the art center, only to find that it is already 1 p.m. Having promised to come by the women's center today, I pull onto the paved road heading south. Just before the asphalt gives way to the tracks leading to Yagga Yagga, I turn left into Kapululangu's short street. I pull up in the heat of the afternoon and park behind a large bush just outside of the barbed-wire fence. When I turn off the engine, I am struck by the silence here, just beyond Balgo's neighborhood camps. I tap the horn twice as lightly as I can, and a minute later, Zohl waves as she walks to the gate with a jangling bundle of keys. As we enter through the house's sliding glass door, the five women Elders are surrounded by family on their single beds in the main living area. In contrast to the usually jovial atmosphere, there is pall in the air. The daughter of Linda, one of the women Elders, tragically died in Broome, and it is now the day before her burial service. The time leading up to a funeral is known as "sorry business," involving weeks of public mourning. I sit with the women while they grieve. Sometimes Linda reaches out to hold hands. After some time, and seemingly out of the blue, she states, "Let's make that film now." Surprised, Zohl and I suggest that there's no need to think of film projects, especially today. However, she, Payi Payi, and Manaya are adamant, and Linda declares, "No, now is the right time."

Shortly afterward, we pack into the troopy and drive a few minutes down the road, pulling just off of the track heading toward Yagga Yagga. Zohl and I place a few blankets on the side of the pindan track and clip a radio mic to the back of Payi Payi's blue hat. With the Elders on camera, we all sit around talking and joking about signs. Having slowly developed this video concept together, this feels less like a film shoot and more like another afternoon at Kapululangu. As much as anything, the video documents our joking relationship, in which my misunderstandings during this learning process are ripe for lighthearted banter.

As the shoot continues, the women Elders are increasingly expressive. Manaya especially enjoys acting out the sign scenarios, while Payi Payi and Linda are determined to get each one exactly right. Having only one camera, we discuss all of the signs while shooting from the front, then again in profile. This perspective is especially important for signs that move forward away from the body, such as marlu (kangaroo). Later that week we attempt another shoot including two additional women Elders. While more cinematic—with the community overlook in the background—it becomes clear that this is not the right moment. We quickly decide to move on, as it was the ineffable feeling of impromptu levity that made the other shoot, and thus the film, feel right.

This seemingly unexpected flash of collective creativity typified Balgo film projects during these months. Over time, *fires* emerged as a useful way of trying to put this creative process into words, and we began using it as a term for discussing creativity. This drew explicitly on previous fire metaphors in Aboriginal media. In the earliest days of video production in Yuendumu, Francis Kelly and others described the need for Warlpiri people to combat outside media with their own through the metaphor of "fighting fire with fire." As Neil Turner recalled:

> I believe [the phrase] came from Warlpiri Media and possibly even Kurt Granites [Yuendumu Elder] has the intellectual property on that slogan, which was directly related to the imminent satellite invasion and the development of community television as a sort of patch burning analogy of creating your own small fire, if you like, to prevent yourself from being engulfed by the bigger fire that would come. (quoted in Guster 2011)

In Balgo, *fires* was both literal and metaphorical. An important aspect of bush shoots was literally lighting numerous fires on our trips as a part of proper land management—what is referred to broadly as "taking care of Country"—through the systematic burning of grasses.[1] Such fires must happen at the right time and under the correct conditions. When lit, they burn brightly and travel quickly. When they are done, they are done. And it can be quite some time before a fire should be lit again in that place. These fires resonate with the brilliant flashes of creativity that regularly occurred in Balgo media projects. The time leading up to a creative fire was typified by a quiet buildup lasting days, weeks, or months. This culminated in an eruption of intense creative group energy, lasting from minutes to weeks, which could neither be fully planned nor delayed. Beyond describing collective media dynamics, *fires* also reframes discussions of creative labor away from individualist discourses around laziness and productivity that are often rendered irreconcilable in Aboriginal community life.[2]

Late one afternoon, Shorty and I were practicing different camera techniques just outside of the radio station and shop. After a few kids came up to us to see what we were doing, interest spread in a matter of minutes. Soon there were dozens of kids passing the camera around and trying it out. They quickly formed various ideas about what to shoot. Over the next two hours, we moved collectively to the playground and the store before driving in the PAKAM troopy all around Balgo. We filmed footy practice and the process of making a slingshot from a balloon and half of a large Coke bottle.[3] We only stopped when the camera battery and its backup ran out. As with most creative fires, this specific blaze was unanticipated and never happened again in a similar way.

Such rhythms of collective Aboriginal action are not new, and often mirror the creative process of ceremonies, rites of passage, and corroborees (regional gatherings involving dancing and important ritual practices) (Berndt 1974). As with filmmaking, these are seasonal. In the Kimberley region from Broome to Balgo there is a stark difference between the wet/hot and dry/cool parts of the year. There is an intensive and busy dry season schedule of shoots from around April to October. During the wet season, people tend to travel and take part in important cultural events. Due to family obligations and practical weather conditions, the wet season tends to be when film projects focus more on video editing, planning, and downtime. It also provides a period for recovery after the back-to-back projects throughout the dry season.

Aboriginal media workers often have to miss work due to obligations, especially in the wet season. Work absence was understood by PAKAM differently than in non-Indigenous organizations. Taking time off to attend a funeral (lasting days or weeks) or to visit a relative was normalized. Neil regularly discussed these seasonal rhythms and social obligations, and the challenges of reconciling this with bureaucratic processes of hiring, employment requirements, and time sheets. *Fires* illustrates that such periodic absences are not just understandable but in fact necessary for the process of collective creativity within palya projects.

As described, based upon my experiences over two years of attending the National Remote Indigenous Media Festival, PAKAM was by all accounts the most productive of all of the Remote Indigenous Media Organizations—contributing a plurality of content to ICTV and related streaming platforms at the time—while somehow also appearing to have the most fun.[4] It seemed to me that PAKAM's unusual combination of productivity and good spirits could be explained, at least partly, by their implicit collective embrace of the *fires* creative process, prioritizing it despite its irreconcilability with bureaucratic norms.

Tire Politics

With the sun piercing the horizon, I awake to the sound of Mark and Larry rolling up their bedding in the shadow of the old Yagga Yagga store. Minutes later, as we get ready to load the troopy, all at once we notice the outcome of two slow leaks, which have turned into total deflations overnight. We are unusually fortunate to have two spares left at the tail end of our trip. Each has been patched multiple times, and we hope that with any luck they will get us back to Balgo. Climbing the

Figure 24. A shredded troopy tire.

skinny ladder onto to the roof, I carefully push both tires off on the side they are not standing. Together, we change them using a faded blue pneumatic jack, pumping it with a makeshift metal lever originally meant for another purpose. The bolts are particularly difficult to remove as they have rusted into place. Loosening them requires standing on the X-shaped spanner, and we have to be careful. One wrong move will strand us. The hardest part is lifting the large, steel-reinforced flat tires to the roof. As Mark and Larry push from the bottom, I pull them up. Only a few hours south of Balgo, Mark steers with an especially keen eye on the track. Driving in Country without a spare is the easiest way to get into trouble or worse.

Throughout all the various bush trips I was a part of, it was never once water, food, injury, or sickness that forced us to turn back, but always tires. Tires were essential. They prevented one from becoming stranded, and enabled travel within and beyond the community to go hunting or visit family members. Yasmine Musharbash (2008b) emphasizes the importance of mobility in Yuendumu, the nearest Aboriginal community of a size similar to Balgo. Describing it as "hithering and thithering," she traces the flow of people within and between communities to demonstrate the complex relational logic of movement, structured within networks of obligation (127). Musharbash notes that the Western conception of a "household" is rendered meaningless in communities due to its boundedness, as people dynamically adjust their housing to their relations (60). In her work with Warlpiri communities in the same region, Melinda Hinkson illustrates that the process of leaving a camp, moving through Country, and returning is one of the most fundamental aspects of Warlpiri social sustenance and world-making (2021, 8).

Tires encompasses interrelated aspects of materiality and mobility in the production process. It includes all of the physical stuff, from film equipment to supplies to troopys. Most vitally, it includes literal tires and is less metaphorical than *fires*. In light of the significance of mobility in Balgo, there were ongoing politics around their possession, exchange, and patching. While vehicle repair was a common skill set, few had access to the tools and equipment needed to fix more than their own vehicles. In Balgo, one community mechanic had both the skill and infrastructural access to fix vehicles. With more requests than anyone could respond to, he had to strategically triage them. These priorities tended to be based on at least two factors. First, since he worked directly for the Balgo community office, he prioritized their official vehicles. Second, the other requests were to some extent ordered based on his own kinship and community relationships. These decisions had more to do with relational obligations than with favoritism.

Knowing that I was working with Mark and other Elders around the community, the mechanic often helped to keep the PAKAM troopys operable through a variety of repairs. His grandmother lived at the women's center and was involved in many of PAKAM's film projects over the years. The mechanic himself, along with his family, took part in the shoot of *Kurrarlkatjanu* in 2013. At various times he patched tires, fixed brakes, and rewired the PAKAM troopys. He specialized in troopys, the preferred Balgo vehicle, and was adept at finding replacement parts in the neatly organized set of broken-down vehicles located just outside of Balgo. While described as the "car dump" by some managers, it contained a plethora of spare parts for those who knew where and how to look. Similar retired car yards can be found along the edges of many Aboriginal communities.

Not all repairs were possible or practical, especially when stranded. For example, when one of the trailers broke an axle during the *Tjawa*

FIGURE 25. Balgo car yard.

Tjawa shoot, we moved its contents of mattresses for Elders onto the roofs of other vehicles. We left the trailer with the hope that it could be repaired and returned to Balgo in the future. However, in light of all of the vehicle work that needed to be done, attempting to weld an axle far away from Balgo was challenging to say the least. Depending on what rumor one believed at the time, the trailer was left as it was, burned, or—and this is perhaps most likely—put on blocks to salvage its most vital components: tires.

Tire politics saturated our film projects. For example, I once arrived in Balgo to discover that the old PAKAM troopy that had retired to the women's center had become embroiled in a minor dispute. One of its tires was borrowed, and its return was overdue. Tires were especially difficult to come by during this period, and not even the mechanic knew of a spare, save for expensive new ones in the shop. Mark suggested that his son-in-law might know someone, who in turn directed me to one of his nephews just around the corner in Kylie Camp. When we went over, they spoke for a while in Kukatja, after which the younger man looked over at the troopy and said, "Oh yeah, it's a Toyota so no worries." Since we did not have a tire-mounting machine, he had to remove and install the new tire on the rim manually with a rubber mallet and crowbar. As he was finishing, the sound of the weekly mail plane buzzed overhead, forming an unlikely sonic symphony along with Tracy Chapman's "Fast Car" playing from a vehicle next door. Hurrying through the final hits, he exclaimed, "My son is coming in! I'll get a compressor and you should be 'right." Jumping into his Nissan, he made a few hand signs to someone across the street, who brought over a compressor and jack so that I could complete the job and return the tire in question.

Tire politics were important, though not because they signaled material possession; it was rather because they enabled the mobility required to move through Country and fulfill relational obligations, in addition to running crucial errands like collecting firewood. Beyond tires, this is true in a broader sense regarding material ownership in communities. While *fires* reframes productivity discussions in Balgo, *tires* upends regular outsider claims about the "irresponsibility" of community members. Such judgments focused on a perceived recklessness with objects and was based on misunderstanding. For material objects such as vehicles, in which safety is a matter of life or death, community members exhibited great care and expertise in their handling. However, there was little sense in trying to retain a new or shiny surface appearance in dusty conditions. Highly skilled bush mechanics often asked me to push-start their car by literally nudging it forward with the troopy's front bumper, or "roo [kangaroo] bar." Dents or bends in the exterior were not relevant to a vehicle's performance, and this method was both effective and efficient.

Irreconcilable sensibilities about material objects existed in ongoing conflict with some whitefella managers. For example, every few years the community purchased a new set of musical instruments for the local bands. As with the vehicles, they operated well, though invariably appeared superficially battered, with chipped paint and wear from sun, dust, and rain. Despite ingenious bush mechanics employed to refashion everything from drum pedals to guitar bridges, the treatment of instruments was a commonly cited example of material irresponsibility. There is also a long regional tradition of using, fixing, and eventually discarding musical instruments rather than immortalizing or guarding them. For example, in the Northern Territory, yidaki (didgeridoos) traditionally were rarely kept, but rather made from termite-hollowed wood, played, and then thrown into the fire. This minimalist logic, so essential to nomadic life, has become distorted through the imposition of Western values around capital accumulation, wage labor, and stationary settlement.

Materialist misunderstandings by whitefellas were perhaps most pronounced in relation to housing. Visiting service providers in Balgo regularly uttered harsh judgments, such as "They don't have any pride in their homes" or "How can they live like that? Those houses should be condemned. People sleep on the floor. There is blood from meat on the wall. Nothing is cared for." Yet, with appropriate context this usage is rendered both logical and responsible. Houses are used in the same way that nomadic camps have been lived in for millennia, and not on the basis of Western conceptions regarding a nuclear family home. As Mary Douglas put it, dirt is matter that is deemed to be out of place based upon "a set of ordered relations and a contravention of that order" ([1966] 2003, 44). Unlike a house, it makes little sense to describe a camp as either dirty or crowded. It was not choice, but the colonial dispossession of land that led to the unprecedented concentration of Aboriginal people into relatively large and sedentary communities, resulting in the very housing concentration and usage that is so often critiqued.

Whitefella perceptions had a profound impact on material access, as most large purchases and allocations of funds were ultimately at the discretion of whitefella managers. Field mates would often comment on the amount of control that whitefellas exerted over items and resources in Balgo. This was epitomized by the "compound," an area near the center of Balgo inhabited by whitefella workers and guarded by large gates that protected various locked-up community assets, including a trove of spare tires.

Issues of material control were often a primary factor in the inaccessibility of community media programs and resources. For example, when I arrived in Balgo the art center's extensive media facilities had lain dormant for years. This included a professional recording studio with high-quality instruments and a video production media center with a gamut of equipment, sitting behind sealed doors. This locked-away phenomenon was common in many communities I worked in. Part of the issue had to do with increasingly dire funding opportunities for remote community art centers. This seemed to be a result of the structure of how such programs were set up in the first place, requiring a dedicated outsider facilitator to manage the space and make sure that the equipment did not leave or get damaged.

Several art center managers in the region noted that it would be challenging for community members to run a music studio because they would be unable to say no to their relatives. Managers often noted that the structure of Aboriginal communities necessitated outside, if not whitefella, managers whose job it was to say no. As one manager phrased it, "The role of whitefellas in communities is to absorb all of the blame. It's important, but it gets tiring." Such comments were frequently made by various managers of Indigenous organizations in communities, and they regularly advised me to blame them in relevant discussions through comments such as "Just tell them *I* said no" and "Just blame it on me," though not all managers agreed with this.[5] These dynamics seemed typified by managers trying to do their best under duress, aiming to continue programs that began before their tenure, with dwindling staff and funding.

More troubling were the many examples in which denial of access was compounded by community CEOs. In one instance I was sent by PAKAM on a crew to assist in getting a community media station up and running again, and upon arrival we were told that the entrance door had been previously pried open and the equipment inside trashed. The door had since been bolted shut by the CEO. When we asked him about it, he said, "Mate, it's effed. You know how they are with this stuff. It's trashed. They didn't look after it. I reckon you oughta just scrap it and start over." When we gained access to the studio we found that in all actuality, it was fine. All that was missing were the headphones, microphones, and cables, which a local band had requisitioned since they were not being used. We located most of these items easily within days, and the studio was soon operational.

In another community, we arrived only to find that the door had been sealed by the CEO with specialized countersunk bolts that were difficult to remove. He had found what he called "illegal paraphernalia" in the radio station, and his response was meant to serve as a punishment, framed through the language of laziness and irresponsibility. He had enacted other penalties as well, including disconnecting the lights at the basketball court for several weeks. When we finally entered the radio station, we saw that the iMac computer was gone. The CEO remarked that someone had stolen it and that we would never see it again. After asking just a few people, we found it twenty minutes later at a house where its residents were using it to watch movies. When we mentioned that we were trying to find the PAKAM computer, the man at the door responded, "No worries, mate. We've been looking after it and using it. I'll go get it now." Such misunderstandings and accusations regarding "theft" were commonplace by CEOs, though most organization managers held more nuanced views.

Many influential whitefellas also held parallel misunderstandings about a perceived lack of technological interest and ability by community members. Yet, throughout the dozens of projects I worked on in communities, I found the opposite to be the case. Whether training to learn radio or video, there tended to be intense interest and quick understanding. Although tasks that required an individual to work alone—like the initial video editing process—rarely elicited excitement, technical processes that were also highly social invited long hours of active engagement.

For example, many in Balgo were particularly savvy in the use of USB drives, which provided a social object and medium for data exchange. Unlike most Western-derived technology, USB sticks align with local material sensibilities. They are durable, portable, inexpensive, and universally operable. They can be tossed, caught, and left baking in the sun or soaking in the mud without breaking. USBs were regularly exchanged in social settings, with people trading music and movies, including locally produced media. Young people made sure to acquire car stereos that had a direct USB plug, providing an easy way of playing music in the moment and on the go. Before each of my return trips to Balgo from Broome, I brought several USBs that contained all of the Balgo-produced media. Not only was this an effective way of ensuring that films remained accessible, but it also provided an object that people would continue to find useful. At media festivals and other events, USBs were the most common and popular items to give, receive, and exchange.

In his chapter "The Aboriginal Laptop," Daniel Miller (2008) argues that a computer could be understood as a metaphorical and literal home for Malcolm, an Aboriginal man who spent much of his life in London. As Miller illustrates, Malcolm used this technology in specifically Aboriginal ways. While remaining cautious about the limits of such a metaphor, USB sticks resonate with the materiality and purpose of message sticks, which are small pieces of wood with etched and painted symbols used to transmit messages over long distances between language groups throughout Australia. Like message sticks, USBs imbue information from the original sender, as well as those who have subsequently passed it along.

Ultimately, community members, while generally excelling with the physical stuff of media-making, are not often in a position to acquire cameras, vehicles, and supplies. By contrast, outsiders often have access to these yet are possessive of their use, largely due to byzantine bureaucratic systems based on power ascribed through *paper*.

Pernicious Paper

While Shorty and I are driving to film a sunset shoot just outside of Balgo, he reaches into his shirt pocket and sighs. "Ah, hold on. I dropped my Centrelink paper. Let's go to the shop." Arriving there a few minutes later, Shorty hops out and says, "I know it's here. Let's have a look." In front of us is a large area of dried spinifex grass surrounding the office and playground. After an afternoon so windy that it overturned a large trash can, there is a confetti of paper scraps blowing around on the ground. With the sun quickly setting, I hold little hope that we have a chance of finding one particular piece. It is only moments later that I hear "Found it, just where I was walking earlier." He shows me a piece of paper folded up to only a couple of inches on each side. "Without it I won't get my payment," he continues. He emphasizes that finding it has saved him long hours of waiting and trying to reproduce the document at the office. While noting its practical power, he describes paper's fragile symbolic qualities too, musing that "With this Centrelink paper, I can get money and go to the shop, but I'll give away most of that anyways. If I didn't have this paper, someone would give me tucker [food]." Holding the object up and staring at it, he continues, "You see, money is nothing to us, just paper. It is nothing."

Paper is the least metaphorical of these three tropes and includes all pieces of paper or its screen simulations. While *fires* distills Aboriginal rhythms of creative production, and *tires* engages material accessibility to enable creativity through mobility, *paper* denaturalizes bureaucratic processes in communities. It aims toward the anthropological truism of "making the familiar strange." Ostensibly banal, paperwork is in practice a primary mechanism by which settler-colonial dispossession continues to operate in Aboriginal communities. Paper is often referred to as "milli milli" in Aboriginal English, and its utterance is usually accompanied by frustration. Of course, not all marked wood pulp sheets carry negative connotations in communities. Many objects, such as artwork, books in Aboriginal languages, and playing cards, are useful and beloved. However, here *paper* refers to the dominant forms of bureaucratic violence that control and limit possibility in Aboriginal communities.

Paper was often as harmful as it was slow, especially when it came to money. Its painfully sluggish pace was especially apparent in Centrelink payments. This system of welfare, available to all low-income Australians, was made especially arduous in remote communities, often requiring recipients to spend many hours sitting in the Balgo office waiting to correct various technical issues with their account. As Musharbash (2007) argues, the recently introduced coalescence of perpetual waiting, settler conceptions of time, and the category of "joblessness" has produced boredom. This is a Western phenomenon that likely did not exist before contact, at least not in the way that it is commonly imagined, as weariness born from a lack of interest. In these ways and more, physical and virtual *paper* has come to influence nearly every aspect of social life (Hull 2012).

"You see, money is nothing to us, just paper. It is nothing." Shorty's comment sticks with me in the following weeks, and speaks to the paradoxes of money in communities. For example, on the first film project I worked on in Balgo, *Kurrarlkatjanu,* Payi Payi's painting sold for five figures. Receiving the money when we returned from the shoot, she noted that by the end of the day the money was "all gone"—and gestured both hands as empty—in that it was distributed throughout her extended family. She described this without resentment, and with a sense of joy in being able to fulfill her relational obligations.

Money, like other resources, is generally shared within family groups. This has worked well for tens of thousands of years, in which tucker (hunted and gathered food) was distributed in prescribed ways throughout small groups. Payi Payi—who like her brother Mark grew up in their Country and came into the Old Balgo Mission as a child—seemed to feel relatively little conflict about money. However, decades of dispossession have fostered increasingly complicated and difficult problems for younger people, many of whom are deeply affected by Stolen Generation policies. At least 100,000 Aboriginal children were forcibly removed from their parents and put into boarding schools from the 1930s until as late as the 1970s. This policy coincided with the forcing of Aboriginal people into stationary communities in order to claim and develop their land. These were systematic processes that the state used to assimilate Aboriginal people and dispossess their Country.

One of their many legacies has been the continual pressure toward individualism, including various incentives to leave communities for towns in order to earn more money.

The shifting dynamics around money have led to what is known in Balgo and other Aboriginal communities as "humbug." This involves requesting money from relatives, usually directed from younger people to their Elders. Humbug is particularly complex. Deriving from long-held traditions of sharing and communal distribution, it has shifted toward an unbalanced generational dynamic. Inverting the structure of providing meat to Elders after a successful hunt, older people tend to have more money from art sales and resource royalties. As Mark often noted, "It used to be that the young fellas would take care of us old fellas. But now everything is backwards, and they humbug us to take care of them. Should be the other way." Humbug was especially apparent during the weekly "money morning" distribution of payments at the art center. On this day, relatives of the women Elders at Kapululangu would sometimes come by to humbug. These visits were seemingly about money, though were much more than that. Sharing has endured as a core social value that creates the context for enacting and reaffirming kinship relationships. Just as there are social taboos against saying "no" to a request, so too is there a lack of the phrase "thank you" in Kukatja. Exchange is not framed in terms of appreciation and indebtedness but through networks of relational obligation. It is money's substance, source, and meaning that render it so irreconcilable with community life.

Money is imagined differently in community media projects than in the acrylic art painting process. Filmmaking and painting share key qualities, including the visual expressions of Country, community, and self through durable mediums. They are also often linked in their funding. Media production was central for the massive culture center expansion built onto Warlayirti (de Ishtar 2005). However, while funding is important at the project and media organization levels in films, there tends to be little (and often zero) income for community participants. This has rarely been the case with painting, which is primarily (though not solely) done to earn money to distribute to relations.[6] As John Carty describes it, this in turn becomes a way of expressing obligation fulfillment throughout kinship networks (2011, 96).

What is it about video production that seems to provide value beyond money in ways that painting does not? One possible answer is media's mobility. Even more so than painting, video production tends to center extended family trips to Country, including access to *tires.* And while painting is at times collaborative, video production tends to be more social, including distributed authorship and roles. There is also a key distinction around imagined audience. Unlike acrylic art, which is usually painted for exhibitions, collectors, and tourists, most community video projects are produced for broader family and friend networks in and beyond Balgo. When filming, participants and collaborators regularly asked, "When will this be on ICTV?" and "Can we get a USB of the footage today?" Even in big-budget projects like *Tjawa Tjawa,* community members themselves are an important audience, along with broader publics. Many show up to community film festivals, though few spend time perusing the art gallery.

Furthermore, the labor of community media-making has not been commodified to the extent that it has in art. This is partly because media cannot be singularly possessed or provide long-term income in the way that art can. While painting did not begin with a profit motive in the 1980s in Balgo, it increasingly shifted that way over decades. The close association of art with humbug and money morning has rendered painting as less of a labor of love over time. I am not suggesting that painting is not a deeply meaningful act, that it is a problem that painting provides income, or that it is a good thing that video production tends not to. Rather, this contrast points to the cascading effects of commodifying creative processes in Aboriginal communities, and the insidious legacies of *paper.* Painting and cinema are not simply representational; they are manifestations of Country, and their processes are conduits for the transmission of generational knowledge (Carty 2021, 1). Thinking of them in relation to one another reveals the counterintuitive and paradoxical impacts of payment and its absence.

Time sheets were one of the most dreaded forms of *paper.* Due by fax once every fortnight (two weeks), these regularly provoked anxiety, as individuals tried to precisely recall the different days and hours that they had worked. These were especially difficult to navigate in situations where distinctions between time spent "on" and "off" the job were ambiguous. For example, should spending time at the women's center hanging out in the week leading up to a shoot be considered media labor? While this may not have involved much time discussing the project, it was necessary for the film to happen and for it to unfold through a palya process. Since PAKAM community workers were part-time and could not exceed twenty hours per week, the calculus of carrying over extra time from a previous busy pay period was confusing. Time sheets also provoked frustration at a material level throughout the process of printing, filling out, and then faxing them in. Workers often felt uncomfortable having to gain access to the fax machine in the busy community office. At the PAKAM headquarters in Broome, the time sheet due date was anticipated and bustling, involving a rush to make everything add up correctly and appropriately.

While much of the *paper* in Balgo was emailed and printed through various offices, it also physically flew in and out on the weekly mail plane. Every Wednesday between the late morning and early afternoon, this plane looped around the community to announce its arrival before landing at the strip at the edge of Balgo. The mail plane provided a consistent unofficial meeting for whitefellas in the community, often including the CEO and most of the managers of various organizations. While waiting under the small area of shade, they sometimes discussed

FIGURE 26. Mail plane being unloaded.

big-picture changes that they expected or hoped for, usually in relation to funding and policies. As a volunteer for the art center, I was occasionally sent to drop off or pick up their large canvas sack of letters and packages. Although it was generally a whitefella ritual, community members sometimes attended, usually to catch a ride on the plane to and from Halls Creek or Kununurra. Such air travel often followed time spent in a hospital recovering from a health issue.

While wages for PAKAM media workers was standard and regular, payment for community film participants sometimes posed irreconcilable problems. This was often more complex than simply paying individuals for their hours of work, as it could seem inappropriate to pay an Elder who shared important knowledge less than a younger person who worked more hours. How does one monetarily value cultural knowledge gained over a lifetime, and which does not belong to a single individual?

Furthermore, there were a variety of bureaucratic barriers regarding payments. For example, anyone receiving more than two hundred dollars for a media project had to complete an increased amount of paperwork. However, the biggest problem with paying people was that—with the rare exception of big-budget productions like *Tjawa Tjawa*—there was relatively little funding in film budgets, generally speaking. While Indigenous media organizations remained *relatively* well funded, this was only in relation to other Aboriginal sectors that were being rapidly defunded. For example, NITV had comparatively scarce funds to acquire programs, often paying less than industry standards out of budgetary necessity. When paying community members, it was noted by many that given the tight funding constraints, it was sometimes more dignified to be unpaid than severely underpaid. This was especially the case for Elders contributing cultural knowledge, where small payments could feel disrespectful (Woods 2014). On the other hand, it follows that participants should be compensated for their time with available funds.

Neil's skills in navigating such bureaucratic realities were finely honed, as he translated irreconcilabilities to render them as more sensible within both communities and bureaucracies. This deft dance occurred at a variety of levels, from complex A–Z budgets to interpersonal meeting dynamics. He remained self-conscious of the various embodied habitus adjustments required from moment to moment to move between the social realms of *fires, tires,* and *paper* (Bourdieu 1977). Neil on occasion related such moments to my own research in our discussions. For example, once when walking from the PAKAM shed to visit with the accountant in the upstairs Goolarri offices, he quipped, "Alright, gotta go put some shoes on to walk over to Goolarri. Hey, that's a good anecdote for your study!" Seasoned hands like Neil developed an intuitive sense for navigating bureaucracy, though he provides an exception that proves the rule of how complex and challenging it is to collaborate on Aboriginal film projects as a whitefella. There were community projects that I heard about or witnessed firsthand in which *paper* drowned them before they could even get started. Broadly speaking, bureaucratic navigation was, at best, characterized by imperfect compromises.

Extinguishing and Sparking

Although *fires, tires,* and *paper* sometimes aligned to foster palya projects, they tended to be at odds, since they involved competing pressures. Often an increase in material *tires* and *paper* funding reduced or even extinguished *fires,* and vice versa. Throughout my fieldwork there were many moments of creative *fires* that provided an abundance of excitement yet did not lead to a palya project. In 2013, for example, I volunteered in Yungngora for five weeks during which we had virtually no *tires* or *paper.* We lacked proper cameras, vehicles, or money. During this time there were several creative *fires,* and we made iPhone videos walking around and on the back of pickup trucks but were unable to complete any projects due to these constraints. I also worked on projects that had plentiful *tires* and *paper* but in which the creative *fire* was extinguished through the process. For example, when a local artist was unable to attend Desert Mob—a major Indigenous arts festival—the art center manager asked Shorty and me if we could make a video sharing her background as an artist and her work. With only a couple of days to complete it, the process was unavoidably rushed. That said, not every project is or needs to be palya. That video, for example, was meant to serve a specific purpose, and ultimately the artist and the art center seemed pleased to have the chance to at least send something through which she could transmit her own words and presence.

In *Tjawa Tjawa* there was more than enough *paper* and *tires*. We literally lit many fires and had moments of inspired creativity, alongside constraints around time frame, budget, and broad audience appeal. Inevitably, these realities of being on a large and logistically complex convoy trip muted creative excitement in some moments. However, what stands out to me is how *fires, tires,* and *paper* generally remained aligned despite these pressures. Only an Indigenous media organization like PAKAM would have been able to negotiate the *tires* and *paper* for such a complicated film process in ways that held enough space for creative *fires*. It certainly achieved palya status, cited as a resounding success not only by NITV and film festivals around the world but also, more importantly, by community members in Balgo.

For whitefellas such as myself, patience and relationship-building were essential for slowly cultivating projects that might become palya. However, there were some who could ignite creative flash *fires* and foster palya media in an instant. This ability was exemplified by Mary Geddarrdyu. More commonly known as Mary G, this character was played by Mark Bin Bakar, a multitalented Broome entertainer who was also the original creative director of Goolarri in its early days. Mary G continues to serve as the host of a popular weekly radio show and was previously the star of a Goolarri TV show. Mark Bin Bakar is a respected Indigenous media veteran and prolific songwriter who often speaks at large events. For example, he gave the keynote talk at the 2015 National Remote Indigenous Media Festival in Lajamanu. In parallel, Mary G is an Elvis-status celebrity in remote communities. In the course of only a few days' visit during the post–*Tjawa Tjawa* period, Mary G lit several creative *fires* in Balgo, including an interactive singing event at the community school. Mary G also hosted a live radio show in the art center that garnered a long line out the door, including local guests and kids singing along to the host's catchy musical hits, which have become standards in Broome and the Kimberley.

Mark Moora especially enjoyed being interviewed on this radio show, as they joked back and forth about him marrying the character. In addition to Mary G's jovial and charming persona, the popularity of the character was based upon carefully crafted songs that conveyed serious colonial critique while drawing upon the power of comedy. In

FIGURE 27. Mary G and I at the Balgo recording studio.

these lyrics from "Poorbala Poorbala Me" (2003), Mary G reveals and critiques whitefella *paper* in relation to well-known government program acronyms:

They give us social security
ATSIC gives us CDEP[7]
Government say "he good now"
They trick us with their money

While the pressures of *tires* and *paper* make achieving a palya film project challenging, the less expensive and technologically complex medium of radio was especially suited to quickly sparking creative *fires*. As an often-improvisational art form, radio programs such as Mary G's illustrated the power of unencumbered creativity (Bessire and Fisher 2013). In between our Balgo video projects, regular moments of creative *fires* occurred during radio programs and in prerecording segments such as station IDs with portable audio recorders.

Music recording provided another mode of capturing *fires*. As a volunteer with the art center, I was asked to assist in revitalizing the music recording studio, which had not been regularly used in years. After a couple of weeks of reconnecting the electronics and becoming familiar with its workings, we let local bands know that the studio was open and ready to record. More than a month later—after attending a weekend footy trip with most of the musicians to the town of Kununurra—I was approached at the store one morning by Quinton Milner, a musician and band leader. "We'll record this afternoon?" he asked. I nodded, and added, "Sounds good, I'll be there." That day we recorded from 3 p.m. to 3 a.m., and this was followed by several long days of recording that went late into the night. The next week we had completed an entire album of nine songs, mostly in Kukatja, with Quinton's band Cliffside Reggae, as well as other recordings by various community members. Rather than going track by track, we set up to capture the whole band at once, adding only some vocals and guitar solos afterward.

In contrast to past music recording that I had been involved with in the United States, band members regularly switched instruments between and even during songs. Younger kids watched the older musicians closely, taking photos and video of the sessions, while practicing on the instruments during breaks. Mark would sometimes come by in the late afternoon to see how the recording sessions were going, and seemed especially pleased that so many young people were involved. Months before, he had mentioned a song he wanted to record. I asked him once if he wanted to do that soon. With a knowing smile, he said "Yuwai, sometime soon, after this mob records and when my band comes through Balgo."

During this period we also recorded over an hour of Dreaming songs by the Elders at the women's center. These recordings were carefully guarded so that only two CDs of their content exist, both of which are at the women's center. The music studio's creative *fires* burned fast and bright, culminating in a concert just outside of the studio, on a stage overlooking the sandy performance area behind the art center. Within a fortnight it ran its course, and as other creative projects emerged we only rarely used the studio in the weeks that followed.

The musicians and I looked into trying to copyright the songs, burn CDs, and distribute or sell them in cases, though barriers of *paper* and *tires* presented themselves through legal and funding issues. However, through the local network of USB drives, the songs were shared across Balgo within days and could be regularly heard in cars and other stereos over the coming months. I still heard these tracks regularly played in 2023. Aware of the long-term patterns of inaccessibility regarding such spaces, Quinton and I recorded extended how-to videos and stored them on the studio computer and in the art center's database. These consisted of conversations between us as we described exactly how the music recording studio worked for the imagined audience of someone who would reignite the studio in future bursts of creative musical *fires*.

Moving the Center

Ngũgĩ wa Thiong'o (1993) suggests that "moving the center" can be more effective at decolonizing than arguing against dominant frameworks. As an example, he notes that engaging the first and third world model, even to dispute it, naturalizes its logic. It reinforces what is assumed and who is imagined at the margins. *Fires, tires,* and *paper* is one of many possible models that aim to move the center from settler logics and assumptions toward those of Balgo and other Aboriginal communities.[8]

The interrelationship between another trinity at the heart of this book—irreconcilability, envisioning, and cinematic social lives—is crucial here. What is it that is irreconcilable between Aboriginal and settler lives? Settler logics, deeply enmeshed through centuries of colonial policies and representations, form a structure that explicitly and implicitly dispossess through Indigenous elimination (Wolfe 2006). It does so in myriad ways, many of them subtle and subconscious. In addition to eliminating people, these foundational logics degrade their movement through Country, their ability to live a dignified life, and the transmission of knowledge across generations. Settlement ultimately aims to dispossess Aboriginal future possibility itself, both for community members and within the popular Australian imaginary.

The extent to which the settler-colonial imagination has become infused within daily life in Aboriginal communities renders it difficult to disentangle and decenter. However, also embedded within the social lives of palya media projects are "glimpses" into refigured centers, which cast imperial imaginaries toward the margin (Bessire 2017). *Fires, tires,* and *paper* aim to further move the center regarding dominant discourses in remote Aboriginal communities.

Fires is symbolized not through Western connotations of destruction and hell but rather as a fundamental mode of productive group action, as it represents the literal means for taking care of Country. It decenters pervasive deficit discourses regarding Aboriginal communities, which moralize individual work ethics through the capitalist framework of productivity. *Fires* speaks to the ways in which even arguing against this can implicitly reinforce the very logic it opposes through its centering of European conceptions of labor, rather than community understandings of collective cultural production. *Tires* encapsulates aspects of infrastructure, materiality, mobility, and kinship. However, it troubles the artificial separation between these realms in Aboriginal community life. It centers local expertise and points toward the critical issue of outsider control over resources. *Paper* includes bureaucracy, institutions, and governmentality. Yet, it unsettles the idea that these are reasonable, and instead decenters them as alien and irrational systems—mind-boggling wastes of time that are inherently disruptive and colonial.

Ultimately, these three analytics emerged from the attempt to understand how palya projects come into being. Each aims to move the analytical center by reframing language in ways that illustrate the positive space of what Indigenous collective creative production *is,* rather than through the negative space of what it *is not.* In addition to understanding palya film processes, I have also come to think of this trinity as a framework for considering how outsiders can most appropriately contribute to Aboriginal community media.

To our great surprise, *Marumpu Wangka* won the NITV Spirit Award at the 2015 NRIMF in Lajamanu, which included funding to extend the project into multiple short films totaling a half hour for broadcast on NITV. In light of my direct experience in *Marumpu Wangka,* I was asked by PAKAM to be the director of these films. I was initially reluctant to serve as a whitefella director for these NITV productions, though I eventually agreed when it seemed that there was not an available alternative for this very niche and time-specific project. Collaborating with crew members I had worked closely with over years on many projects, I drew upon this trinity as a guiding framework throughout many decisions in the social life of these films. While this was a larger project, we were grounded in the knowledge that *Marumpu Wangka* resonated largely because the creative fire that represented a normal day in Balgo was spontaneously recorded and not extinguished through the process. We aimed to facilitate *paper* and make *tires* as available as possible, while remaining patient and ready to catch unexpected *fires* in real time as they lit.[9]

Film Families

It is the day after Shorty improbably found his Centrelink paper near the shop, and we are driving the PAKAM troopy with his wife, Allison, toward the pound. Named after areas where community members kept livestock in decades past, the pound is a visually striking, extended overlook along the edge of Balgo and is especially popular with visitors for its desert sunsets of long shadows and burnt sienna hues painting the landscapes below. "I have had this in my mind already, for years now," Shorty reiterates as we pull toward the edge of the drop-off. It is over an hour before sunset when we arrive, as the three of us discuss the best angle and then set up two cameras and multiple mics. Shorty has told me about his idea for a film titled *For Young Futures* for several weeks while waiting patiently for his Elders to finish their projects. Double-checking his background and how he is sitting within the frame, Shorty confidently signs and states, "Roll 'em." Over the next twenty minutes he details the importance of supporting community youth, personified in their son, Eli, who is in much of the footage. He describes how to guide youth away from addiction and help them to "look at the good future in the front" so that "moms and dads, aunties, uncles, grandmas, and grandpas might be a proud family." It is clear that Shorty has practiced this many times in his mind. He does not need a second take, and as soon as he is done he signs "nyamu" and then "palya."

To visualize the metaphor of family relations in these film projects, I often imagine a kinship chart with *Tjawa Tjawa* as the ego. The represented kinship relations are—like *fires, tires,* and *paper*—both metaphorical and literal. One way of understanding the cinematic kinship of *Tjawa Tjawa* is to imagine its parent as the 2013 film *Kurrarlkatjanu,* which served as its direct precursor, itself a child of the other films produced in partnership with the women's center in prior years. In many ways, *Marumpu Wangka* became a sister project to *Tjawa Tjawa.* In a literal sense, it starred Mark's sister Payi Payi and his half sister Linda. *Marumpu Wangka* was specifically made possible through Mark's support following *Tjawa Tjawa,* and it subsequently gave birth to two nieces of *Tjawa Tjawa—Hand Talk Trilogy* and *Bush Hunt Hand Talk* (2016)—as well as a dictionary of more than three hundred signs that Mark and I recorded throughout the hand sign projects in front of a bright green container near the airstrip.

For several weeks, Mark's nephew Shorty and Shorty's wife, Allison, were ready to shoot *For Young Futures,* a child of *Tjawa Tjawa.* However, it became apparent that we should first shoot *Jimmy Tchooga: Painting Two Snakes,* as Jimmy was their Elder (this was the film from chapter 2 when we got bogged and Jimmy's son rescued us after seeing our signal fire). When Bob Dingle unexpectedly decided he wanted to film, Shorty and Allison again delayed their project, seemingly without a second thought. In other words, we were appropriately obliged to prioritize filming projects based upon respect for Elder relationality in Balgo. *Mangkayi Calling* was the longest wait of all, unique in that it was both grandfather and grandson to *Tjawa Tjawa.* This mirrors the multigenerational repetition of kinship skin-name categories. For example, because Mark is a Tjapangarti (by skin name), his grandsons are also Tjapangarti. While there are limits to this kinship analogy, it conveys how the social lives of palya Aboriginal films extend to other projects and relatives.

It is through this cinematic kinship relationship that I came to better understand the roll of *Tjawa Tjawa* as both *fire* starter and family member to other films. The Songlines on Screen program required tight constraints around both time and topic, centering documented precontact cultural knowledge. However, beyond the primary short film, NITV encouraged communities to use the associated equipment and expertise to produce whatever was locally valued. They also reiterated that all footage and films should ultimately be archived within communities. In addition to stoking local *fires,* this institutional openness also contributed *tires,* providing long-term project equipment that enhanced the Balgo PAKAM projects following *Tjawa Tjawa*. The Songlines on Screen films were meant to serve as inspirational and material catalysts for community media productions moving forward. The program's status and funding facilitated community members like Mark to travel with their films—in his case to Broome, Lajamanu, and Sydney—where he made an impassioned case that was explicitly political, integrating his own plans to return to Country. *Tjawa Tjawa* and the films in its wake fostered the creative collaborative process that transformed Mark's understanding of cinema from one more way to *visit* his Country to a powerful mode of radical political transformation for *returning* to his Country. It was toward the end of this creative post–*Tjawa Tjawa* period that he and I would have a short yet transformative conversation near the community store.

5

After-Images

A thing is mighty big when time and distance cannot shrink it.

—Zora Neale Hurston, *Tell My Horse*

While preparing to travel to Balgo after a brief visit to Broome, I call Mark to let him know that I have just come across some old photos of him in the digital archives at the Sisters of St. John of God. These include images of him as a young man living in the Old Balgo Mission. After a pregnant pause, he asks, "Any photos of my wife?" When I reply "Yes, I think there was one," I can hear the smile in his response. "I lost all of my photos of her and now I don't have any. See if you can get one." Days later, I make the sunrise to sunset drive to Balgo. I quickly drop my faded olive-green backpack in the shared volunteer housing and drive the PAKAM troopy to see Mark. He moves with uncharacteristic speed from the front door of his house, and after a brief greeting he flips swiftly through the eight-by-ten thinly laminated photos, before suddenly stopping. Taken on their wedding day just after they were married, the black-and-white image shows her next to him in a dress, beaming, and with a flower in her hair. Mark examines the photo closely for a long moment, then folds it into quarters and carefully places it into his front left blue jean pocket. Sighing slowly, he turns inward and slowly says, "She was a good woman."

In the wake of his wife's death, Mark had destroyed all of her photos as a way of honoring important restrictions against speaking about or seeing recently deceased family members. However, things had changed. Not only had time passed, but there had also been shifts in Balgo regarding these practices. And since this and other photos had been digitized and archived, they could dematerialize and rematerialize.

As a perceptual phenomenon, an after-image persists within the retina following a flash of light, or when it is cast into sudden darkness. This lingering impression floats amid the blackness of one's eyelid. It can at times retain aspects of image fidelity, invert its colors, or even provide a sense of continued movement. Building upon previous anthropological engagements with after-images, I have come to think of the echoes, reverberations, and cinematic relatives of our films as metaphorically unfolding in such a way. Like cinema itself, an after-image simultaneously conveys multiple meanings. It speaks to what endures after images are created, shared, and destroyed. I also consider after-images in terms of the processes that layer upon previous cinematic envisionings—visual palimpsests that conjure the past into moments of creative presence, opening toward the future. Unlike "postproduction" or "circulation," after-images extend beyond the explicit realm of a project's own life cycle. Palya films give birth to a variety of after-images, from archives, to other films, to this very book, as well as to the numerous quiet moments of reuniting and remembering images.

The after-image of *Tjawa Tjawa* that most animated Mark was *Mangkayi Calling,* an expansive project and film though which he envisioned returning with his family to their Country and restarting the community of Yagga Yagga. This chapter illuminates a variety of after-images in the wake of *Tjawa Tjawa.* It traces ongoing shifts in protocols regarding images of the deceased and within media archiving. It illustrates how projects such as *Mangkayi Calling* can act as temporal and spatial portals that collapse pasts and futures into the present through moving images. It concludes by considering the limits of after-images and ethnographic engagement, as well as the opening potential of cinematic co-creation toward gaining insight into the dynamic process of culture itself.

Images of the Deceased, Archives of the Future

Aboriginal taboos against viewing images of the deceased have been well documented since the earliest records of missionaries and anthropologists, including shifting perspectives regarding visual media (Michaels 1994). Along with hearing the names of the deceased, viewing their images has been prohibited for months and even years. The death of an individual imbues an after-image with enduring agency from which the bereaved distance themselves—abandoning the deceased's camp, possessions, name, and image by extension. This is softened over time, as memories become increasingly ambiguous. Such practices bolster boundaries between the spirit and human realms, though powerful healers sometimes carefully engage with the recently departed. For a variety of reasons, these practices have changed in recent decades.[1] For example, Balgo community members often noted that while the placing of photos on funeral notices remained somewhat controversial, it had become increasingly less so. Understanding these shifting perceptions was paramount for the film projects I collaborated on. As recently as a few years prior to *Tjawa Tjawa,* it was common for films to be delayed for years following the death of someone featured in a project.

NITV was acutely aware of these dynamics in their Songlines on Screen program. To account for such eventualities, they included a relevant section within every release form for the films in the series. There, participants could explicitly agree (or not) to allow their images to be used in the event of their own passing. Neil described his surprise that every single person in the *Tjawa Tjawa* shoot checked this box, and how unlikely that would have been in past years. In a strict legal sense, this form would be technically adequate, since individuals control their own image release. However, in practice Aboriginal family members could still decide that they would not like the film to continue, regardless of the permission form. As Neil put it, "That could come up and likely will in the future with such releases. That checked box is really just to confirm the wishes of the individual. After that, it's a conversation to figure out what the right thing to do is, as far as PAKAM is concerned."

At the 2015 National Remote Indigenous Media Festival in Lajamanu, Mark greeted me one morning as I was emerging from my tent. With a heavy heart, he told me that one of the Elders at Kapululangu had passed away overnight. I called the women's center to send my condolences and to say yowie (sorry),[2] speaking with several of the Elders. At the end of my discussion with Zohl, I mentioned that I should talk with ICTV about pulling *Marumpu Wangka* from screening that evening. We had completed this film just a few months earlier, and the recently passed Elder was featured throughout. I was surprised when Zohl responded, "Hmm, I'm not totally sure, but I think it might be alright to show it. The Elders worked hard on that one, and my sense is that they want it out there. I'll go and talk with the families about this and see what they think. In the meanwhile, ask Mark what he thinks."

When I asked Mark, he thought about it and started looking around the festival. He seemed to consider every individual who was there. After a long pause, he said, "It's alright. It's not a problem for anyone here. No families." Zohl confirmed that everyone she spoke with in Balgo wanted it to be shown, and so we left it in the screening schedule. My sense in hindsight is that this decision was partly made because of the starting assumption that we would *not* show it. Indeed, had I left the film in the screenings or pulled it without consulting them, this would likely (and quite rightly) have been upsetting for family members in Balgo. Ultimately, it was the open discussion that led to the decision to screen it. This seemed to create a precedent, and when a similar situation came up in our hand sign projects in 2017 there was again a consensus to release the films.[3]

One interpretation of shifting protocols regarding images of the deceased is that they are the result of an insidious decline in adherence to traditional Law—the outcome of increasing assimilation into settler Australian society. I regularly heard whitefella managers bemoan that "Aboriginal people are losing their culture." Implicit in such comments is the assumption that changing one's ideas necessarily implies degradation. As Fred Myers (2004) argues in relation to Aboriginal acrylic painting, such judgments reveal that for many whitefella Australians, Aboriginality is static and archaic. While all communities and traditions shift, there is often a double standard regarding the imposition of a temporally frozen cultural purity for Aboriginal communities.

My fieldwork suggests that such changes are not well explained as a "loss" of traditional culture but rather as nuanced shifts stemming from deepening relationships with the processes of image creation and preservation. Legacies of Aboriginal images being taken and stored without consent or transparency have until recently resulted in cautionary approaches (Michaels 1994, 10), though as technological familiarity has increased, so too has community control over media creation and the movement and storage of images (Deger 2006, 109). Unsurprisingly, the more that community members directly control the representational process, the more permissive such image circulation seems to become. As Jennifer Deger points out, one key change over time is that photos are not only "taken" but increasingly given, exchanged, and shared (98).

Current decisions regarding such images seem to reflect shifts in practices of selective concealment. For example, in the Coen region of Cape York, access to cameras has meant not only that the vast majority of images of Aboriginal people are now taken by Aboriginal people, but also their display of photos has come to far exceed that of non-Aboriginal households (B. Smith 2003, 20). This proliferation reflects the regular movement of images through extensive networks of relations. After varying periods of time following the death of loved ones, those images, hidden though not destroyed, are now often unboxed and returned to household walls. The COVID quarantine era further shifted these practices in Balgo. In 2023, one manager in Balgo noted that especially in relation to community films, "After-death images are changing a lot. There has been so much trauma since 2020 that people seem to be okay with the potential downsides in order to see and be inspired by their Elders, which they need now more than ever."

In decades past, Aboriginal archives existed largely to salvage information for settler posterity. This is changing quickly due to technological innovations and collective actions within the Indigenous Australian mediascape. Archives are increasingly located in and run by communities. For example, when Warlayirti Artists built their Culture Centre expansion in 2000, much of this funding went toward creating a community archive for cultural objects, paintings, and digital media. The relatively low cost of digital storage has transformed community archiving, which can now be achieved with a few encrypted hard drives paired with robust cultural protocols. Throughout my fieldwork, I attended various well-funded archival workshops and programs. There was a particular emphasis on digitizing tape-based media, as these were reaching the end of their stable lifespan. These events were part of Indigenous Remote Communications Association's Remote Media National Archiving Strategy, initiated in 2014 in partnership with the National Film and Sound Archive of Australia and the Australian

Institute of Aboriginal and Torres Strait Islander Studies in Canberra. Archiving was a regular topic of discussion at media organizations, from national festival roundtables to production meetings in the PAKAM shed, which itself held a particularly vibrant archive featuring decades of Kimberley Aboriginal media.[4]

Many organizations, including the Sisters of St. John of God Heritage Center (SSJG) in Broome, had begun using Ara Irititja software, which later became the Keeping Culture Knowledge Management System (Thorner 2010). Issues of access in such systems were often debated in archive meetings as stakeholders navigated the balance between competing goals of accessibility, security, and community practices. Such balance was crucial. If trust was lost around any of these three elements, a system would quickly lose traction. However, if trust was earned, it could build momentum for many years. As Jacques Derrida put it, an openly accepted archive "produces more archive, and that is why the archive is never closed. It opens out of the future" (1995, 68). Meetings on archiving imagined the long-term futures of archives by and for Aboriginal people, made especially challenging due to rapidly changing media formats and cultural protocols.

FIGURE 28. Archive room at PAKAM.

Such practical concerns about archive programs continue to be widely discussed, as the "technical structure of the archiving archive also determines the structure of the archivable content even in its relationship to the future. The archivization produces as much as it records the event" (17). In other words, an archive's interface shapes what will be in it, who will use it, and to what ends.

While driving together around Broome on a balmy morning, Mark suggests that we stop at the place where I found the photo of his wife. It is only a few blocks away, and when we pull into the SSJG the flags lining its meticulously manicured pathway signal that it is open. Mark is greeted by friendly faces that he already knows, including Exhibition and Engagement Officer Sarah Keenan and a notable volunteer, the late Bardi singer and performer Stephen "Baamba" Albert—a musical legend who was integral to the formation of PAKAM and Goolarri. We catch up over a long cup of tea on the porch and then down with Sarah at one of the two Keeping Culture Knowledge photo archive stations within their exhibition space. As Mark guides us through the archives—his index finger often lingering over an individual on the screen—the images from the Old Balgo Mission ignite story after story from this era. In light of his knowledge, the SSJG staff ask if he might like to contribute to the archives, since many of the people he is discussing from the mission are not currently identified in the system. Mark agrees without pause, and we move to a room with a larger screen where he spends over an hour identifying dozens of people.

The intersection of content, systems, and discussions facilitated this spontaneous and open moment of collective archiving. Receiving photos (especially the one of his wife) initiated a relationship between Mark and these archives.[5] The welcoming and unrushed visit extended this relationship to the organization that held them. Furthermore, the accessible yet secure system facilitated kinship-oriented pathways for exploring the images, leading Mark to contribute so that others might revisit and rematerialize photos of their own loved ones. Not only have the once guarded images from Kimberley missions become more accessible, but the archive has been transformed into a locus of collective remembering.

The archiving process itself is crucial. Derrida (1995) describes this as the process of inscription. Archives have tended to emphasize written documents and photos that implicitly center colonial imaginaries, even as Aboriginal people have resisted this process since at least the 1860s (Lydon 2006). As Michel-Rolph Trouillot (1995) argues in relation to Haitian colonial history, archives and the histories they imply consist of "a particular bundle of silences" that provides an illusion of completeness while furthering imperial narratives. The SSJG archives also exist in inevitable tension with the complex (and often tragic) histories of missionization described in the very exhibition that surrounds these computers. At the same time, such archives serve as a "colonial witness" in the "complex process of seeing and overlooking, remembering and forgetting" of times that are often too difficult to either remember or forget (Lydon 2010, 234). Increasingly, communities hold secure archives that contain both outsider images and Aboriginal media, operating through locally defined protocols whereby community members are "calling the shots" (Lydon 2014). The constellation of an archive's system, content, and location fosters possibilities for engaging the past in the future and the future in the past, while accounting for changes in the present.

In the archive workshops I attended, motivations for archiving seemed to both confirm and contradict Derrida's declaration that there is "a compulsive, repetitive, and nostalgic desire for the archive, an irrepressible desire to return to the origin, a homesickness, a nostalgia for return to the most archaic place of absolute commencement" (1995, 91). While archaic nostalgia remains a motivating force for many colonial archives, Indigenous media organizations' desire to archive seemed animated by other sensibilities. At times they engaged through what Faye Ginsburg (2002, 40) calls "screen memories," which "recuperate their own collective stories and histories—some of them traumatic—that have been erased in the national narratives of the dominant culture and are in danger of being forgotten within local worlds as well." Mark's naming of the unidentified in the Old Balgo Mission seemed like such an act in that back room at the SSJG.

The motivations of Indigenous media organizations to archive also stemmed from the desire to honor the work of current and past media workers, especially in relation to lineages of creative work within organizations. During moments of video rendering or other downtime processes, PAKAM workers often rewatched old videos together as they recounted stories from past shoots and reflected on the creative arc of workmates. Deceased individuals in these films were sometimes fellow media workers, and watching their films at times felt like a commemoration. Media archives provided a chronicle of and for the media workers themselves, serving as much as a family album as an institutional record. In the face of the broader defunding of Aboriginal organizations and communities, archives also provided crucial evidence for the importance of Indigenous media and affirmed the case for its continued funding. Archival discussions often emphasized their value for younger generations, as workshop attendees imaginatively projected why youth might interact with archives in the future. So, while Derrida's "fever" might not capture these archival motivations, perhaps *fires* can—slow-burning coals that gently warm swags on cool desert nights, ready to burst back into brightness with a bit of care and attention.

Mangkayi Calling

This book began at the turning point of this story, following the completion of *Tjawa Tjawa*. On a sunny morning, in his cowboy hat and with a smoldering Winfield Red in hand, Mark declared, "Let's make a film about going back to Country, about the future. Let's make the real film." For Mark, a catalyst for this moment had recently occurred. A few mornings earlier at the store, Mark pulled me aside and told me, "There's going to be a men's meeting this afternoon. You should come. I've been thinking about something to tell the young people." Hours later, sitting in a large circle not far from the store, community members and managers discussed various aspects of men's health. When Mark spoke toward the end of the meeting, there was a palpable shift in the air, and a gravity to his words in Kukatja. He spoke widely about problems in Balgo, how they were bound up within the history of being forced off of Country, about how this brought multiple language groups into the Old Balgo Mission and then to its current location. He emphasized the importance of young people having a clear vision to see that right path forward. This was fresh in his mind when Mark asserted that we should make the "real" film about going back to Country in the future. He already had thoughts and audiences in mind, and when he declared that we should start "tomorrow, first thing early morning," he knew exactly what the initial shoot would entail.

Just after sunrise, Mark, Shorty, Allison, and I climb into the troopy. This first trip is not a long one, as we drive just beyond the edge of Balgo's soundscape. As Mark eases himself down onto soft terra-cotta sand in front of a spinifex-covered hill, the three of us set up the equipment. In synchronized coordination, we place the camera, plug in cords, and clip the radio mic to Mark's flannel shirt just below his beard. We balance the boom mic on a small case within the wind shadow of the troopy and set the tripod to its lowest height, which requires us to dig a shallow hole for the center pole to descend into. Having been filmed throughout *Kurrarlkatjanu* and *Tjawa Tjawa*, Mark seems increasingly accustomed to this process. Testing the mic levels, he repeats "1 2 3." Finally satisfied with the setup, Shorty turns to Mark and gives him the signs for palya and roll 'em. Subtly nodding, Mark looks into the camera and, without delay, begins:

> It's very important for me to tell you what is in my head, in my mind, and my heart. Taking people back to Country. Changing the idea that there is no future for our young people. Yeah, when you take them out and show them hunting and freedom, they can enjoy life in the bush and know their own Country, where they come from. Earlier, I spoke in languages in the community. But I want to tell you in English, about leading young people to their future in Country. My heart aches for my people. My heart. Yeah. This is what I'm telling you. Some of us are getting older and we want to put these messages in the pictures so you can understand what we are saying. You can see and hear me very clearly, what sort of problems we have in our community, and what I'm thinking now.

Mark speaks for over an hour, pausing only to roll a cigarette halfway through. As he had told us before we began, Mark shares what he said at the men's meeting, but in English and on camera. His final words are specifically meant for Kukatja youth:

> I want you to become somebody in the future, not only me Moora, Moora, Mark, Mark. I talk all the time. I won't last long. I won't last forever anyway. What do you think? You are the one who's gotta learn to change if you want to become someone or learn to run Yagga. That's why I'm making this film story. For a better place for you, for your future with your grandchildren. For your great-grandparents, for the future to come. That's all. That is my aim. I hope in the future I see you there. Thank you. Good luck.

These were only some of the many messages he conveyed for a variety of audiences, including Balgo, other communities, politicians, and the Australian general public. For Mark, these messages were encapsulated within the broader project of *Mangkayi Calling* that he, Warwick Nieass, and their families had been working toward for decades. The two had remained close ever since Warwick arrived in Balgo as a cook in the 1980s, after which he lived in Yagga Yagga and married into Mark's extended family.

Figure 29. Warwick Nieass and Mark Moora. Photograph by PAKAM crew; courtesy of Pilbara and Kimberley Aboriginal Media, copyright 2014.

Sitting next to Warwick in a shoot about his life story, Mark said, "He's a friend of mine because he lived in Yagga. And a very good friend to me. Yeah, every time I go to Broome I go to his place and sit down and eat and sleep." As Mark reached down for a cigarette, Warwick had already begun to pass him a lighter. The depth of their friendship was illustrated in many small moments. As they discussed their lives, Warwick noted: "My time is still here with my friend, and we enjoy working together. And when distant we talk on the phone. As Mark has been saying, it's very difficult. It's slow. It's very slow. And yeah, we've found that we're in a position where we're getting old and it's time for the younger people to take over."

I serendipitously got to know Warwick during my first trip to Balgo in 2013. Working separately and together with Warwick and Mark throughout my fieldwork, it felt momentous when the three of us collaborated in person. While Warwick often could not be in Balgo during the *Mangkayi Calling* shoots, he remained at the heart of the project throughout.

FIGURE 30. Larry Gundora. Photograph by Joe Pickering; courtesy of Pilbara and Kimberley Aboriginal Media, copyright 2014.

Over the next few months, Mark and I made regular trips south of Balgo, each usually for a few nights, and always with Mark's relation and closest mate, Larry Gundora. During these trips we would spend the first night in Yagga Yagga. It was there, near the sacred site of Mangkayi, that Mark envisioned a home base for their future plans. The site of Mangkayi carried particular significance. When attacked by outsiders, Kukatja people would retreat to this hill, which rose up into the sky, protecting them from their enemies. It was more than a metaphor in the larger project of going back to Country. Witnessing the devastation of diabetes, drugs, and suicide on the younger generations in Balgo, Mark envisioned a community of small family groups that was culturally, environmentally, and financially sustainable and which would welcome intercultural exchange through bush tourism and media projects. *Mangkayi Calling* followed Mark from sun-drenched deserts to the Sydney Film Festival stage in his larger mission to foster a new generation of Aboriginal leaders.

This project has not only engaged the future; it has embodied it through a film process that bridged the past and present as Mark and his family planned to return to their Country. Mark's deepest cinematic awakening was not that he had something important to communicate. It was not that Mangkayi was calling his family home. It was not about the specific ways that he planned to return to Country. These had all been gestating for years. It was that cinema itself was a crucial component for answering Mangkayi's call, communicating each of these previous insights from Country across time and space.

Biographical Backtracking in Mark's Life Story

Toward the end of the *Mangkayi Calling* filming period of several months, Warwick arrived in Balgo. He, Mark, and I quickly settled into a daily rhythm at the art center volunteer house, located near the community store. Every morning at eight, Mark would come over for tea and toast and we would review film footage and make plans at a metal table on the large porch overlooking the center of Balgo. During one of these morning discussions, Warwick suggested that Mark tell his life story, specifically at the Old Balgo Mission where he had spent much of his childhood. For a long moment, Mark was quiet as he gazed at the overcast sky. Finally, he said, "Yuwai, that's good. I'm going to start thinking about my life. I want people to know all of the things that I've done and what has happened to Aboriginal people. It's time I told my story." Over the next few days, Mark discussed and considered his life story with us and others as we went through the social process of purchasing a patched spare tire.

On a cloudless morning, we made the drive to the Old Balgo Mission —two hours west from the crossroads in front of Mark's house. Months earlier, we had visited as part of Balgo's golden jubilee celebration. At that time, Shorty and I filmed Mark amidst rocky remains, where he described the mission days and pointed out specific places, from the dormitories to the bread oven. However, on this trip he did not want to film in the mission but rather along the road leading out, with its structures faintly visible in the background. When Mark spoke about the mission it seemed all at once to represent history and nostalgia, tragedy and trauma, and rubble and ruin (Gordillo 2014). It was already hot when we began, and no words were required in the setup process.

Mark told the story of being hidden in spinifex grass as a baby when his parents witnessed their first airplane, though he did not begin there. He did not tell a linear story. It began in the present and slowly moved deeper into time, though not in reverse order either. Mirroring the process of finding his way through Country that he had not been to in years, I have come to think of this as biographical backtracking, as he narratively circled pastward in widening loops to move forward in his story.

The social life of *Mangkayi Calling* was embedded within multiple layers of after-images. That was never more apparent than in this shoot, as Mark sank into the depths of his life story just beyond the remnants of the mission he grew up in. Writing this section felt much like the process of film editing, as I intercut his life story and footage alongside personal and regional histories.[6] In my first drafts I attempted to place events in chronological order, thinking that this would provide clarity, but it ultimately felt untrue. Here I aim to honor the discursive and relational way that Mark told the story of his life.

Mark's life was as atypical as it was emblematic. From being born in the bush to growing up in a mission. From Balgo to Broome. From shell shucking to horse whispering. From starting Yagga Yagga to witnessing its decline. From becoming lost to guiding others home, on- and off-screen. It is the unusual and eclectic trajectory of his life that interconnects worlds that too often remain disconnected within national imaginaries of Aboriginal life. Mark's story encapsulates a multitude of Kimberley Aboriginal experiences across time and space, and disrupts the narrow limitations that are often imposed upon Indigenous possibility.

The Rise and Decline of Yagga Yagga

Understanding the need for intros and transitions in a film edit, Mark began his life story by introducing himself and describing the larger purpose of the film, stating that "the reason why we're making this film is going back to Country, returning to the desert, our Country. And this film's name is *Mangkayi Calling*." He started, as he often did, by focusing on Yagga Yagga. This particular shoot, however, was more temporally expansive than others. He centered his dreams, both literal and figurative, as a motivating force in his life:

> Yagga Yagga was set up because of the story of my people. Old people told me story about the Country where they came from. They told me story when I was about that high [gestures the height of young boy]. I kept telling that story when I became a man, and I thought about my Country when I went away in the Kimberly where I was a stockman. I had dreams about my Country. It was calling me back. That's how I started up Yagga, by story, it came true. I'm still telling stories about it. I want to go back to Yagga, to lead my people to a better life.

Throughout his life story, Mark connected the pieces that made Mangkayi's calling so vital for him. He spoke in reference to previous films and the shoots we had completed with Larry over the previous months in their Country. In this moment, I thought back to our previous trip to Yagga Yagga and the words he spoke there.

We stop in Yagga Yagga on our way back to Balgo. Mark directs me to set up a shot of him and Larry sitting in sun-soaked red plastic chairs in front of the abandoned community store. As we begin rolling, Mark

FIGURE 31. Mark Moora and Larry Gundora on a *Mangkayi Calling* shoot.

does not waste a moment of our limited battery life and speaks directly into the lens. He starts by introducing himself and describing a deeper purpose of the film:

> I was born in the desert, and me and Warwick have plans for going back to Country. You can call it Mangkayi Calling or your Country calling back, or your parents, your family calling back. Your grandmother. That's what it is. That's why I keep coming back here and making films, for one good reason: to lead people back here to the good, peaceful Country. My vision, my heart, my soul is out here. In the future I want to settle down. Go back and start developing this dream, this community, this home right here, right through this Country. In the past we lived in small family groups, which was good. They enjoyed life. They had a good life. They had a happy life.

Mark seems to imagine this past as he tells it, and conversationally notes that "people were talking about the homeland movement. Scott

Cane helped us and we settled in Yagga. We studied the land and landscape stories and everything. We got the well, I got a gun, then we moved out, living in Yagga. It was a good life." Mark pauses and looks toward the disheveled community store with its shattered windows. After a moment he continues, "But when you start something good somebody or the government is going to come along and try and stop it or steal it. They ran away with the money and whatever else they did." Seeming to turn inward, he adds, "Then I lost . . . my partner, and I'm on my own now. I used to be sad, but now I feel good and I get along with my life." As he often does when his story becomes somber, he snaps back to the present moment and smiles. "Anyway, I want to lead you to a better world. A better future. We want to go back and be free people in our own Country. That is my aim. Yuwai."

Before leaving for Balgo, we stop at the Yagga Yagga water tank. As we fill up, Mark examines the intermittent drip from the faucet that feeds a tiny oasis of moss below. Staring at the verdant scene, Mark recalls, "When I first moved back to Yagga I got a rifle and only a couple of old people followed me down. I had to go out hunting and I used to fill the water tank up and leave them with plenty of water. Water is important. That's why I want to find that water hole by the airstrip and in Mindirr. This tank is still important. People use it. It saves lives." As he speaks, I consider just how right he is. I remember back to the *Tjawa Tjawa* shoot, when his son Eric and I filled the water trailer here with what felt like endless buckets under moonlight. With one patched tire to spare, we begin the drive back north to Balgo.

As Zora Neale Hurston wrote, "There are years that ask questions and years that answer" ([1937] 1998, 21). The year 1979 answered, following a lengthy period of Aboriginal sovereign assertions. Amid a zenith of activism at Noonkanbah Station and the creation of the Kimberley Land Council (KLC), Mark wrote to the director of the Western Australia Aboriginal Lands Trust to apply for rights for Mangkayi—his Country—which extended from Lake Mackay up to Yagga Yagga (Cane 2016). Increasing activity in oil exploration brought in anthropologists Scott Cane and Sylvie Poirier, who both spent years at Yagga Yagga with Mark and Warwick. Desert homeland outstation settlements expanded from five in 1975 to five hundred by 1986 and to one thousand by the late 1990s (Myers and Peterson 2016, 13). As many noted about this era, they did not need governmental programs; all they needed were "diesel, water, and bullets."

Having received the water well in 1984—which tapped into a high-quality and plentiful aquifer—Mark led the establishment of Yagga Yagga. Unlike most outstations, it was created with little governmental funding and involvement. It inspired and was inspired by other desert communities, such the Pintupi community of Yayayi (Myers 2016). Reflecting on his years there, Cane writes:

> The name Yagga Yagga is taken from the Wati Kutjarra ("Two Men") *Tjukurrpa* (Dreaming) and means "to be quiet" (in the context of the Two Men walking quietly across the plains to avoid waking a large sleeping snake). The name was applied to the small settlement and was indicative of the circumstances that gave rise to it: a place of intended peace and tranquility. Yagga Yagga was not, in this sense, a product of nostalgic desire for a return to the past, nor a confused attempt to mix the past with the present or amalgamate traditions with modernity. It was a local solution to the terrible social problems at Balgo. (2016, 260)

Many sought refuge in Yagga Yagga in the late 1980s from the troubles of Balgo life, which stemmed from the unprecedented number of people, mix of language groups, and lack of mobility—further exacerbated by counterproductive governmental policies.

The early success at Yagga Yagga, which is located a few hours south of Balgo along an unpaved road, was due to its *lack* of governmental involvement. By 1986, Mark secured funding for significant infrastructure, including refrigerators, upgrades to roads and the airstrip, and a used four-wheel-drive vehicle. Approximately sixty community members lived there in corrugated iron shelters and had access to fresh water, which was pumped into a water tower that provided sufficient pressure for house plumbing and gardening. Over the following years the community prospered, bolstered by regular supply runs, nurse visits, and a part-time school. The acrylic painting movement that began in Balgo blossomed in Yagga Yagga, with most of the area artists living and painting in its relative peace (Tjama et al. 1997). By comparison, the primary change in Balgo during this period was the establishment of a police station to address increasing social tension.

As was often the case with outstations, the problems of Yagga Yagga began with a sharp influx of governmental money and, by extension, control. The community received a lump sum of $4.5 million in 1989 for infrastructure. Due to bureaucratic stipulations, the community had to use or lose $3.7 million of this funding during a four-month period in 1990. In this rush to spend money, Yagga Yagga community members established smaller outstations within a fifty-mile radius at Walkali, Lamanpanta, and Piparr. However, no meaningful funding followed in the years after this surge. This left those in the smaller communities little choice except to return to Yagga Yagga, which came to average around 150 residents. Despite such fluctuations, the government lauded Yagga Yagga as an exemplary community, with low levels of conflict and only two whitefella workers employed there. Order was largely maintained by consensus, kinship networks, and Law enforced by Elders.

Unfortunately, the ever-changing government bureaucracies did not leave well enough alone. In 1990 the newly minted Aboriginal and Torres Strait Islander Commission (ATSIC) began exerting control over Yagga Yagga through their funding requirements, which became further complicated by their byzantine bureaucracy. ATSIC funded the community, adding significant infrastructure and machinery, though their perhaps well-meaning policies were shortsighted, extending the community beyond its ability to self-manage. Ultimately, Yagga Yagga became a victim of its own success, and by the mid-1990s it attracted agencies and people who sought to impose their ideas about the best way to run it. This was why Mark remained adamant that Yagga Yagga be redeveloped slowly: "We'll start with a few, maybe ten or twenty people. It will build up like when you plant a tree. It grows. You look after that tree with water. Maybe it will grow big with a lot of roots. We don't know what's going to happen in the future."

The 1990s were also an especially vibrant era for Yagga Yagga artists. However, the six-figure income of many top artists and their regular travels to Balgo further destabilized Yagga Yagga, in addition to the large sums of royalty money from mines coming in through family networks. The new whitefella staff and community members also became increasingly combative. Meanwhile, Mark was elected to the ATSIC Regional Council, leading him to travel around Australia to attend meetings, which resulted in a leadership vacuum. All of this contributed to the rise of general discontent.

By 2000 the population had fallen to under forty people, many of them children. The overextended infrastructure became unmanageable, with regular supply shortages and road maintenance issues, leading to a downward spiral. Mark would often recount—with great drama and a dash of humor—the story of when he led a group of men to the regional town of Kununurra to visit ATSIC. After politely asking its workers to leave the building, the men smashed their computers with clubs, since that was where they were told that the money and problems were located. While the magistrate was sympathetic—dismissing the charges and suggesting nonviolent protest—there was little recourse to save the community. Describing this event in his life story, Mark thanked the magistrate directly and described how it led to his awakening to the idea of protest, which they began to engage in from that point forward.

Yagga Yagga's decline resulted from a national trend toward "streamlining" services away from outstations and toward larger community hubs such as Balgo. Governmental agencies also began taking a harder line on policy rules, citing technical breaches of contract to withhold funds and exert top-down changes. Yagga Yagga was abandoned by the very government agencies that had inflated it beyond its ability to sustain itself. The few who remained faced isolation in addition to a lack of services, leading many to refer to this as the sad period of moving to regional towns, including Halls Creek and Broome.

As Yagga Yagga declined, so too did Mark's health. The combination of stresses in the community and his family took a toll. As Cane notes, Mark

> began to suffer extreme anxiety and depression: he was, quite literally, being driven mad. His mental state was aggravated by the development of cataracts and increasing blindness, by the manslaughter of his daughter-in-law, and his wife's cancer and subsequent death. Mark believed his wife had been "sung" and he told me he had "spirits in his head" after she died. He was so disturbed he went to the Balgo cemetery one night,

> where he was found by his family trying to retrieve her body and bring her back to life. Mark continued to live at Yagga Yagga and speak at meetings, pursuing his aspirations for native title commandeered by the KLC some 13 years previously. But he was a shadow of himself, under heavy medication and otherwise catatonic—and spent most of the day sitting alone in front of the Yagga store staring into space. (2016, 269)

The breaking point for Yagga Yagga was when a young man hung himself in the school playground. As Mark recounted, after that everyone walked out, leaving the community for Balgo. Shortly thereafter, the road to Yagga Yagga was gated and locked, and everything that could be sold was auctioned off in 2006. Around that time some of the buildings were burned down, possibly to dissuade whitefellas from living there (Cane 2016, 270).

Ultimately, even Mark was left with little choice but to move back to Balgo, which was embroiled in increased policing to deal with community disputes that had escalated over decades. After the closing of Yagga Yagga, Balgo's suicide rates climbed to catastrophic levels. As Mark continued to struggle in Balgo, Peter Njamme—an influential Yagga Yagga community member—was found dead on a street in Broome in 2013. The fate of Yagga Yagga was mirrored in Aboriginal outstations across Australia. Recent threats to the remaining Aboriginal communities are an extension of these policies of abandonment spanning the past few decades.

It was in the aftermath of Yagga Yagga's decline that I first met Mark in 2013. And yet, the man I got to know over several years was quick to laugh, a captivating storyteller, and a gifted leader. I came to understand that in the wake of Yagga Yagga's closing and a series of deaths, including his wife's, he had felt profoundly lost in Balgo and in himself. As he told me once, "I've done a lot of hard things in my life, but the hardest is going back to Country." Over the years I have met several people who lived in Balgo during the early 2000s, and each described Mark as Cane does above, in a state of profound anguish. As one field mate described it, "His heart was broken. He would grind his teeth and sit next to the store, so I never got to know him, though his legend loomed large." If the depth of one's grief is the measure of one's love, Mark's love for what he and his family had lost was immeasurable.

This could have been the end of Mark's story. That would have been more than understandable, and enough for most people to give up. Yet it was not the end. His late-life enthusiasm for making films about going back to Country was made all the more powerful because it involved him climbing out of an abyss. As much a doer as a dreamer, Mark was not an unshakable optimist. He knew what it was to experience devastating loss, to endure that for as long as it took, and to try again. In this way, his story speaks to more than the power of strength and leadership. It also speaks to those for whom hope seems all but lost.

Kimberley Walkabout

While Mark only alluded to the exact reasons why he left Balgo to travel throughout the Kimberley as a young man, he once described this time away as an unconventional sort of walkabout.[7] First working in cattle stations near Balgo, Mark eventually made his way across the Kimberley, working from station to station. After heading north to the town of Halls Creek, he drifted west, working in the Fitzroy Valley and eventually making his way toward the Indian Ocean and Broome,

FIGURE 32. Mark Moora on a horse as a stockman.

before being called by a dream and his promised wife back to his Country.

Mark had ridden horses since he was a child in the Old Balgo Mission, and by the time he was a young adult he was a first-rate stockman, renowned for his ability to drove cattle and to calm the wildest of stallions. It was this skill set that provided his initial means for working beyond Balgo. As we traveled around the region, Mark often recalled stories of his treatment at different stations. Once, while on a back road near the meteor site of Wolf Creek, we passed an old house that evoked a story about a boss there who used to threaten him with the six-shooter displayed prominently in his holster. Such experiences of rough station managers inevitably ended with Mark leaving to find a better situation. He preferred to drove cattle under moonlight, often recalling childhood memories of walking with his family through Country at night. He emphasized that this was the *only* sensible time to travel during the hot season.

The role of the stockman is crucial in Kimberley Aboriginal history. Like the deep-sea pearl-diving "saltwater cowboys" in Broome, stockmen commanded respect for their bold mastery of a dangerous profession. For decades, station life served as a way for Aboriginal people to live in *relative* peace with whitefellas while remaining on or near their Country and without relying on inconsistent governmental funding. In a cruel irony, many from that era point out the unintended consequences of laws guaranteeing fair and equal wages in late 1968 as leading to the end of that lifestyle (Jebb 2002; Skyring 2012). As former Kimberley Land Council executive director Peter Yu argues, this policy allowed little time for adjustment and in one fell swoop "broke the back of the feudal relationship between station managers and Aboriginal families. Pastoralists began to force Aboriginal people to leave the stations, which precipitated a refugee crisis of enormous proportions" (1994, 19). While skilled stockmen like Mark could still find work, it was increasingly difficult and initiated the migratory dynamic that exists up to the present, with many Aboriginal people from communities moving to the fringes of regional towns like Broome, where they are often treated as second-class citizens. Even Mark found it difficult to find a station job with a reasonable manager and eventually ended up in Broome. Elders sometimes describe Aboriginal history as having three distinct eras: the killing time, the pastoral time, and the welfare time. If the beginning of the stockman era marked the end of the time of mass violence, its end marked the start of the era of forced dependence.

Walking past the oval in downtown Broome with Mark and Warwick on a sunny afternoon, we sat down in the shade of the "Balgo tree," which oriented toward Balgo from the center of the oval—much like how camps in Balgo spatially gesture toward the Country of their inhabitants. After signing and saying hi to friends and family, Mark described his first day in Broome as though it were yesterday. He reminisced that initially he knew no one and sat down in this very area, quickly realizing that it was a meeting place for Aboriginal people throughout the Kimberley. The Balgo tree was a beacon that immediately oriented him and placed him in relation to others. Noticing pathways, Mark had walked the short distance to Kennedy Hill—a small neighborhood community in downtown Broome near culturally significant places overlooking Roebuck Bay's mudflats—looking for a place to rest on his blanket. Just then, an older Aboriginal woman called out to him, asking if he wanted to stay with her family. Happy to see a welcoming face, he agreed and had a meal with them. As Mark described, in the following weeks it became clear that he had entered into a relationship with this family, and he was determined to find a job so that he could contribute to their funds.

Like many young Aboriginal men of this era, he quickly found employment within the world's premiere pearling town, shucking (cleaning) raw pearl shells as they were brought into the port. Having worked hard his whole life for little money, he recalled being overwhelmed by the amount he was earning. It allowed him to buy whatever he wanted, including an occasional carton of beer to share. Rather than saving his income, he insisted on contributing all of his money to the family he stayed with. He spoke with pride about being able to help support the household and how the woman of the house gave him just the right amount of money back for him to spend so that he wouldn't have to worry about food or shelter.

This continued for some time. He enjoyed life in Broome, but it was difficult to sustain. While he had a relational network, it was not *his* family or Country. Ultimately, he yearned to return to a quieter life and escape the daily realities of racial strife in Broome. He noted that leaving ultimately boiled down to the fact that "I'm not a saltwater blackfella. I'm a freshwater blackfella from the desert. That's my Country." For a time, Mark returned to the life of a stockman in nearby communities including Beagle Bay, north of Broome along the coast. He met and came to know Dunba Nunju (whose film he watched with great nostalgia). This was also where he received word that his promised wife (arranged marriage based on skin-name kinship relations) was waiting for him in Balgo. This prompted him to slowly make his way back home, working station to station along the way. Just before this journey home, Mark experienced a crucial moment just after waking one morning, "I had a dream. Mangkayi was calling me back, and I knew straight away I better go back to my people. From that dream, we built the community."

Sitting near the Old Balgo Mission telling his life story, Mark seemed to have become transfixed in time while discussing this period. He was suddenly aware of this as he turned to the camera and smiled, now back in the present moment. With his characteristic levity following a serious topic, Mark finalized his thoughts: "But anyway, a real good life in the Kimberley, and I met a lot of good people, good tribal people."

Mark often recounted with humor how he was a stranger when he first returned to Balgo after many years away. While he knew everyone right away, Mark had changed so much in appearance and demeanor that at first no one recognized him. It was only after introducing himself that he was warmly welcomed home. Previously he had wanted to see the larger world, but now he wanted nothing more than to be near his family. Furthermore, his travels had reignited in him a desire and plan to return home—not simply to Balgo, but to the Country that he walked with his family in the moonlight of his youth. This dream was deepened by his wedding and the three children that followed. Mark had changed during his absence, and so had Balgo. Indigenous activism across the continent had resulted in national policy shifts toward increasing Aboriginal control of communities.

In 1984 the Old Balgo Mission was formally transferred to community members as an independent body. It was renamed the Wirrimanu Aboriginal Corporation, based on the Luurnpa (Kingfisher) Dreaming embedded within its location, though it is still generally known as Balgo

(Carty 2021, 47). However, as with the implementation of fair wages on cattle stations, this was part of a policy shift that included unintended consequences due to its rushed execution by the government. There was not enough training or preparation for what this transition would entail, leading to years of increased tension between different language group camps who were not accustomed to the unprecedented reality of living permanently in a shared community. Although Kukatja people held the majority population and influence—and their language was the local lingua franca—Balgo's new location placed it squarely in Jaru Country. By Law, Kukatja people were therefore guests who should have deferred to Jaru Elders. As Mark put it, "We were living in the wrong land because people came and built Wirrimanu. Kukatja people are not from that Country. How can you fix that problem? No one can fix that. Nobody. That's why I want to move back here [Yagga Yagga] with my people. So they could have a better future." Mark described bureaucrats who wanted to fix Balgo as being similar to a non-mechanic trying to fix a motor, liable simply to further damage it.

Meanwhile, the political changes in the 1980s coincided with the rise of a local painting cooperative initiated by Warwick, which was quickly followed by missionary involvement (Carty 2011; Healy 2014). Unfortunately, such whitefellas carefully engaging in Balgo life were few and far between. While the control of the church declined, missionaries were often replaced by increasingly less scrupulous kartiya and an influx of mercenaries and misfits led to unchecked alcohol smuggling (Mahood 2012, 27). As Mark often distilled it, "big community, big problems." Such structurally induced dysfunctions were sometimes referred to as "the troubles" (Hinkson 2021, 12). These problems were exacerbated by the dramatic dismissal of Father Ray Hevern in 1984, leading to rising discontent in Balgo that continued throughout the decade. During that fateful year, ever watchful for something more, Mark and his family were able to acquire a water point (well) established by Mobil Oil in his Country that would become the foundation for Yagga Yagga.

Of Beginnings and Balgos

Toward the end of his life story shoot, Mark was winding down to his final comments, noting, "I was born in Emily Springs, and I was a baby in the bush and in a coolamon [elongated wooden container]. I was brought in with my parents, and my family walked into the mission." He suddenly stopped and said:

> Oh, sorry. I forgot about something. About a place called Mindirr. One day I'll get there and get a film about that Country. It's got a water hole. One day there, my family hears this sound coming. WOOOH, looong way and they look and ask, "Where is this sound?" It is coming from the south, low like a bush fire. They chuck me in the spinifex and run for their lives. Yeah, and that's the first time they saw an apple and orange. They didn't eat it, and when they came here into the mission, they knew that food. They didn't know that was kartiya food, whitefella food. All they knew was blackfella food.

Mark was born around 1945 near Kiyarr in the Great Sandy Desert to the south of Balgo. He was born into the Kukatja people as a Tjapangarti within the desert Dravidian skin-name kinship system. He often recounted this story of being hidden as a baby when aircraft first flew overhead. He spent his early years with his family in Mangkayi, not imagining himself as either "Aboriginal" or as part of one of the "world's oldest continuous societies."

Mark and his family lived their lives through what anthropologists have long described as a nomadic hunter/gatherer lifestyle, following Songlines in accordance with Law and in relation to Tjukurrpa, or Dreaming. Despite occasional interruptions and the increasing knowledge of whitefellas in their Country, life continued. However, a combination of pressures—including leprosy epidemics and the intrusion of water-seeking cattle drovers along the Canning Stock Route (Carty 2010)—led many to walk into local missions, what is often described as "coming out of the desert."

In the early 1950s, when Mark was a child, he and his family walked into what was then called the Balgo Hills Mission. Now known simply as the Old Balgo Mission, it was established in 1942 by Pallottine missionaries after years of searching for suitable sites following the failure of missions to the north. This site was important, as it had previously been used for initiation ceremonies and corroborees. The mission's name, like many in this era, was based on a misunderstanding. On one of our visits there, Mark joked about how the missionaries pointed to the nearby hills to try to understand the area's name, asking, "What is that called?" A Kukatja man responded that they contained a grass called *palkurr-palkurr,* which sounds roughly similar to "Balgo Balgo." Mark laughed and nodded his head when he told this story, continuing, "It's a bush tucker where you grind 'em in the rock, cook it, and make a damper out of it. Yeah, I grew up on that anyway."

The Pallottine missionaries, joined by St. John of God sisters, were tough taskmasters by all accounts. Isolated during World War II, the mission had to be virtually self-sustaining. Aboriginal men worked long hours in construction and as stockmen, while women tended gardens and made clothing. Mark and others who grew up here emphasized the impractical and uncomfortable life of being locked inside mud-and-brick dormitories at night, which were freezing in the winter and sweltering in the summer. It was here that he was given his English biblical first name the last name of "Moora," inspired by the way he was known to be aspirational, regularly asking for "more." He often noted how he wished he could have learned to write, but he was deemed too old for this when he came into the mission: "I only went to school in Old Balgo for five years. I was going to be a young man, so they told me no more." While at the mission, Mark continued through his now-disrupted process of Law. Due to negative attitudes toward these practices, they were often carried out in secret and he was not able to complete all of the initiation rites. He emphasized that he nonetheless listened carefully to the old people in his youth, whose stories guide him still.

> I grew up with the old people. I was a good listener. I used to listen to old people's story about a lot of things around the campfire and they used to camp in Old Balgo. Yeah, that's what I did. I was a good listener to the old people who passed away a long time, a long time ago. They were always sitting down and telling story. It was the good old days. Yeah, good old days. I still think about them.

Mark looked over his shoulder toward the mission, and then ran his hand through the pindan, before continuing directly into the lens,

> Wisdom and knowledge come from old people, not from young people. You've got to learn to talk to the old people and get to know them. Because

> they're the ones who will give you good knowledge. Yeah. The ones who can tell stories. They can give you something good in your heart and your mind. Law was very strong when people lived in Mangkayi. I had that story about that place when I was a kid growing up. I used to ask a lot of questions to old people. They told me this area is yours. Your tribe's Country. It's the right one.

When the Old Balgo Mission came up over the years, Mark spoke of both the good of that era and its tragedies. At other times he would make then break a long silence to say that he preferred to not even think about it, stating, "Those days are hard to talk about. Those times left scars on my heart."

For Balgo's 2015 golden jubilee, a series of small paintings were completed for visitors to buy. One of the most discussed depicted Aboriginal people carrying wheelbarrows full of rocks around the Old Balgo Mission. It was stared at, picked up, and pondered over, yet it was also one of the very few that did not sell that week. It was as if the

FIGURE 33. Mark Moora interview at the Old Balgo Mission.

FIGURE 34. Dormitories in the Old Balgo Mission.

artist had violated an unspoken code about concealing the stark realities of mission life to tourists. Tellingly, its companion painting sold quickly. Made by the same artist in the same style, it depicted community members praying in white clothing. When visitors romanticized mission life, Mark was quick to note how hard it had been, shaking his head slowly and bemoaning that "it was a *hard* life. Hard work."

Over the decades, Old Balgo Mission grew to more than two hundred people. In response to the insufficient water supply, Father John McGuire sought to establish a new mission in 1965. The vast majority of this labor was done by Aboriginal people, including Mark. Consisting of three thousand acres of freehold land twenty miles east of the Old Balgo Mission, the newly reestablished Balgo quickly doubled to nearly four hundred Aboriginal residents and thirty whitefellas by 1969, when McGuire took ill and was replaced by Father Ray Hevern and Father Anthony Peile. That same year, Balgo became an incorporated Aboriginal entity, granting at least theoretical decision-making power to community members under the national leadership of the progressive prime minister Gough Whitlam, who shifted control of Aboriginal affairs from states to the federal government (which would become a critically relevant detail in the recent community funding crisis).

Community members in the 1970s lived in single-room stone houses and small scrap metal shacks known as "humpys," while constructing a variety of buildings in the community to house a clinic, a school, and a stone oven producing one hundred loaves of bread per day. They also established larger ventures like the airstrip and an accompanying plane service. Balgo supported a population of up to seven hundred with huge gardens; over a thousand head of cattle, in addition to other animals; and heavy machinery to construct roads, dams, and water bores. These early days of this newly formed Balgo community are celebrated by many in the church. However, as with Old Balgo Mission, they are not glamorized by most community members, who were paid meager amounts of sugar, tea, flour, and tobacco, along with occasional one-dollar payments for hard labor.

While the Old Balgo Mission had a predominance of Kukatja people, this new mission included higher proportions of four other primary language groups: Ngarti, Jaru, Warlpiri, and Pintupi (as well as a smaller number of Walmajarri, Wangkajunga, and Ngaatjatjara people). This regionally unprecedented mix of tribal groups led inevitably to increased tensions. After Mark had helped to build Balgo, the combination of low wages, social division, and increasing conflict led him to search for a life beyond Balgo throughout the Kimberley.

Mark's story is in many ways the story of the Kimberley. He has lived a life full of remarkably varied experiences that integrate regional distinctions and historical shifts over the past seven decades. Although I first met Mark in the aftermath of Yagga Yagga's decline, this difficult period was not the end of his story. It was only the beginning of his cinematic renaissance, becoming a film director and broadly asserting messages born from hard-earned experiences.

In the final words of his life story shoot, Mark mused on the broader arc of his experiences. After seeming to reflect on whether he had covered everything he wanted to, he smiled to himself and looked directly into the camera. "That's my life. I've been around in the Kimberley and Australia. I worked very hard in my time just for a little bit of money or tucker. But no worries. I enjoyed it. It was a good life. I hope you like my story. Yuwai, that's a true story about my life. Nyamu."

Envisioning After-Images

What remains within images after they circulate? Here, I consider how after-images carry forth the multitudes that cinema contains. Due to this compression, there are limits to how much context can be conveyed. As Michael Taussig argues, there are also dangers in interpreting after-images through Western frameworks, which are embedded within various hierarchies of difference. Irreconcilabilities can further result in what Taussig describes as a "chamber of mirrors" feedback loop, leading to "an after-image of an after-image receding to a limitless horizon," where at best we can catch only "cascading glimpses of splintered Othernesses on the world screen of mechanically reproduced imagery" (1993, 249).

Yet there is also something grounded and enduring in after-images. Lucas Bessire builds upon the potential power and meaning of "glimpses" within experimental workshops though the Ayoreo Video Project in Paraguay. He develops the glimpse as an analytic, method, and writing style that "is aimed against alterity known in advance . . . attuned to the incipience of open-ended subjects, affective surges, and possibilities falling apart or taking shape." Bessire's consideration of "glimpses" engages in a co-creative process that "begins by surrendering ethnographic authority to flashes of an unfinished present" (2017, 121). Such moments of surrender mark the opening of ethnographic possibility, which is as relational as it is unpredictable.

Co-creation is crucial to the promise of after-images, as well as ethnographic engagements with Indigenous media more broadly. Miyarrka Media's *Phone & Spear* (2019) provides a model for co-creation that resists the assumptions of what Linda Tuhiwai Smith (Ngāti Awa and Ngāti Porou, Māori) distills as the "imperial imagination" (1999, 23). Proposing a Yuṯa, or "new," anthropology grounded in Yolngu frameworks, the full-color pages interweave an energetic collage of images, artwork, commentary, dialogue, and analysis. The two most prominent voices in the book are Yolngu Elder Paul Gurrumuruwuy and anthropologist Jennifer Deger. Deger describes their decade of collaboration in art, filmmaking, and writing as an anthropology that aims to "bring different worlds into relationship" rather than what she notes is the more common ethnographic goal of "revealing one world to another" (Miyarrka Media 2019, 11). This seemingly subtle difference is profound in its deceptive simplicity, with implications about the foundations of anthropology itself—where anthropologists and community members are "together, but not mixed up" (56).

It is within the space of what Maya Haviland (2016) develops as "co-creativity" that such glimpses become possible and meaningful. Sarah Elder describes the "collaborative space between image maker and media subject" that fosters a moral and open space for meaning making in ethnographic film (1995, 94). Such dialogic openness is especially fostered when the project itself is co-created. This is also apparent in the emerging genre of interactive documentary, in which access, authority, and audiences are shared between co-creators and their various communities (Ryan and Staton 2022, 11). Rather than polyvocality, such documentaries imagine collaboration through metaphorical musical "polyphony" by which voices interact through harmony and dissonance. This cinematic form "is in a constant process of becoming and . . . is not so much a genre as a set of possibilities and practices that are constantly evolving in response to not only technological developments but also the cultural specificities within which these technologies unfold" (Aston and Odorico 2022, 20). In the rest of this chapter I reflect upon *Mangkayi Calling* as an after-image that illustrates how co-creative processes can transcend and interweave time and space to envision future possibilities.

Slipstream Media Portals

Mark's engagement with futurity resonates with its recent ascendancy as a central theme in Indigenous intellectual and political movements across the globe (Estes 2019; Medak-Saltzman 2017; D. H. Taylor 2021; Weiss 2018). In *Walking the Clouds,* Grace Dillon (Anishinaabe) establishes Indigenous futurisms and defines *slipstream* as a subgenre of Native science fiction, with "pasts, presents, and futures that flow together like currents in a navigable stream" (2012, 3). Such temporal currents open rich avenues for co-creative cinematic envisioning. This is the case not only in Balgo but also within the broader international Indigenous mediascape where futurist parallels abound, including and extending beyond science fiction genres (Ginsburg 2018; Lempert 2014, 2018b; Medak-Saltzman 2017).

While I was attending the imagineNATIVE Film + Media Arts Festival in 2018—only three years after it screened *Tjawa Tjawa*—there was a buzz in Toronto surrounding two innovative Indigenous futurist media premiering at the festival, each bearing the title *Biidaaban. Biidaaban (The Dawn Comes)* was a short film by Amanda Strong (Métis/Cree), whose characteristic stop-motion artistry and soundscape brought to life writings by Leanne Simpson (Michi Saagiig Nishnaabeg). As within Strong's previous shorts, such as *Four Faces of the Moon,* in *Biidaaban* "a piece of media technology becomes the portal or mechanism through which these Native currents of time flow and out of which an empowered Indigenous cultural future emerges"—in this case, a round organic tablet (Dowell 2018, 191).

As this premiered, the other *Biidaaban* was playing downstairs in the experimental media area, which included games, virtual reality (VR), and even cookies being laser-etched with festival logos in real time. Featured within this space was *Biidaaban: First Light,* an immersive VR experience created by Lisa Jackson (Anishinaabe) through which the viewer explored a high-fidelity re-creation of a future Toronto reclaimed by plant life and First Nations people and languages (Monani et al. 2021). Both of these media developed out of organizations engaging at the intersection of futurity and Indigenous media in Canada, including imagineNATIVE, the Initiative for Indigenous Futures at Concordia University, and the National Film Board. While Toronto was half the world away from the Kimberley, imagineNATIVE was unanimously considered to be the favorite festival by the Aboriginal filmmakers I worked with, and great excitement was expressed for the 2016 launch of its sister event, the Winda Film Festival in Sydney.

As defined within *Biidaaban: First Light,* "Biidaaban is an Anishinaabe word. It refers to the past and the future collapsing in on the present. It is the moment of first light before dawn." By highlighting the simultaneous expansiveness and collapse of time within the present moment, Indigenous slipstream media provide a powerful framework through which such narrative and form emerge through a collective process. Rather than simply describing futures, these projects unfold through a constitutive process.

Phone & Spear centers collaborative process as the foundation for analytical insight, highlighting the participatory aspects of poiesis, a concept developed by ancient Greek philosophers. Heidegger rendered this as "a bringing-forth . . . the arising of something from out of itself . . . the bursting of a blossom into bloom," which, when embodied by artists, carries the potential to burst not only into itself but also into its creators and audiences (1977, 10–11). It is therefore fitting that *poetry* is derived from *poiesis*. Poiesis collapses boundaries not only between people, processes, and products of creation but also between the past and future within a present presence—where "the old and the new are made co-constitutive: the new renews the old; the old is manifest as the source of the new" (Miyarrka Media 2019, 11). It provides a temporal portal across time and space through which the creative process brings itself into being. This is especially the case for Aboriginal connections with their Country, which animate and inhabit virtually every aspect of life. As Zora Neale Hurston put it, "A thing is mighty big when time and distance cannot shrink it" ([1938] 1991, 245). Plato imagined that such poiesis exists along thresholds of emergence, such as the gathering of nighttime and the moments before sunrise—where it is neither light nor dark, day nor night—at the merging of something into another along a horizon.

"I didn't know I would say that, but we did it right, palya," Mark said after we finished watching the previous trip's footage at the Balgo radio station. Mark often responded this way and was sometimes even surprised at what he said. In the *Mangkayi Calling* shoots, it was not simply that Mark was collecting his thoughts or summarizing his ideas. Rather, he was considering how to best summon the right words in Country. Depending on where we were going, he would have us pick up specific people to come along before we drove hours out of Balgo toward that particular place. When we arrived at the right location, he would stop and say, "Here, now, this is what we need to film and this is where we need to talk." After a quick setup, Mark and the rest of us would have a conversation on film. He was moved to speak when we were in the right place, in the right way, at the right time, and for the right reason. On the other hand, Mark described his frustration at speaking at meetings across Australia, noting that "When I'm in a city, I think differently. Too much traffic, too loud. I'm rushing and I think like a whitefella. When I'm out here in the desert, I think like a blackfella." As in Strong's films, cinema itself provided a portal which transported Mark's messages across time and space from his Country, where he could see the personal and political horizons with clarity and purpose.

Constitutive Cinema

Creative acts have long been understood to be constitutive of their own process. As novelist Edward Morgan Forster once put it, "How can I tell what I think till I see what I say?" (1927, 152). Mark implicitly reimagined this question as "How can I tell what I think until I'm in my Country?" The issue, then, is not simply what community members such as Mark think, but also the extent to which they are able to be in the proper places to properly do so. Sylvie Poirier, an anthropologist who lived with Warwick and Mark in Yagga Yagga, writes that "places and the sentient land can offer messages and novel information to those willing to listen, information that may influence important decisions, trigger processes of negotiation of varying scope, change the course of events, or be called upon in the interpretation of events" ([1996] 2005, 243). In Balgo, speaking and thinking are not precursors to action, but are rather the outcome of being in the right place in the right way. This involves both sitting on and moving through Country.

Aboriginal/anthropologist collaborations have often provided generative partnerships in communicating such embodied and placed knowledge, especially in relation to varying forms of displacement. Melinda Hinkson's *See How We Roll* (2021) provides a model for sensitively navigating such a partnership. Drawing upon a long-term relationship with Nungarrayi, a Warlpiri woman, Hinkson describes Nungarrayi's exile from her community not far from Balgo. While Mark is displaced from his Country among his family, Nungarrayi's urban exile paints an intimate portrait of complex and shifting settler state relations.

Over many years, Stephen Muecke recorded and co-wrote Elder Patty Roe's stories about Law and culture in the Country north of Broome. In their work, the displacement was of knowledge itself, as they navigated the contested politics of kinship and cultural lineage. Their partnership is particularly relevant, as it laid the groundwork for the Lurujarri Heritage Trail—a nine-day, fifty-mile walk from Broome north along the coast that is run and led by Goolarabooloo people, including the Roe family. Muecke notes that as they considered writing a follow-up to their first book (Roe and Muecke 1983), Roe had an idea that was "much better than a book" (Muecke and Roe 2020, xxiii). This idea was the trail itself, which Muecke frames as functioning through collective attention to subtleties while walking through Country (xxiv). As Muecke put it to me on a different walk in Broome, this way of thinking takes seriously the reality that "intelligence is beyond the brain. That it is in the body and in Country." Therefore, moving one's body through Country is not simply a rejuvenating experience; it is paramount for thinking, understanding, and communicating.

Goolarri's film *Naji* (2014)—part of the same Songlines on Screen series as *Tjawa Tjawa*—became an integral part of this trail. On one of the last evenings on the trip, after days of buildup by our Goolarabooloo guide and one of the film's stars, Terry Hunter, we watched *Naji* projected onto the side of a white supply truck. Terry emphasized media's role in understanding the meaning of Country, noting that "to fully understand it, you need to walk this Country, hear the story, and then see this film." He believed the film to have value not only in being able to see Country and hear the story from traditional owners, but also as an imaginative production that was uniquely capable of further communicating the power of the story of the trail. As John Carty illustrates in relation to Balgo acrylic art, serious creative practice on Country is not simply representational: "It means everything. Literally, everything. It is not a retelling of a Dreamtime story. It is not a picture of a place, or a representation of it. It *is* Country" (2021, 1). So too are films such as *Naji* and *Tjawa Tjawa* for their creators and communities.

Anthropologists working in creative collectives also demonstrate the power of collaborative co-creativity. Miyarrka Media is emblematic of this. Kayleen Djingadjingawuy—a coauthor of *Phone & Spear*—asserts that the "Yolngu way of life is to make it real. Not talk-talk. Action has to happen. To make it alive" (2019, 134). As Taussig describes it, "In this world, the glimpse, like the . . . after-image, is where the action is" (1993, 249). Another prominent and inspiring group is the grassroots film collective Karrabing (which translates as "low tide turning"), consisting of dozens of Aboriginal filmmakers and anthropologist Elizabeth Povinelli. They use "film to analyze contemporary settler colonialism and, through these depictions, challenge its grip" (Lea and Povinelli 2018, 37). Collectives such as Miyarrka Media and Karrabing do not rely on formalized institutional structure as much as they do on "a mode of copresence that would otherwise not exist but for the deliberate intention of working together. . . . Like the tides, [they] come together and move apart as different functions of their lives converge and dissipate, neither as a once-off nor as a constant steady state, but as a continuation of relational practices" (41). Their work embodies the reality of Aboriginal/state irreconciliation and the inseparability of art and life in the process of experimental creation "under occupation" (Biddle 2016). One of Neil Turner's most noteworthy skills has been navigating institutional bureaucracies in ways that allow PAKAM to function as much as possible as such a collective.

Co-creation is not only relevant for creative projects. At a broad level, culture—that elusive and complex anthropological whole—is itself an ongoing series of co-creative actions that foster continual renewal within established systems. Scholars have alluded to this in various ways over time. In *The Anthropology of Poiesis,* Mihai Popa (2022) argues that creativity and culture operate between the immanent and the transcendent. After-images reveal such concurrent layers as "two conterminous levels of immediacy—the latent and the manifest" (Sheehi 2012, 406). Culture solidifies and ruptures in unpredictable rhythms, what Gregory Bateson described as schizmogenesis, "a process of differentiation in the norms of individual behaviour resulting from cumulative interaction between individuals" ([1936] 1958, 175). Heidegger argued that being and becoming are themselves inseparable—two sides of the same coin of human existence through which being becomes, and vice versa.

The imposition of stasis onto people inflicts profound representational, material, and spiritual violence. Yet this is the settler-colonial pretext for the treatment of Indigenous communities within and beyond Australia. It seeks to symbolically exorcise the very act of becoming, leaving only a narrowly defined state of being. From Native Title land rights to the Stolen Generation to defunding communities to popular film representations, Aboriginal people are popularly imagined as static windows into the past—and by extension, presently brittle and futureless. This is why the role of Indigenous media is so crucial. It is not simply a matter of pushing back against negative stereotypes, but also of asserting the most fundamental of life's qualities: change. Indigenous media are especially meaningful for the creators themselves, who through collective poiesis are changing and becoming throughout the process.

A crucial distinction here concerns whether a medium engages culture as representational or constitutive. At their conceptual extremes, a representational model frames people as their preexisting qualities of being, while a constitutive model understands people as only their present moment of becoming. While human life invariably exists between being and becoming, the process of writing tends toward ossified representations. As Marshall McLuhan asserted, "The medium is the message," that is, the qualities of a medium shape its content and perceived meaning. There is something about the finality of symbolic marks etched into stone, inked on paper, or pixelated in screens that implies permanence—what Lucien Taylor (1996) notes is partly due to an anthropological "iconophobia" driven by fears that the ambivalent qualities of images may undermine ethnographic authority.

Cinema, on the other hand, lends itself to the process of dynamic becoming. As ethnographic filmmaker David MacDougall argues, video communicates in ways that writing does not, particularly in relation to corporeal subjects that open up questions, rather than the tendency of writing to focus on answers (2006). Engaging classical anthropologists including Claude Lévi-Strauss and Marcel Mauss, Derrida ([1967] 1993) wrestles with the dangers of irreconcilable dead ends or unbounded complexities in the process of trying to escape the limits of language through language. This is similar to the chamber of mirrors of after-images that Taussig alludes to (1993, 249). Derrida suggests that the way beyond this is neither nihilism nor obfuscation, but "freeplay"—the active disruption of and alternative to the already known. In other words, the embracing of poiesis.

Another way of engaging the enigma of emergence is through Miyarrka Media's deceptively simple question, "Can a book hum?" It builds upon Taussig's description of humming as "central to language . . .

being neither conscious or unconscious, neither singing nor saying, but rather the sound where the moving mind meets the moving body" (2015, 41). Deger describes how this question attempts to get at the difficulty of "animat[ing] the gaps between words and images, digital and analogue, English language and Yolŋu concepts, between past and present, past and future, us and them, here and there. . . . How to set up a field of resonance between worlds coming ever more into relation, and yet still, distinctly, far apart?" (2006, 32). While writing's linear inscription lies in tension with freeplay, cinema tends toward embracing it. Since filmmaking is a social and relational process, creative differences continually reinforce an unavoidable fact: there are innumerable ways that any film could have turned out. Jean Rouch embraced such ideas within anthropology decades before others, largely because he leaned into the constitutive freeplay embedded within co-creative filmmaking.[8]

Cinema, like the ethnographic process—if not always its products—unfolds itself through its own unfolding. Bessire describes emergent glimpses through the unpredictable process of experimental film workshops, which he worried would fail:

> To my surprise, something else started to happen. By the second week of the workshop, a peculiar momentum had started to build. No one could articulate it, but everyone felt it like a shift in pressure. . . . Within two weeks, people began inhabiting this set and acting out collective visions and dreams for the camera. This raises questions: What did the process of collaborative video production open up? What characters—and what ethnography—did its openings refuse, summon, or create? (2017, 120)

These questions emerge from the process itself and could not have been formulated beforehand. They lead to different types of understandings, opening inquiries that co-creative cinema facilitates—releasing control of the process and the search for definitive conclusions.

My own co-creative experiences led down unexpected pathways through collective processes that would have been extinguished through attempts to control them. Creative *fires* of collective poiesis were emergent within their own process. Dancing flames shape one another, becoming transformed as they change the landscapes they move through, leaving behind the promise of renewal—as individual as they are collective, as tangible as they are immaterial, and as inevitable as they are unpredictable. As Heraclitus is said to have uttered, "The meaning of the river flowing is not that all things are changing so that we cannot encounter them twice, but that some things stay the same only by changing" (Kirk 1962, 369). While this continuity through change emphasized water, it is perhaps telling that he viewed fire as the essential uniting element, believing that the nature of the universe was animated by "ever-living fire kindling in measures and going out in measures" (326).

In this project, ethnographic knowledge was most meaningfully generated by working together in the service of collective projects, rather than in its direct pursuit. Co-creative filmmaking conveys, and engages in, collective action within social worlds, though I do not mean to suggest that cinema somehow escapes the many traps of representation. Quite the opposite. As Bill Nichols notes, documentary realism itself can at times engage in a sort of "epistephilia," or pleasure in understanding the sensory world (1991, 178). However, an open co-creative approach to filmmaking demands movement and confronts the inescapable limits of the knowable, collapsing time and space into a present where after-images may provide glimpses.

Water and Fire

Mark seemed reinvigorated in the days following his life story shoot. While he was previously ambivalent about going on upcoming trips, he insisted that we drive around Balgo and talk to people who knew about the location of a water hole near the Yagga Yagga airstrip. The next week, we traveled there with a few of his family members. We lit fires across the area and sat down for packed lamb-chop sandwiches and tea upwind from the flames.

Most consequentially, we stopped by the Yagga Yagga water tank, only to find that the crucial power converter box connecting the solar panels with the well pump had been stolen. This was a shocking and troubling revelation. It was a life-and-death problem, as people relied on this tank. There had even been a few recent deaths in the region due to a lack of water after becoming stranded. We reflected on what would have happened if the tank had been empty during the *Tjawa Tjawa* shoot when we had to make the emergency water run. Mark made sure that we took extensive photos of the damage and components, as well as images of him and others sitting in front of the tank as he gazed into the lens, back at the tank, then down in sadness. Mark choreographed these photo details to serve as supplementary materials for a letter he dictated to me the next day. Before sending it to the relevant bureaucrats in Perth, he had me carefully read it back several times to make sure that it was just right and that we were including the most evocative photos.

The water tank issue seemed to serve as a moment of redemptive failure. Mark and his extended family engaged in various discussions about it that extended far beyond the tank itself, leading to renewed plans for ensuring that someone was regularly camped in Yagga Yagga. There was a suggestion by some that the tank could be sold back to the government so that they could make sure it was always running. Providing a bigger-picture analysis, Mark responded:

> We don't want to think the government way. We need to think about what's going to happen in the long haul. If we sell the water tanks to the government, they will take it over. Then the government will say "We are the boss," and then it's all over. We need to be down there so that the government can understand that we will be strong there in the future. If the government sees that it's an empty place, they will think "We can do what we like." If we live here in Balgo too long, people won't worry about going back. They will forget. But anyway, in the future we'll be back here, so we can run our own community and find jobs and everything. I hope so. I hope we will.

The future imaginary that he described in such moments was based on his long and hard-earned experiences at Yagga Yagga, and demonstrated his ability to articulate a vision of his family back on Country that also anticipated state responses.

It was often said by those who had known Mark over the years that the films had catalyzed a deep change within him. His attitude about filmmaking shifted from viewing projects as a way to get back to Country, to reestablishing himself as a community leader, to a means for broadly communicating Aboriginal life, to a platform for creating future imaginaries for his family. Mark's transformation in the wake of these trips reiterates the importance of traveling to Country and the self-reflexive qualities of the filmmaking process itself. It also highlights both the durability and the fragility of hope. Its simultaneous resilience and vulnerability. Its wellspring and leaky cracks. How quickly it can light, cool to embers, and rekindle. How the winds of change are just as able to blow it out as they are to set it ablaze.

6

The Visibility Paradox

> Power largely consists in the ability to make others inhabit your story of their reality.
>
> —Philip Gourevitch, *We Wish to Inform You That Tomorrow We Will Be Killed with Our Families*

It was on a late March evening in 2015 that I found myself stranded while house-sitting during an unseasonably late Broome wet season storm. I spent much of the afternoon flipping between the four Indigenous TV channels, when an NITV news segment caught my attention. The announcer began, "It's been dubbed the Indigenous Annihilation Strategy, as communities across Australia feel the full impact of the massive funding cuts. Communities . . . are asking, where is the advancement?" "Indigenous Annihilation Strategy" was an ominous nickname given to the recently implemented Indigenous Advancement Strategy (IAS), which had cut roughly 40 percent of the national funding for Indigenous organizations. Yet the Indigenous media sector was spared virtually any funding cuts, and in some cases its funding was even increased.

The story went on to describe how Tennant Creek—a remote town of three thousand in the Northern Territory, composed of approximately 50 percent Aboriginal people—just had twenty-six employees cut from its already limited after-school programs as a result of the IAS. Community members described the negative effects that would result from this, including increases in youth suicide, substance abuse, and financial precarity. The piece intercut positive images of the sports and creative arts activities with community members personalizing what would be lost for them and their families. The significance of this segment being presented nationally by an Indigenous broadcaster was demonstrated in such visuals, and centered Aboriginal viewpoints within mainstream news production values. As the announcer declared, "The artistic heart of the community is now struggling to beat. With what many are calling a fatal cut to the public service system, the mob is asking, 'Where do we go from here?'" He even positioned himself empathetically in the first person, closing the segment, "Danny Teece-Johnson, feeling the pain, for NITV news."

This segment, in which the peak national broadcasting network in a burgeoning Indigenous mediascape covered this story about widespread funding cuts to Aboriginal organizations, cuts to the heart of this chapter. NITV helped to publicize this issue, which contributed to the subsequent reinstatement of Tennant Creek funding. Meanwhile, virtually all other cuts were maintained. Here, I unpack the stark contrast between two seemingly contradictory funding realities that I have come to think of as a "visibility paradox": the unprecedented support of Indigenous Australian media and the devastating defunding of Aboriginal organizations and communities more broadly. The process of trying to unravel this enigma reveals some of the broader dynamics around funding and state relations for Indigenous Australians, as well as the myriad impacts of media-making. After unpacking various forms of bureaucratic *paper* violence and policies of cultural annihilation, I describe the ways in which sovereign envisionings hold transformative political potential.

The Visibility Paradox in a Golden Age of Aboriginal Media

In February 2015, Indigenous Community Television (ICTV) began broadcasting in Broome. Due to an unusual set of circumstances, Goolarri held the rights to three TV channels in this market. They used the first two for their own content, leaving an additional channel to broadcast ICTV. This was particularly exciting as it made Broome one of only a handful of towns in Australia—not classified as "remote communities"—to receive it. As Neil Turner said shortly after it came online in Broome, "I'm in media heaven." The addition of ICTV meant that anyone with basic TV in town could now watch four Indigenous channels: two Goolarri (GTV) channels, ICTV, and NITV. This was in addition to hours of weekly Indigenous-focused content on the national flagship Australian Broadcasting Corporation (ABC) and Special Broadcasting

Service (SBS) channels. Radio was also rich with Indigenous content, including Goolarri Radio in Broome, analogous stations in other regional towns, and the PAKAM network in Kimberley Aboriginal communities. There was an even deeper well of content online, with NITV, ICTV, and virtually every Indigenous radio station streaming content, often on demand. Meanwhile, the peak regional and national film-funding bodies were making unprecedented investments through programs such as Songlines on Screen, which funded *Tjawa Tjawa*. Furthermore, there was an increasing amount of Indigenous Australian content at major film festivals within and beyond the continent, including the establishment of the Winda Film Festival, an Australian offshoot of the Canadian imagineNATIVE Film + Media Arts Festival (imagineNATIVE).

Viewed from outside of the larger political context, this period through the present represents a golden age of Indigenous media in Australia, relatively speaking.[1] The United States, by comparison, has a loose network of Indigenous film festivals and radio stations, yet there is comparatively little integration, infrastructure, or consistent institutional funding for these endeavors.[2] Canada has a dynamic Indigenous mediascape, including the Aboriginal Peoples Television Network (Roth 2005) and imagineNATIVE. New Zealand features two vibrant Indigenous television networks, Māori TV and Te Reo. In this settler state global media context, Australia has relatively strong funding and support infrastructure for a diversity of Indigenous media forms and content—a lineage that can be traced back to the birth of the moving image.[3]

The ascension of Indigenous Australian media began to gain momentum in the 1980s. The launch of satellite television in 1985 provoked concerns that mainstream media would destroy Aboriginal culture, though Eric Michaels (1986) provided compelling and nuanced evidence to the contrary. In the decades since, Aboriginal activists and advocates have voiced concerns about programming that violated cultural protocols, especially regarding taboos around viewing the deceased (Michaels 1994, 73). In parallel with the influx of outside media to Aboriginal communities in the 1980s, several Aboriginal communities, including Yuendumu and Ernabella, began realizing the potential of producing alternate media to amplify their voices within and beyond their communities. This sentiment was part of a larger global phenomenon, with the concurrent and subsequent rise of Indigenous video production including the Video in the Villages project in Brazil (Aufderheide 1995), Zapatista media in Mexico (Halkin 2008), and Igloolik Isuma in the Arctic (Huhndorf 2003).

The Central Australian Aboriginal Media Association (CAAMA) started on a shoestring budget in 1980 as the "world's first Aboriginal radio station" and the first to broadcast in Aboriginal languages (Molnar 1990, 156). The station lacked its own radio license until 1985, when they won an unexpectedly successful bid for what became Imparja Television in 1987. By 1988 they featured thirty Aboriginal-themed community radio programs, aided by a network of audiotape mailings (154). CAAMA experienced resounding success in their Aboriginal-run radio station, though Imparja faced challenges due to the general lack of training in television and the medium's associated high costs (Bell 2008).

The rising dominance of the left-leaning Labor Party in the 1980s provided a largely unexpected turn toward more support for Aboriginal media licenses and funding (Bell 2008; Morrison 2000, 140). Some Indigenous organizations, including Goolarri, began receiving semi-commercial licenses (Forde, Foxwell, and Meadows 2009, 63), which allowed them to engage relatively freely in media markets. A watershed event occurred in 1989 with the formation of the Broadcasting for Remote Aboriginal Communities Scheme (BRACS). It was later renamed the Remote Indigenous Broadcasting Service (RIBS), though I generally use BRACS, since it is the more commonly used term in practice. This continues to provide a national structure for Indigenous remote community media, which has expanded across the continent. In 1992 the program was moved to the Indigenous-operated National Indigenous Media Association of Australia. While radio continues to receive steady funding, there has been relatively less financial stability for Indigenous television programming (Deger 2006, 170).[4] In the 1990s, in tandem with the *Wik* and *Mabo* court victories, Aboriginal media expanded. In 1996 the National Indigenous Radio Service (NIRS) was launched with the goal of providing Aboriginal radio and video content throughout Australia. Many BRACS units continue to produce content for the NIRS network and are able to broadcast over satellite, in addition to local radio towers.

This golden age positions Indigenous media as a powerful force, potentially able to communicate with Australian general audiences who often have few meaningful experiences with Aboriginal people. Media representations—hopeful, dystopian, or otherwise—largely construct the ideological and rhetorical frameworks through which politicians and bureaucrats navigate key policy decisions, including the recent mass defunding of Indigenous communities and organizations.[5] Bleak portrayals also contribute to negative self-perceptions that lead to diseases and acts of desperation, especially for Aboriginal youth. As Philip Gourevitch wrote in relation to the Rwandan genocide, "Power largely consists in the ability to make others inhabit your story of their reality" (1998, 48). In the increasingly ominous times regarding Aboriginal sovereignty, these media are on the front lines of representational battles for national future imaginaries that will affect the fate of their communities.

Irreconcilable Mediations

At the heart of the visibility paradox in Australia is the tension between this burgeoning mediascape and the lack of any Aboriginal treaties.[6] Unlike other major settler states such as New Zealand, Canada, and the United States, Australia was claimed not through treaty making and breaking but through the logic of *terra nullius*. In the absence of treaties, the fight for land rights over the past few decades has provided a double-edged sword. Elizabeth Povinelli (2002) articulates "the cunning of recognition," in which to gain Native Title land rights, Aboriginal people are required to demonstrate—to the very government that has spent centuries attempting to assimilate and erase them—an unbroken and unchanged precontact relationship with their Country. This cunning asserts a false reconciliation that relies on imagining both colonization and Aboriginal people as fundamentally of the past: faint and fading echoes of inevitable, if regrettable, Australian history.

It is challenging to break out of this cunning dynamic in land rights, due to its embeddedness within legal structures. Indigenous media have a more enigmatic relationship with recognition frameworks that depend on tropes of Aboriginal purity. Media provide a landscape where irreconcilable realities can be, and often are, confronted. The vast majority of the media projects I worked on did so, often implicitly and sometimes explicitly. Still, the mediascape is not free of the forces that emphasize a pure and past Aboriginality. The Songlines on Screens program itself—the first Aboriginal community documentary funding program of its scope—focused on precontact conceptions of culture. At the same time, beyond the delivered films, the program provided ample and thoughtful flexibility for community-defined process and outcomes.

Part of the reason why Aboriginal media have managed to maintain relative success and creative freedom is because they are seemingly not perceived as a threat to state governments. Broadcasting Aboriginal media through NITV to potentially millions of people throughout the country might at first appear to be a watershed moment of distribution. However, although virtually all households receive NITV, its viewership is relatively low—and ICTV is only available in Aboriginal communities and select small towns. In the context of the decades of dominant misrepresentation, their programs represent a small percentage of overall Indigenous representations. Therefore, a cynic might be inclined to dismiss the political potential of these media as naive.

This would be a mistake. Australia is the settler state in which Indigenous media have perhaps the greatest potential for meaningful policy impacts. While Aboriginal Australians in many ways have the most tenuous Indigenous land rights when compared to other major settler states—due to their lack of treaties—they are also among the most visible. Aboriginal people are the subject of regular front-page news articles and lead TV stories. Left-wing groups publicly defend them. Hate groups decry them. The civil rights politics of the 1960s and 1970s centered them. While their mainstream representations are highly distorted, they loom large in the national conversation. As I will illustrate, it is *because of* the depth of Aboriginal tropes and their lack of treaties that the state underestimates these media despite the political potential for "cultural activism" (Ginsburg 1997). While most Australians may not regularly watch Aboriginal media, many Aboriginal people and a significant minority of the general public do. In crucial political moments, these media and the political coalitions they foster continue to make crucial differences when it matters most.

Dystopian Depictions

One evening, after a long day of filming in Balgo, a few community members and I turned on a much-anticipated episode of the Australian Broadcasting Corporation's flagship current affairs documentary series *Four Corners* (2015), which that night featured Aboriginal communities in the region. This broadcast aired at the height of a nationally polarizing debate about Western Australia's plans to defund approximately half of the 274 Aboriginal communities in the state. While we watched the episode titled "Remote Hope" (2015), the atmosphere in the room sank from curiosity to despondency. The program quickly revealed that it was not about hope in Aboriginal communities but rather about hope itself being remote in communities. An opening line declared, "These dysfunctional communities have the most depressing living conditions imaginable. They are a disgrace to Australia and all those who have a prosperous way of life."

While the episode presented itself as a balanced debate on "the future of Australia's remote and Indigenous communities," even the supposedly neutral narrator described them broadly as "blighted by grinding poverty, with few job opportunities, chronic alcohol and drug abuse, and in some cases, endemic sexual and physical violence, including against children." Accompanied by ominous soundscapes, these morose narratives continued throughout its forty-four minutes. The joyless program framed itself through derisive, unsupported, and often disproved accusations made by governmental representatives. While the fault for alleged community failures was debated, the overall message was unambiguous: remote Aboriginal communities were miserable and futureless.[7]

There are indeed instances of despair in communities. Many, including Balgo, have some of the highest rates of suicide in the world (Campbell et al. 2016). However, the deeper deception is enacted through the glaring and one-sided omission of everything *except* for suffering, as well as the colonial causes of these problems. The deficit discourses that dominate such popular representations and corresponding policy rhetoric are not representative of the sanguine register that often characterizes everyday community life. The dystopian vision of Aboriginal communities that "Remote Hope" depicted was unrecognizable to community members I spoke with, and it ran counter to my own experiences.

This episode was emblematic of the broader representations and discourses around Aboriginal communities seen in nightly news stories and journalism. A particularly egregious example was a cartoon by prominent Australian cartoonist Bill Leak, which depicted an Aboriginal policeman returning an Aboriginal child to his father. Holding the youth by his shirt, he says, "You'll have to sit down and talk to your son about personal responsibility," to which the father replies, "Yeah, righto, what's his name then?" It was printed in *The Australian*—the most widely circulated national daily newspaper—which vehemently defended it as "confronting and insightful" (Whittaker 2016).

Even celebrated big-budget films such as *Rabbit-Proof Fence* (2002) and *Samson and Delilah* (2009) are not free from this representational context. While these are powerful and moving films, it is worth considering why stories emphasizing tragedy, drug use, and abuse have received a disproportionate amount of funding, distribution, and critical acclaim. *Samson and Delilah* is an example of what Faye Ginsburg (2012) describes as the "Indigenous New Wave," including talented filmmakers such as Warwick Thornton, Beck Cole, and Ivan Sen.[8] Their films are often "concerned with how young Indigenous Australians might carve out culture futures for themselves. Their protagonists not only suffer but also survive and take on the task of imagining possible lives despite the clear challenges that lie before them" (4).

In contrast to the subtle shades of hope in such somber films, Rachel Perkins's *Brand New Day* (2010) stands out within popular film representations of Aboriginal Australians. Based upon Jimmy Chi's Broome-based musical hit *Bran Nue Dae,* it speaks to a broader Kimberley cinema aesthetic of jovial realism. As Audra Simpson argues, such Indigenous projects subvert expectations by the Australian settler public "to see 'difference' in ways that are comfortable, to know, to consume a difference of diminishing and soon-to-be-disappearing culture" (2018, 64). The seeming paradox of joy amidst hardship in Aboriginal communities remains difficult for most Australians to imagine, let alone see. Complex representations of Aboriginal life have primarily arisen via Indigenous media makers, often within networks centered beyond Australia's largest cities.

Closing the Gap and the Politics of Suffering

During one of the post–*Tjawa Tjawa* trips to Balgo in 2015, our PAKAM crew was tasked with making a short video encouraging increased school attendance for a government agency. The shoot seemed initially to have the potential makings of a palya project that integrated *fires, tires,* and *paper.* Titled *Yarra Ninytirri Kuurlta* (2015), it starred David Young, who was the actual local school attendance officer, as he gathered students to go to school in the morning. In the video, he found the boys and girls playing footy and basketball, respectively. He explained to them the importance of education before driving them to school in the school troopy. It was an organic and playful process that developed smoothly in a single day. The edit furthered the humorous tone by contrasting upbeat music when the kids were playing with exuberant metal guitar music from David's point of view as he looked for the kids. This contrast received a laugh every time we screened it in Balgo, not because David was viewed as a frightening disciplinarian but because of the absurdity that such police-style enforcement would be necessary. As in his actual daily job, all he had to do was ask, and most of the time kids would happily go with him to school.

This seemingly palya video went well and was engaged positively in Balgo, so I was surprised when the video was rejected upon submission. As a project directly funded under a Closing the Gap program focused on "Children and Schooling," it seemed to me to be an ideal fit with a resonating message communicated with a bit of humor. However, it was judged that the children were *too* happy to be in the community outside of school. After a few re-edit attempts, it was clear that there was no practical way to address this feedback. The kids *were* happy to be playing with each other in the community, and they were also happy to go to school if encouraged by their Elders.

To receive this grant, PAKAM had to quickly produce the alternative video *Staying at School in Bidyadanga,* which showed footage of kids deeply struggling in school and mentors trying to help them. In contrast with *Yarra Ninytirri Kuurlta,* it featured somber music and muted color grading. Watching these videos consecutively provided me with a stark reminder of the affective impact of current funding policies that emphasize deficit frameworks. While such explicit impacts on film projects were rare, when they did happen they were directly tied to such governmental programs. Because of PAKAM's relative independence and core funding, although *Yarra Ninytirri Kuurlta* did not receive that grant, it was still broadcast and streamed through Indigenous media networks.

The broader stakes of retaining such independence are particularly high in the current political moment. The last decade has seen a resurgence of neoliberal policies that have sought to dismantle decades of slow but meaningful progress around Indigenous rights in Australia. The recent emphasis on the politics of Aboriginal suffering (Sutton 2009) is the result of an insidious rhetorical reframing of Aboriginal communities since the 1970s. Deficit-oriented mass-media representations carry grave policy implications for communities. This is also the case in some ethnographic representations.[9]

A consequential example of the impact of dystopian policy assumptions was the Northern Territory National Emergency Response Act of 2007, commonly referred to as "the intervention." This was a governmental program enacted to address allegations of child abuse in Aboriginal communities in the Northern Territory. A variety of experts have dismissed the alleged high rates of sexual assault as misinformation in the years following these policies (Dodson 2007). The intervention exacerbated negative moralizing narratives about Aboriginal people while also giving rise to a new Stolen Generation of children who were taken, ostensibly to protect them from abuse. It even suspended protections afforded by the Racial Discrimination Act, the Aboriginal Land Rights Act, and the Native Title Act. High-level rights commissioners have decried the intervention as violating human rights, noting that the metrics they were meant to address have generally stayed the same or gotten worse.[10]

These policy moves have been couched through Closing the Gap, a broad constellation of umbrella policies that were formally established in 2007. This initiative has flooded Australians with dismal images and statistics (such as "Remote Hope") regarding well-being in remote communities. The metaphor of the "gap" provides an ideological euphemism for assimilation by the governmental bodies and policymakers that passed it. Framed through relative deficit, Closing the Gap does not—as it would at first appear—refer to the mutual bridging of two social worlds toward a shared middle ground. Rather, it single-mindedly aims to reduce the relative disparities of Aboriginal people, as defined mathematically through the lens of settler values.

As with the intervention—or symbolic "wars" on drugs and poverty waged by nation-states—Closing the Gap is framed within a deficit model that narrowly engages symptoms without considering the larger causal forces of ongoing settler colonialism. Through this logic, defunding anything that gets in the way of aligning Aboriginal statistics with the Australian mean is warranted. This not only justifies myriad policies of assimilation and urbanization but cloaks them within virtues of multicultural equality that fundamentally undermine sovereignty, to be carried out by well-meaning bureaucrats (Kowal 2015; Lea 2008). It was within this policy framework that the Indigenous Advancement Strategy was proposed and deployed during my fieldwork.

The "Indigenous Annihilation Strategy"

"We all knew it was buggered," she said about the IAS, shaking her head. Sitting in her office in Balgo, the manager leans her back against the wall and sighs, adding, "Even with two helpers, I didn't have time to apply. We are taking care of the Elders. And anyways, it would have been a waste of time. The application was as confusing as it gets. Just more Closing the Gap nonsense." Later that week, an art center manager put it similarly:

> The IAS is a disaster. How could it not be when putting 150 programs into one without any real consultation or planning? Case in point, not only did we not get funded, but no art center in the country did. I've written successful grants for years, and even to me it was incredibly confusing. There was no time to develop it. They told us to write and submit our wildest dreams, and then they went and cut nearly half of all the funding. Look at all of the medical and youth services they cut. Barkly Arts got refunded after the NITV story, but most don't have resources to do that. They are vulnerable.[11]

Unfortunately, this drastic funding shift remains a familiar dynamic for Aboriginal art centers. For example, Warlayirti Artists in Balgo had to close their newly built culture center just three weeks after it opened in 2001 due to the sudden cut of more than 50 percent of funding for the Aboriginal and Torres Strait Islander Commission.

Even successful recipients of IAS funding were quick to note that this system was deeply flawed, since its application process was in conflict with that of organizations in Aboriginal communities. Such resignation was typical of virtually every conversation I had in communities about the IAS, with some echoing NITV's description of the program as the "Indigenous Annihilation Strategy." While "annihilation" may at first seem like an overstatement, it aligns with both patterns of policy and public statements by the most powerful people in the Australian state. Instituted by the newly elected coalition headed by Prime Minister Tony Abbott and the Liberal Party, the IAS demonstrated policies of cultural annihilation, implicitly and at times even explicitly. In an ABC Radio interview in March 2015, Abbott infamously proclaimed that "What we can't do is endlessly subsidize lifestyle choices if those lifestyle choices are not conducive to the kind of full participation in Australian society that everyone should have." In addition to this statement's deceptive framework, it is worth noting that he was referencing a tiny sliver of one of the biggest per capita budgets in the world. At a broader level, this relatively small amount was to fund basic services for the peoples whose dispossession has provided the entire basis for Australian territory and wealth.

Abbott's comments speak to state attitudes toward Aboriginal communities that have resulted in real-world impacts. Framed as a way of reducing bureaucratic waste, the IAS proved to be one more form of whitefella pernicious *paper* and coalesced almost all of the funding for Indigenous organizations from various programs into a single application system. When all was said and done, it reduced the total funding for Aboriginal organizations and services by approximately 40 percent. Through this program, no Aboriginal organization, no matter how crucial or long-standing, was guaranteed any funding. All had to competitively apply for funding. To describe the IAS as rushed would be an understatement, as applicants only had six weeks for the entire process of preparation and submission. Furthermore, dozens of applicants I talked with described it as overly convoluted in its questions while at the same time limited in its scope (Scott 2015).

In the end, the IAS resulted in a substantial reduction of funding for the vast majority of Indigenous sectors.[12] In this way, it fulfilled its reputation as the “Indigenous Annihilation Strategy.” Yet, Indigenous media generally met or exceeded previous funding. Why would this be the case? There are multiple reasons for this. PAKAM and Goolarri, like most such Indigenous media outlets, were left with about the same amount of funding through the IAS.[13] A key factor is that these media organizations had seasoned and experienced grant writers, as media makers are routinely proposing projects to a variety of funding agencies.

However, the process was not easy or simple for them either. For example, several executives at Goolarri stayed up late into the night working to refine their application as the deadline approached. As Goolarri CEO Jodie Bell describes:

> The whole application process was hard. Compared to others we didn’t struggle as much, but it was very time consuming and I have a lot of sympathy for those organizations that don’t have three experienced grant writers to spend a full week doing it ten hours a day. If you think about a community organization that doesn’t know how to polish this for the government, they’ve got almost no chance. That’s what I think is the biggest danger of the IAS. If this kind of thing continues, they are not going to get funded. That may not be this year, but eventually.

As with all Closing the Gap programs, IAS applicants had to appeal to one or (ideally) more of the following five categories: (1) Jobs, Land and Economy, (2) Children and Schooling, (3) Safety and Wellbeing, (4) Culture and Capability, and (5) Remote Australia Strategies. However, years of experience in Closing the Gap funding made it clear to Aboriginal community organization applicants in Balgo that these categories were not as they first appeared. For example, many noted that as described through the IAS, “Culture and Capability” did not seem to apply to their organizations even though they were explicitly oriented toward cultural activities. This funding tended to be awarded to non-Indigenous organizations that had professional grant writers proposing quantitative outcomes that were perceived as more objective through the language of "assessment tools."

In conversations on the IAS there was a consensus that funding success often related to who could "check the most boxes" rather than supporting Indigenous organizations with long-term relationships and experience in communities. In other words, in the framework of Closing the Gap and the IAS, culture was rendered fundable through the dominant logic of bureaucratic *paper,* not creative *fires*—and without this *paper* funding, there would be little to no material *tires* to keep such organizations afloat.

Another reason why Indigenous media organizations fared relatively well under the IAS relates to the innate flexibility of content inclusion within video and radio. In effect, media can address virtually any topic, including these five categories. Media exist fundamentally as form, with malleable content. While media have been adaptive to changing funding frameworks, the increasing focus on "checking boxes" nonetheless had concrete impacts on content, as with the rejection and reshooting of *Yarra Ninytirri Kuurlta.*[14] Overall, such examples were exceptions that proved the rule of *relative* topical freedom in media, as such censoring was relatively rare. However, media makers were often aware of these constraints in grants, and they had a subtle impact on which projects were prioritized and how they were framed.

It became clearer over time that there was also a deeper reason beyond funding experience and content flexibility for why the Indigenous media sector retained its governmental support. The 2014 National Remote Indigenous Media Festival opened with a keynote by John, a consultant who had worked for years at the highest levels of government. He foresaw the coming IAS cuts, as well as the potential for media to nevertheless succeed. He opened his address with a warning:

> I look around, and I'm worried that you're not worried. There is a new wave of grant changes that could leave you penniless, but that doesn't need to happen, and if you play your cards right you can get even more. No one punches above their weight more than you all. No one can do what you do better, if at all. Tell your story effectively, and you will be in a great position. But, if you don't, it can go very badly. Do not be passive. They *will* defund you if you don't do it properly.

For such veterans of governmental programs, it was clear early in the IAS process that, even amid massive cuts, the media sector could thrive. This was partly due to media's advantage of national integration via savvy umbrella organizations that efficiently disseminated and translated funding strategies, including this keynote. While most Indigenous community organizations were on their own to submit IAS proposals, IRCA provided a support network for even the smallest organizations to understand and receive guidance on how to navigate the process.

Indigenous media had another advantage in retaining funding; it was relatively inexpensive compared to viable alternatives. A staff member at IRCA put it this way: "Remote media is a great bargain compared to other options, and there would have been a huge backlash if it was defunded. It's visible and inexpensive in the grand scheme of things." The two most common phrases I heard used by policymakers I interviewed about why Indigenous media would remain funded were that it "punched above its weight" but cost "pennies on the dollar" in comparison to non-Indigenous media organizations. For other sectors, such as medicine and education, Indigenous community organizations had to compete with large organizations that leveraged economies of scale and were well practiced at making the case on paper that they presented a better value.

However, mainstream TV networks cannot pragmatically compete with Indigenous media organizations that run on comparatively tiny budgets with mostly part-time workers. In addition to their established community trust and track record of producing and circulating a large amount of content, their developed infrastructure and social network allows them to flexibly adjust to ever-changing scenarios. Some directors and managers of Indigenous media national organizations I interviewed made the case that it was this ability of media to adapt that enabled its continued funding. Its nimble qualities around training, products, and relative low cost resulted in media being better able to adapt to the IAS model than other Indigenous sectors. Through media-making it could be clearly documented that workers received training toward objectives that improved their earning potential. Media projects are also able to be quantified in terms of their productivity as measured by project output and job creation. Since Indigenous media is widespread through multiple national networks while remaining comparatively inexpensive, it translates well into grant productivity models of capital efficiency.

After speaking with various policymakers, I have come to better understand this paradox through the banal and bureaucratic logic of the state. As Goolarri COO Kira Fong described it, "Media does better than the other Indigenous sectors in the current funding situation largely because it has a commercial component." In relation to the rise of the Bollywood industry, Tejaswini Ganti (2012) illustrates how media production sometimes happens to work well within neoliberal parameters of defining success through specific outputs. For a relatively small investment, Indigenous media has "paid off" through a disproportionate amount of national prestige via the circulation of award-winning films and programs at prestigious events around the world, in addition to the global streaming of media highlighting Australia. In this way, there is a certain logic of calculated national utility, which tends to be carried out by politically indifferent mid-level bureaucrats who view the cost/benefit accomplishments of media as sufficiently efficient. Tragically, this same logic also underwrites the IAS's severe reduction in funding for the vast majority of most other Indigenous organizations, programs, and services.

Here lies the question at the heart of the visibility paradox: What dynamics enable the thriving of Indigenous media within broader policies of defunding Aboriginal organizations and communities? At first glance, one might arrive at a pessimistic conclusion regarding the funding of inexpensive Indigenous media. It could even be suggested that this highly visible sector stands in for deeper policies of justice—including land rights and substantial spending on community infrastructure and health—that would cost the government millions if not billions of dollars. However, this misses the ways in which these media emerge and disseminate meaningful content. Indigenous media are certainly not complicit in governmental plans to undermine Aboriginal life. Rather, their programs are often the only ones presenting nuanced and futured representations in a representational sea of dystopian images. To better understand the dynamics of this visibility paradox, I unpack other policies of annihilation that unfolded during the IAS's implementation—namely, the aggressive and wide-scale governmental attempt to effectively close most Western Australian Aboriginal communities in 2014 and 2015.

Closing Communities and Perpetual Precarity

Sitting at the radio desk in the BRACS trailer in Beagle Bay, I am reminded of Henry's understated and intrepid skill. No one I knew was surprised when Henry received the award for "remote radio broadcaster of the year" at the 2014 National Remote Indigenous Media Festival. Over the hum of fluorescent lights and an air conditioner, he improvises jokes, gives personalized shout-outs, and reorders songs, all the while interviewing me as though nothing else is happening. We chat for several minutes about the process of filming *Dunba*, which we are editing in that same room. After playing an upbeat song by his cousin Albert, he takes an uncharacteristic pause. Deep in thought, his smile fades as he speaks to his audience across the Kimberley and beyond,

> Hey folks, this next one is called "Listen to the News" from the legendary Broome musical and movie Bran Nue Dae. Like in this song, you "listen to the news talking about the blues of our people." Yeah, across the internet people are very worried about the closures of the communities. Before playing it, I just want to say that I believe no communities should be closed down. There is a protest this Thursday. You are welcome to come, especially Beagle Bay people. It affects us all. We are all worried about our future. Keep your head up, and together we'll stand or divided we'll fall. Be strong. Governments come and go.

Throughout this Broome classic, Henry listens closely, and nods solemnly along with the lyrics. His focus tightens further in the final lines of the song, which are repeated several times. Contrasting with its major-key joviality, the song ends with an observation on media coverage and an existential question that seems as relevant as when it was written decades earlier:

> Listen to the news talking 'bout the blues of our people
> Is this the end, is this the end of our people?

While managers in Balgo and elsewhere bemoaned the futility of applying for the IAS, this was far from their primary concern at the time. Looming larger in Aboriginal politics across the state was a profound uncertainty about the very existence of their communities into even the near future. This fear was provoked months earlier. In November 2014 the premier of Western Australia, Colin Barnett, announced without warning or consultation, that the majority of the over 270 Aboriginal communities in Western Australia would be defunded, with their members being relocated to larger regional communities or towns. Balgo was one of the communities possibly designated to become a larger regional community, with expanded housing, services, and even a swimming pool. At a bureaucratic level this was the result of a budgetary game of hot potato between the national government and the state of Western Australia. The former handed over remote community funding responsibilities to the latter, while including a one-time budget of ninety million dollars—enough for only three years of funding.

Shortly after this announcement, a leaked 2010 government document was widely circulated by Aboriginal activists which demonstrated that the state government had long been preparing for such an action. Titled "Priority Investment Communities—WA," it categorized 192 communities as "unsustainable," 160 of which were located in the Kimberley. In what quickly become known simply as "the list," this file was quickly disseminated through Balgo by community members through USB drives, phone Bluetooth sharing, and folded pieces of printed paper. Balgo was listed in the ambiguous Category B, which was identified as neither sustainable (Class A) nor unsustainable (Class C). The ambiguity of this classification only intensified anxieties. After reading the list of Class C communities slated for potential closure, people would often voice concerns such as "My cousin lives there. He can't leave his Country. Where would he go?" This was far from the first time that federal and state governments had initiated large-scale plans to defund Aboriginal communities. The decline of Yagga Yagga itself was part of a broad policy to close outstations in the early 2000s (Peterson and Myers 2016). Having experienced the community closure of Yagga Yagga firsthand, Mark Moora was disappointed by the list yet unsurprised. He emphasized that this is how it goes when the government is involved, and it only increased his confidence in the long-term imperative to develop communities that were not reliant on governmental support.

One might reasonably ask how exactly the government can *close* long-standing Indigenous communities, especially at this scale. The answer begins with understanding how Aboriginal communities were initially established by the government. In the expansive deserts that make up much of the continent, Aboriginal people lived a largely nomadic lifestyle before colonization. They tended to travel for most of the year in small family groups, meeting in larger numbers for cultural events such as corroborees. Most currently existing communities were established during the twentieth century as either missions or pastoral stations (cattle ranches). The process of colonization made living in these communities nearly unavoidable through the forced movement of people and by the destruction and gating of water sources by pastoralists.

Communities have been set up in unsustainable ways that necessitate constant governmental funding. While many are located in some of the best places in the world for solar panels, nearly all remain powered by expensive fossil fuels. Electricity is precarious not only because of its means of generation, but also because it has to be continually recredited through "power cards" in each house or it simply shuts off. The vast majority of the houses and other buildings are not owned by community members and are technically governmental properties. Compounding this is the expense associated with mobility. Travel between communities requires four-wheel-drive vehicles as well as intensive and irregular road maintenance. Community members often joke about how the government cares deeply about road maintenance for every community that is on the way to a lucrative mine.

Since the IAS and threat of mass community closures were instigated under the Liberal coalition led by Prime Minister Abbott, it is tempting to view these policies as the result of right-wing political ideologies. However, many of the policies that led to the closing of Yagga Yagga and other outstations occurred under Labor governments. The "intervention" and Closing the Gap policies were enacted by the Labor prime minister Kevin Rudd, who even publicly apologized for the Stolen Generation on behalf of the Australian government. In a cynical deployment of futurity, the 2012 Labor government, headed by Prime Minister Julia Gillard, passed the Stronger Futures in the Northern Territory Act, which extended many of the disastrous intervention policies through 2022. Particularly harmful are the "child protection" policies, which often result in the removal of Aboriginal children from their families and communities by the government—a continuation of "stolen generation" policies. Unfortunately, outside of occasional left-wing political allies, such destructive policies have largely been a bipartisan affair since the 1970s.

I am not arguing that there is a mass governmental conspiracy to cause Aboriginal communities to fail. While some officials may (and likely do) orchestrate their failure, such intent is not necessary. Similarly to Bruno Latour's (1996) description of the Parisian Aramis transportation system's demise, all that is required is sustained neglect paired with a disinterest in understanding and implementing long-term strategies. As Teresa Montoya (2016) asserts, such neglect inflicts violence upon the land itself. The explicit and implicit forces of financial interests in the extraction of natural resources further encourage this systemic disinterest.

As Patrick Wolfe (2006) has established, colonization consists most fundamentally of structures rather than individual events. Povinelli (2011) describes these structures of neglect as "economies of abandonment" in which Aboriginal people are sacrificed for the greater national good because they are not viewed as producing in the way "good" citizens should. This is used as a justification for allowing the slow-motion violence of abandonment to become normalized and made to seem inevitable. Ironically, the same productivity-oriented forces that are causing such abandonment are also sustaining the very Aboriginal media that has been instrumental in resisting community closures.

This most recent push to close communities has not yet succeeded, though not because of any official legal protection. Rather, closures have been prevented by the mass public response of many urban whitefellas—led and bolstered by Indigenous media and activists—which at its zenith resulted in large protests in every major city across the continent as well as in regional towns (see photos of Neil Turner and other PAKAM members marching in a protest in Broome). However, while the state has momentarily backed away from these plans, Aboriginal people in communities like Balgo remain at the mercy of bureaucrats. Seemingly aware of their PR misstep of saying the quiet part out loud, the state government reframed their language on the issue just a few years later. Their updated approach avoids the framing of "closure" and rebrands their plans in the positive sense on the building up of larger remote community centers, such as Balgo. The new language is careful to note that people would be allowed to remain in their communities if their "services are reduced," even though that is nearly impossible in practice due to infrastructural realities. While public opinion has prevented the state government's attempt to defund communities for the time being, subtler policy decisions are in the pipeline and suggest that defunding may be pushed through by other means.

A vocal minority of media producers, politicians, and bureaucrats have been active advocates for Aboriginal rights. However, it is not enough that some have generally opposed policies of annihilation. Internal government audits of the intervention, Closing the Gap, and the IAS have concluded that each one lacked meaningful consultation in their implementation and failed to reach their own self-defined metrics of success. These audits have been highly publicized by major

FIGURE 35. Signs at the Broome protest against closing communities.

FIGURE 36. PAKAM flag at the Broome protest against closing communities.

news organizations and the political advocates of Aboriginal rights who pushed for the audits to take place. However, attempts to demonstrate the failure of these policies have not prevented further iterations. For many journalists on the right, the dysfunction of these programs provides tautological evidence that the real problem is having *any* Indigenous funding in the first place.

The paradox between the golden age of Aboriginal media and mass defunding also resonates with a deeper existential crisis regarding Australian culture and whiteness. Australia has only been a nation since the beginning of the twentieth century, and throughout most of this short period White Australia policies were enforced to keep out immigrants deemed to lie beyond contemporaneous conceptions of whiteness. And yet, unlike the heroic origin mythos of the American independence movement—as tenuous as that narrative is—white Australians are often at odds with their own history as a penal colony of criminals forced from their homelands.[15] Although Australia is often deemed "the lucky country" because of its low population and vast resources, many white Australians I spoke with bemoaned its lack of cultural roots. This was somewhat less the case in Broome, with its long-standing exceptions to White Australia immigration policies.

Within this broader settler-colonial context, Aboriginal Australians simultaneously represent both a fundamental problem and its solution. On the one hand, their status as the oldest continuing societies quenches the nationalist thirst of the young nation for a meaningful temporal and spatial connection to place. On the other hand, the existence of Aboriginal people and the unjust dispossession of their Country simultaneously undermines the legal legitimacy of the nation itself. This is made all the more salient by the increasingly acknowledged illegitimacy of *terra nullius* and continued lack of treaties. Therefore, it remains important for the national imaginary that Aboriginal people are symbolically engaged and narratively absorbed, while at the same time it is paramount that they be removed from their Country and assimilated so as to legitimize Australia's very existence. This speaks to a profound settler ambivalence toward Aboriginality that animates irreconcilable motivations for fostering Indigenous presence and absence.

It is in the context of the visibility paradox of irreconcilable national tensions that Indigenous media remain too often underestimated. At a superficial level it aligns with settler logics and desires as a relatively inexpensive, productive, and visible sector. And yet, these qualities do not corrupt it, but rather provide a Trojan horse for disrupting and reimagining the representational forces of dispossession at the heart of Aboriginal survivance. While not a panacea, Aboriginal media challenges the dominant images of dystopian communities falling into inevitable dysfunction, painting vivid portraits of complex lives that have endured unspeakable tragedies with dignity. Just as importantly, Aboriginal cinema provides a constitutive process by which media makers come to articulate the immemorial and unfolding aspects of what it means to be Indigenous, what their social world is like, and what they aspire for in the future.

Sovereign Envisionings

Sovereignty is a crucial concept that has been engaged deeply in critical Native studies and anthropology (Cattelino and Simpson 2022).

Unlike other marginalized groups, Indigenous communities often prioritize sovereignty *from,* rather than equality *within,* multiculturalist settler states. To this end, it is difficult to overstate the significance of treaty relationships. As much as treaties in the United States, Canada, and New Zealand have been violated, they have nevertheless provided at least a benchmark for long-term land claims and self-government. In contrast with Australia, it would be difficult for the governments of these three countries to compel Indigenous people out of most of their communities in a short period of time.

Discussions of sovereignty quickly lose significance if they are not grounded within relationships to Country. From this foundation, sovereignty integrates into other realms of Aboriginal life, including kinship, language, and Dreaming. Through the lens of "sovereign envisionings," here I discuss the assertion of visual and temporal sovereignties. I illustrate how they are embedded within Mark's cinematic awakenings and in the renewed movement for developing treaty relationships across Australia.

"Visual sovereignty" (Raheja 2010; Rickard 2011) articulates how the rise of Indigenous filmmaking has been instrumental in challenging and refusing dominant stereotypical representations, while also asserting increased control over representation. In light of their continued slotting into primordial pasts, for Aboriginal people, visual sovereignty is inextricably tied to the temporal. "Temporal sovereignty" resists the ways that settler conceptions of time have become imposed (Rifkin 2017). Futures, like land, have been structurally dispossessed, and offer a parallel framework for thinking through the dispossession of temporal territory. Theresa McCarthy articulates how Haudenosaunee regularly draw "upon frames of reference derived from intellectual traditions oriented toward [their] futurity. Since land, political difference, and 'knowing' are the moving targets in settler colonial efforts to eliminate and replace Indigenous peoples on their territories" (2016, 277). Temporal sovereignty provides an analytic for enacting such Indigenous futures within and beyond Australia.

This ethnography has converged at the nexus of these two aspects of sovereignty, through what I have come to think of as *sovereign envisionings.* It encapsulates the integration of visual and temporal sovereignty while also emphasizing active processes of doing rather than being.

I draw on Grace Dillon's (2012) intentionally plural conception of Indigenous futurisms and Joseph Weiss's (2018) articulation of active "future-making." Sovereign envisionings exist as a multiplicity within and between people and communities. They are characterized not by singularity or solidity but by the continuous adaptation to shifting landscapes of power toward the collective imaginings of returning to Country in new ways. These envisionings are not only *of* sovereign futures, but the acts themselves *are* sovereign assertions. They are as much promise as plan, and their success is based on their ability to spark and cultivate the dreams of younger generations.

Like cinema itself, sovereign envisionings integrate product, process, and place. Among the most envisioned of mainstream media, films embody the social lives through which these come into being and move through the world. Sovereign envisionings engage the ways in which media can reimagine not only *how* Aboriginal people are imagined and represented but also *when* and *where*. They unsettle futures and naturalized relationships through which Aboriginality is rendered temporally and spatially "remote" through the projection of a mythic past.

On one of our many three-person film shoots with Larry, Mark Moora proclaimed:

> Media is good. It can go out and tell all the mob what is going on. People in Canberra and everywhere might think bad things about us blackfellas. They don't know the truth, so I have to tell them what is true. In my Country, in the bush, I think about my people and the future. If I go to Sydney or another Country I think differently and get mixed up. I want to talk to Canberra and tell them what I think about politics. If they argue that's alright, but they should come to my Country to argue.

As Mark implies, sovereign envisionings are not simply messages about the future to be communicated. They are constitutive, not only between people but in relation to Country. Unlike other forms of media, cinema provides a process to communicate envisionings from Country. It does not simply assert, but transports and connects. The medium is more than the message—a portal of potentiality that honors Country as an active presence and precursor to meaningful communication.

The importance of decolonizing temporal mediation is embedded within Audra Lorde's (1984) solemn declaration that dispossessed people "were never meant to survive." As is often asserted in protector movements such as Standing Rock, Indigenous existence is resistance. Anishinaabe cultural theorist Gerald Vizenor reimagines the notion of Indigenous survival through his articulation of *survivance,* which he defines as "an active sense of presence over absence, deracination, and oblivion; survivance is the continuance of stories, not a mere reaction. . . . [Survivance stories] are renunciations of dominance, detractions, obtrusions, the unbearable sentiments of tragedy, and the legacy of victimry" (2008, 1). Far from being guaranteed, Indigenous survivance has been largely the result of steadfast activism by Aboriginal people, in addition to the meaningful though perhaps overstated role of non-Indigenous allies (Horner and Langton 1987).

Geoffrey Stokes (1997) reaffirms the fact that Aboriginal people have not been passive victims of settler-colonial domination. Since colonial contact they have demanded change. Notably, this included the formation of the U.S.-inspired Black Panther Party of Australia in the late 1960s, a story chronicled in Darlene Johnson's (2014) documentary, *The Redfern Story*. Aboriginal celebrities—such as the musician Jimmy Little and world champion tennis star Evonne Goolagong—have further shifted white Australians' views of Aboriginal people within popular culture.

In the 1970s, counterculture movements motivated waves of hippies to live in Aboriginal communities. Despite their attempts to support Aboriginal rights, cultural miscommunication often rendered such efforts ineffective or even counterproductive (Henry 2012). Furthermore, it took decades of losing battles over land rights, such as the 1980 dispute over gas mining in sacred sites near Noonkanbah Station in the Kimberley (P. Vincent 1983), for enough momentum to build for the legislative watershed of the 1990s, with victories in *Mabo v. Queensland* in 1992 (overturning *terra nullius*), the Native Title Act in 1993, and *Wik Peoples v. The State of Queensland* in 1996 (Cosgrove and Kliger 1997).[16]

After many years of grassroots pressure and federal committee meetings, Aboriginal sovereignty has returned to the national spotlight. Between 2015 and 2017 there was a strong push to hold a referendum vote to amend the Australian constitution to formally recognize Aboriginal people as the first to live in Australia. The last such major referendum, in 1967, passed overwhelmingly and changed policies in which many Aboriginal people were still legally classified as fauna. The recent proposed referendum was highly controversial. Ironically, most right-wing politicians and Indigenous activists generally opposed it, though for markedly different reasons. While many on the right saw it as a slippery slope toward Indigenous land reclamation, most Aboriginal activists I spoke with viewed it as representing a tacit acceptance of British colonization as well as providing a publicized gesture without concrete policy gains. Instead, they preferred and advocated for treaty making.

The debate came to a head in May 2017 in the community of Mutitjulu near the iconic Aboriginal site of Uluru (Ayers Rock), five hundred kilometers south of Alice Springs. Over four days, more than 250 Indigenous Australian leaders from across the continent met for the First Nations National Constitutional Convention to discuss the merits and future of the constitutional referendum. By the end of these meetings, they rejected it and released what has come to be known as the "Uluru Statement from the Heart." It argues for inherent Aboriginal sovereignty as described in the following passage:

> Our Aboriginal and Torres Strait Islander tribes were the first sovereign Nations of the Australian continent and its adjacent islands, and possessed it under our own laws and customs. This our ancestors did, according to the reckoning of our culture, from the Creation, according to the common law from "time immemorial," and according to science more than 60,000 years ago.
>
> This sovereignty is a *spiritual notion: the ancestral tie between the land, or "mother nature," and the Aboriginal and Torres Strait Islander peoples who were born therefrom, remain attached thereto, and must one day return thither to be united with our ancestors. This link is the basis of the ownership*

> *of the soil, or better, of sovereignty.* It has never been ceded or extinguished, and co-exists with the sovereignty of the Crown.

As Audra Simpson (2014) argues regarding Mohawk relations with the state, when presented with an either/or choice, Aboriginal leaders refused the premise. They demanded an altogether different option that was consistent with historical fact beyond the imperial imagination of settler-colonial inevitability. They demanded treaties and to be treated as equals through international law. Implicit in this statement was not simply the point that sovereignty has never been ceded but that sovereignty itself is not something that *can* be given or taken. It is a relationship with Country. While this seemed overly idealistic to some, for these Aboriginal leaders it was a pragmatic move necessary for survivance amidst escalating policies of annihilation. This statement by leadership from remote communities resonated deeply in urban protest camps I spent time in, including the Aboriginal Tent Embassy in Canberra. Situated directly in front of the Old Parliament House, this constellation of tents and a central fire has endured continuously since 1972.

Walking into the Aboriginal Tent Embassy on a chilly, overcast day in March 2016, I approach the fire at the center nexus within the grassy

FIGURE 37. The Aboriginal Tent Embassy and the Old Parliament House in Canberra.

rectangle. Stepping back, I take in the large bold letters planted firmly in the ground proclaiming "SOVEREIGNTY NEVER CEDED." This phrase long precedes the language of the "Uluru Statement from the Heart," and it is far from the first time I have seen this phrase. I recall a similar display at the Redfern Aboriginal Tent Embassy, known as "The Block," a long-standing protest camp in the historically Aboriginal Sydney suburb of Redfern. The Canberra letters form a concave arc which, from above, focuses like a satellite dish onto the front steps of the old Parliament House, whose white Roman architecture stands in stark contrast to the embassy's grouping of tents. I enter the primary structure, a yurt that contains a welcome booth, a kitchen area for making a "cuppa" tea, and interspersed piles of books. Chatting with people I have met in previous visits, it is again emphasized to me by lawyers, activists, and advocates that constitutional recognition is simply one more imperial tool of dispossession. Yet, the feeling in the room is far from hopeless.

While sitting on a battered yellow couch and sipping a mug of English breakfast tea, someone asks me what I do. When I get to the word "anthropologist," we all laugh. "A dime a dozen in Australia!" one activist jokes. However, as the afternoon rolls along it becomes clear that they are interested in media work in Balgo and other communities. Many know Mark Moora well, given his various roles across the continent.

FIGURE 38. The Redfern Aboriginal Tent Embassy protest camp in the Sydney suburb of Redfern.

After considering Mark's history and current film projects, a prominent activist notes, "Australians need to hear and see people like Mark. That is how we will have a future—by seeing it, not by asking for it." He continues, describing why the Tent Embassy and Aboriginal activists are increasingly producing and circulating media, reiterating the fact that Indigenous media have been established as a right through Article 16 of the United Nations Declaration on the Rights of Indigenous Peoples.

Assertions of sovereignty in Aboriginal media projects often gesture toward issues beyond Australia. While the pitfalls of leveraging Indigenous wisdom as a path toward settler healing are notable, global issues of justice and environmental degradation are also vitally relevant to Aboriginal futures. They are the result of colonial processes, and Aboriginal Australians have sophisticated analyses that draw upon thousands of years of knowledge (Liboiron 2021; Yunkaporta 2019).

It is the day before a Broome protest in solidarity with the 2015 Paris Climate Accords, and I am sitting on Michelle (Mitch) Torres's front porch, mixing dried green and black acrylic paint with water. While I am working out the clumps in the dried paint with a steel potato masher, her family stops by. We discuss Mitch's new film about Indigenous Kimberley perspectives on climate change and the frustrating difficulty in funding such politically charged projects. With the paint ready, we consider what to write on a poster. As Mitch is thinking out loud about the history of Aboriginal people since time immemorial, she suddenly exclaims, "You know what, we've already lived through two ice ages. I think we know a thing or two about climate change!" This garners a laugh all around, though it is a serious point as well. Asserting the past in this way is to claim the future too. The next day, the sign (see Figure 39) stands prominently in the front of the protest at Town Beach and is highlighted in photos that are being shared globally through social media about the accords.

Many politicians expressed shock over the "Uluru Statement from the Heart," which in no uncertain terms rejected symbolic constitutional

FIGURE 39. Poster in the center at the protest near Town Beach. Photograph by Martin Pritchard; courtesy of Environs Kimberley.

acknowledgment. After centuries of sustained dispossession and a lack of any treaties, mass-scale Aboriginal disenchantment would be more than understandable, as would a general desire for a framework of non-sovereign futures that abandons land rights for tactical economic benefits (Bonilla 2015). However, this statement was representative of broadly held community commitments to sovereignty despite historical precedent. It reframed the issue as one of an illegitimate constitution imposed through invasion. While initially decried by the mainstream press as a pipe dream, in the months after the statement was released serious treaty negotiations began progressing in every single Australian state and territory. There remains an unprecedented political momentum for treaty agreements to be reached, with the most progress having been made in Victoria, led by the First Peoples' Assembly. Negotiations with this state began in November of 2024 and are currently in process as of early 2025.

Throughout 2023 a revised referendum was debated which proposed the inclusion of a new body for Aboriginal representation in Parliament. Indigenous media played a meaningful role in engaging community members in this process, even if it was overshadowed by mainstream media that often bolstered the opposition. In September of that year, the national peak organizational body, First Nations Media Australia, released a mass email communication that highlighted

> the significance of the ongoing discussions surrounding a referendum to recognise First Nations independently in the nation's constitution and to establish a Voice to Parliament representing First Nations peoples . . . [and seeks] to contribute to the national conversation by providing accurate information, context, and relevant insights on the potential impacts of constitutional recognition and the Voice to Parliament. . . . Above all, First Nations Media Australia remains steadfast in our mission to empower First Nations voices through media and to ensure recognition of their significance in the ongoing national conversation.

Ultimately, after being placed on the ballot that October, the referendum was decisively voted down. This felt like—and in ways was—a profound failure for many people deeply engaged in Aboriginal rights. At the same time, few of my field mates seemed surprised or discouraged by the outcome. Some even suggested that demands were not high *enough,* and that regardless, the process represented a refusal to endorse empty platitudes, to demonstrate that the Emperor's reconciliation wore no clothes. It forced Australians and the state to explicitly acknowledge or deny fundamental Aboriginal history and political representation on the global stage. It shone a spotlight upon the realities of ongoing irreconciliation. This way of thinking resists what Chloe Ahmann (2019) describes as a tranquilizing "subjunctive politics" that narrowly winnow and foreclose future possibilities. It refuses any reconciliation that lacks meaningful truth and justice (A. Simpson 2014; Weiss 2025).

Aboriginal communities continue to be underestimated by government agencies and officials. After generations of dispossession and dystopian portrayals of these communities in popular media, most politicians, bureaucrats, and citizens display hubris regarding the totality of settler-colonial victory, even as the legitimacy of Australian territorial possession is increasingly cast into doubt. Paradoxically, it is the very discounting of Indigenous media's political potential that facilitates its transformational possibilities. Even though—and perhaps because—it is a cost-effective sector that assuages settler guilt through its seemingly innocuous visibility, the Aboriginal mediascape serves as a crucial platform for envisioning and enacting sovereign futures.

I sometimes return in my mind to the end of a long red carpet at the Sydney Film Festival, where Mark introduced *Tjawa Tjawa* and the Songlines on Screen series to industry titans and film aficionados. Mark was featured, made visible, celebrated even. And yet I cannot help but wonder whether, in that moment and at the rarified after-party where he passed out his single-page summary for going back to Yagga Yagga, if he was being seen, being heard. I got the sense that Mark wondered about this too, though it did not seem to overly concern him. He pragmatically made the most of this visibility. As the party wound down, we sat in an oddly textured couch at the center of the bustling space. Turning to me, he said, "All we need is a bit of money," and then, after a long and considered look around the room, continued, "You never know."

CONCLUSION

Twilights

> Do you know why I'm making films?
> It's to keep the story alive.
>
> —Mark Moora

Mark and I have a full morning ahead of us. First, we search for his cousin to repair a flat tire, before trying to have his Centrelink payment sent to the community office. The tire trip is successful. The paper task will take a few more attempts. As usual, we stop at the women's center to spend time with his sisters before I drop Mark off in the early afternoon. As we pull up to his house, I mention that Mary G (Mark Bin Barker) is visiting Balgo in the coming days. Multiple bands have been recorded in the previous weeks, so the studio equipment is ready for the event. Just before climbing out of the troopy, Mark says, "That reminds me. My band Desert Scorpions is in Balgo this weekend. Let's record my song properly." "Tonight?" I ask. "Yuwai, come around after dinner and we'll pick 'em up."

Mark has talked about this song since I first met him. However, I am surprised by this suggestion, since we already recorded it with PAKAM in a nearby community some months back. He notes that while the track sounds technically proficient, he has become increasingly dissatisfied with it. "It's too slow and sad. It should be faster and happier. It should be a rock and roll song with my band." As with the other music recordings in Balgo, this promises to be a late-night marathon session. We pick up Larry, and Mark's band members from around Balgo. Each hops in knowingly, without discussion.

Beginning after dark, we record from seven to midnight. Unlike this song's previous recording, Mark's vision for the sonic choices is crystal clear. He explains this to the band and has them practice it several times, making periodic arrangement notes through hand signs and comments such as "Pick 'em up" and "Pull back the drums." Watching through the mixing-booth glass, I balance the levels. When Mark is satisfied that the band had nailed it, they record it in a single take. This would have astonished me had I not already witnessed several first-take band recordings over the previous weeks. Through studio headphones, Mark listens to it carefully with his closed eyes. "From the beginning" he directs, before listening to it a few more times. "Yuwai, now we just need more voices in the main part. Big mob." Over the next hour, we layer on a literal chorus including his overdubs and the voices of Larry and the band members.

It is getting late, and Mark seems to be willing himself to stay sharp in this pivotal moment. Listening again, his eyes narrow as he adds, "One more thing, and it's very important. We need Larry to cry at the end." Larry, his true-blue mate, seems unfazed by this suggestion. Mark discusses this with him for a few minutes, before looking over and signing "Roll 'em." During the final thirty seconds of the song, while Mark and the chorus repeat "Ngurra" (Country), Larry makes weeping sounds that are gentle yet somehow able to cut through the mix. Mark puts the headphones back on and closes his eyes, this time uncharacteristically and subtly dancing in his seat. When it ends, he smiles in a way I have not seen before or since. Then after a deep exhale, he declares, "Palya, time to fix 'em up."

Sitting around the fire during the evenings of the *Tjawa Tjawa* shoot, Mark would often talk about Songlines at a more expansive level than in the Songlines on Screen program. He once noted, "There are old songs. That's right. But there are new songs too. Sometimes one comes to me." The song "Ngurra Yulparirra (This Country South)" came to Mark in a dream years earlier in the wake of Yagga Yagga's closing. He described how he did not "write" the melody, lyrics, or structure, but rather received the song as a whole. It centered around a melodic polyvocal chorus, which translates as "I have seen this Country south in my dream." The verse sections included his non-melodic stating of seventeen places in Country beginning with Yagga Yagga, nearly all of which we had visited in film trips over the previous years. The ending included an extended chorus with the following lines, ending with Larry's weeping:

I have seen this Country south in my dream
The old people left this Country with strong culture and history,
  left this good Country
I'm going to sit down here and pass away, poor me
I have seen this Country south in my dream

The morning after this recording, Mark and I listened to the song together several times, after which he suggested that we should film him singing it in Country. On our next *Mangkayi Calling* shoot with Larry, Mark directed us to a particular area of golden grasses, where he chose a spot and described the story of the song on camera:

> I had a dream about that song, about when I was in Yagga, when I was in Country, after all of that traveling in the Kimberley. I was thinking about my Country south and water holes and all the names of other places. Yeah, that's a song I dreamt. And the other day I told the boys to play guitar and tune them up and there it is. Now it can go on NITV and USB, anywhere. It's all from dreams and stories. That's what it is. When we dream we make songs, it's from a dream. Tribal people don't go out and dream music like those days, but one day it's going to happen again. We'll be making more music and telling stories in the future.

Just then, Mark nodded to me to begin playing the song on the portable music player. He sang along with it twice before singing several versions of the chorus by himself so his voice could begin the song in the film a cappella. Consistently, and increasingly, he was "directing for the edit," which filmmakers describe as the ability to imagine shots within the postproduction timeline. Over the coming weeks his song traveled across Australia, playing on Radio Goolarri in Broome, throughout the Kimberley over the PAKAM radio network, and throughout Australia on the National Indigenous Radio Service (NIRS). On our next trip to Broome, Goolarri's Sandy Dann invited him back on to her NIRS-broadcast show, where she played the song and they discussed its deeper meaning on-air.

In an image, sunrise and sunset appear virtually indistinguishable. For practical considerations around setup and framing, sunset often serves as the cinematic sunrise. So too did Mark employ cinema to transpose dawns and dusks of dreams and despair. In spite of a lifetime of being confronted by myriad forces of dispossession—or perhaps because of this—he envisioned a world that would become increasingly brighter for his family and Aboriginal communities across Australia. His desire to re-record "Ngurra Yulparirra" was about remaining true to a song imbued with both heartache and its shadow, hope. So often, tomorrow's promise grows in sorrow's soil. This has remained true throughout Mark's life, his cinematic awakenings, and his dreams of going back to Country, each presenting uneven tracks reaching out toward shifting horizons.

Dawn

Dust seeps through the rusted undercarriage while exposed yellow ignition wires bounce against Mark's dusty blue jeans, as he suddenly

Figure 40. Mark Moora and band recording "Ngurra Yulparirra" in the Balgo recording studio.

turns off of the corrugated road toward Mindirr. Sitting next to him, Larry strokes his beard and points to something I cannot see in the distance. Acknowledging this, Mark raises his left index finger, which bounces sporadically on the stick, as he prepares to downshift the aging transmission. Despite outward appearances, one battered spare tire left, and no satellite phone, we are not off-road "in the middle of nowhere." As community members often assert, we are "right in the middle of everywhere." Mark navigates termite mounds while sputtering down a track that, although invisible to me, he sees "as clearly as when I first walked it in the moonlight as a young fella with Larry and all our mob." And yet, driving through Country poses new challenges to old pathways, as we backtrack, break down, light rescue fires, and try again while improvising new ways forward, anchored by their knowledge and determination, through attempts that are at least as significant as arriving.

In some cases, not arriving seemed most meaningful, as it offered the immediate promise of return. On several *Mangkayi Calling* trips with Mark and Larry we unsuccessfully attempted to make it to Mindirr, an important site near Mark's birthplace. Each time, we got closer, though while Mark knew how to walk there, he had never driven. Running low on tires, we would invariably have to turn back. As we did, he provided assuring declarations such as "Next time we'll make it to Mindirr! I know a better track." As within the social life of cinema, the *process* of locating specific sites was often more motivating than actually finding them, partly because it fostered purpose for another imminent bush trip. Country, Dreaming, and Songlines themselves are not destinations, but exist as living paths that people move within and through. While driving back after one attempt to reach Mindirr, Mark smiled and said, "When you go back to a place where you've never been for a long time, it brings back good memories. Mangkayi, yeah, she's calling alright."

While the social life of *Tjawa Tjawa* lasted years, *Mangkayi Calling* represents a process that has spanned Mark's lifetime, as he has worked again and again to return to his Country with his family. It included the film, but it was most simply and deeply a calling to go home. The social life of *Mangkayi Calling* parallels the vacillating history of victories and setbacks in remote Aboriginal Australia more broadly, from initial land dispossession to the successful development, tragic closure, and potential resurrection of outstations like Yagga Yagga. This project serves as a microcosm for the precarity of movements back to Country, where nightmares of the past, dreams for the future, and perpetual desires for one more bush trip coalesce into a film whose completion seems as urgent as its resolution is unimaginable.

Mark's active engagement with his family's future was not only reflected in large projects but was also embedded within his daily activities. In one characteristic example, I called him from Broome to say hi. When he answered, I could barely hear him over the roar of machinery. "Hey, mate!" he shouted through the noise; "I'm just on a grader now." "You mean those giant road-flattening construction trucks?" I ask loudly. "Yeah. I think if the young fellas see this old fella doing it, they might think 'I should do more too,' hah. Well, gotta run. Anyways, just practicing for grading the road to Yagga. See you."

I returned to Balgo in 2019 to deliver my PhD dissertation to the organizations and individuals in this project. As usual, when I arrived in Balgo I went to Mark's house at sunset after the long day's drive. He greeted me with an enthusiasm that seemed to paper over weariness. Unfortunately, his health had declined and he could no longer drive on bumpy roads without pain. "No more bush trips for me, mate," he sighed as he sat down in a chair on the porch the next morning. As the sun continued to rise in silence, his eyes brightened and he gently proclaimed, "Let's sit down at the airport and do one more film trip." That afternoon we drove the short and smooth drive to the shade of a bright green shipping container next to the airport. It was a familiar place to both of us. Only a few years earlier it had served as a vivid backdrop for a visual dictionary of hundreds of hand signs that he demonstrated in a three-camera shoot.

As the camera's red light lit up, so too did Mark, and his previously fatigued demeanor vanished. He began the way he often did, discussing *Mangkayi Calling,* kids, Balgo, the future. He spoke directly to Balgo youth about his late stage in life. "Going here and there in the desert. I can't do that. I'm getting old now. I'd like to go back, back to visiting that Country. Yeah, but now I'm on tablets. I want to relax my mind. I'm not getting younger, and so you're the one that's gotta take over my job." As he talked, he provided introductions and conclusions that he knew would work in the film edit. He described a new song he had received, and how he wanted to record it with his band when they came back through.

After a few minutes, he slowed down, paused, and thought for a long moment. Then he shifted his gaze from the camera lens to me and said, "You've been filming and going bush here for years. What have you learned? What do you think about it?" As in our first discussion six years earlier during the *Tjawa Tjawa* shoot, I was momentarily speechless. While we regularly shared lengthy chats—often on the concrete square at the foot of his front door—my own views had never been captured in a shoot, nor had it crossed my mind to include them. His question was a doorway that opened to others. He asked about my book and the film, and described how he hoped that they would reach the right people. We talked until the camera battery died and the red light dimmed along with the fading early evening. As we packed up the troopy to leave, and with an air of finality he said, "Time for me to retire, I'll spend time with my grandkids now that I'm an old man. Time to finish that film and fix 'em up."

Dusk

The last time I spoke with Mark was in May 2020. For some time, Warwick had been updating me about Mark's health, which was quickly declining. Doctors suggested that he now might only have weeks, or perhaps even days. Mark did not have a phone at the time, though I was eventually able to get a hold of him through his daughters, whom he was staying with. While he sounded weak, his spirits were high. Mark made jokes, and we asked about each other's family. We both seemed to sense that this would be the last time we would speak. I told him that I hoped to see him again next visit. He responded with a thoughtful "Yuwai, palya," and after a pause added, "I might not see you again, mate, but I'll be here alright."

Just weeks later, in the early morning, Mark's daughter Sophie called to tell me that he had passed. Even though this was anticipated, I turned cold when I received the call. It overwhelmed me for days. For lack of a better word, it was heartbreaking. Because we were in the throes of a global pandemic, it was impossible for me to attend Mark's funeral period later that year, or in the foreseeable future. And this was not the only heartbreak. Sadly, many other Elders I had worked closely with also passed during this period, including Larry, Payi Payi, Linda, Bob, and, most tragically, Clint Dixon, a talented PAKAM filmmaker my own age whom I had the fortunate chance to work with on several projects.

Reflecting on her own fieldwork, Ruth Behar (1996) suggests that anthropology worth doing can and does break your heart. As with methodology, heartbreak is usually hidden in ethnography, and for understandable reasons. It runs the danger of diverting too much attention to the author or overstating fieldwork relationships. These are real risks, though so too are those of dispassionate detachment. I include it in an attempt to convey the weight of Mark's passing for so many.

Throughout this book, I have aimed for Mark to remain as alive for you throughout the social lives of his films as he was while they were unfolding. To illustrate that his passing is not simply an end, but part of a process of continued beginnings that carry his many after-images down the track. That he remains alive within his films, family, and Country.

Unfinished. This is a seemingly counterintuitive concept to include in a book's conclusion. Yet, even as you hold this *paper,* its own social life continues. To be unfinished "is both [a] precondition and [a] product of becoming" (Biehl and Locke 2017). In other words, a palya process, like a family, endures. Mangkayi is still calling, as are Mark's plans, and as is the future itself. Within these unfinished processes are the whispers of tomorrow. Of more movements of *tires,* and of *fires* to be lit anew. Communities, individuals, films, and books precede and outlive themselves through rich and interconnected social lives. They reverberate beyond their own release—complete, yet ever unfinished.

For a long time following Mark's death, unfinished is how I imagined that this book and the *Mangkayi Calling* film might indefinitely remain. It was nearly two years until I could bring myself to revisit them. During that time, I questioned much about them—my role, the purpose of ethnography, the trust that Mark seemed to have put in me. I wondered, was this misplaced? Had I failed? I sat uneasily with the irreconcilabilities of these projects. I sit with them still.

It was in the first few days of 2022 that this abruptly shifted. While backing up and reorganizing my laptop, I unintentionally double-clicked a footage file for *Mangkayi Calling.* Sitting in front of tall columns of smoke rising from the fires he had lit that morning, and with kangaroo tails cooking underground nearby, Mark spoke from his Country with clarity and with an assuredness that Mangkayi's calling would be answered. That his family would return home. This accident led to my watching another clip, and then another, and then another. Between that day and the next, I watched all sixteen hours of footage, as well as Mark's other films. Through cinema, I was transported across time and space back to Mark and Mangkayi. To our trips dense with movement: fastening mics, lighting fires, changing tires. Throughout this footage he spoke again to Balgo, kids, his family, politicians, and future community members—of a resurrected Yagga Yagga yet to be, down the track.

Through fragmented footage, Mark reminded me of things I thought I had come to know, though had already begun to forget. He reminded me to go *slowly, slowly*. That part of the process is having to stop and reorient. That sometimes moving down the track means backtracking too. That cinema is a time machine, a portal that carries its makers and viewers to its moments of creation and back again. That after-images contain afterlives, like an acrylic painting that never dries. More than anything, watching these reminded me of all of the time and energy Mark had devoted to these projects.

As I sat for months with how to write about the dreams of someone who had passed, the sitting with it changed it. The greater risk, it seemed to me, was in *not* conveying his story as best as I could. During one of my last mornings in Balgo with Mark, an anthropologist and mate of his, John Carty, was visiting the community and joined us for breakfast. Walking into the kitchen, Mark posed a rhetorical question to him, "Do you know why I'm making films?" After a pregnant pause, he continued, standing tall with his right hand characteristically holding his left arm behind his back, "It's to keep the story alive."

After years of pandemic restrictions, I was finally able to return to Balgo in 2023. In light of the many deaths since my last visit, I anticipated that this would be a trip defined by mourning. I was surprised when it was animated more by sunrise than sunset. I spent time with Mark's three children—Eric, Andrea, and Sophie—and their extended family. They spoke about his final days. My remaining doubts about completing these projects were cast away when each of them responded to the topic with comments such as "You should finish them up. That was the whole point. That's why he spent so much time on them with you."

That week, I visited a field mate living in the house where Mark, Warwick, and I used to spend early mornings sitting on the porch. Instead of housing volunteers, the art center was now renting it to a newer organization, the Ngururrpa Rangers. At the very table where Mark pondered how to convey his life story, I learned that some of his dreams had already come into being. After years of efforts led by Mark, the Ngururrpa Indigenous Protected Area was now established, serving as an extension of past successful land rights in this Country. It included this ranger program, which created high-quality jobs for people from a large area of Country that encompassed Mangkayi. I learned that Mark passed away after it was publicly announced, though just two days before its signing ceremony in Balgo. I learned that his son, Eric, had signed in his absence, and that he and his sisters had been deeply involved in the ranger program since, regularly moving through Yagga Yagga and Mangkayi. Burning, taking care of, and being on Country.

While Mark was usually the first person I visited with in Balgo, I waited until my last day to visit his grave, which was just a short walk from the art center on the way to the airstrip. It was my first time there. His children had described exactly where he was buried, yet I was surprised by my own shock when I arrived finally at his gravesite. It was different from those nearby. It was sort of hidden, and with a smooth, unpebbled surface that had become a bustling pathway for ants. A small bed of fading roses lay under a single vertical plant that seemed too tall for its age. Visiting Payi Payi's grave as well, I was reminded that his sister passed away only two months before him—that Mark died in the wake of both heartache and hope, with his children positioned at the dawn of a new chapter in answering Mangkayi's call.

There have been several doubles in this project, each with their own irreconcilabilities: cinema, the photorealistic portal of life captured and reordered, though for all of its fidelity, never life itself; the visibility paradox, an ascendant Indigenous mediascape amid an era of annihilative policies; Mark and my relationship, bound by a sense of shared purpose and process, intimate yet infused with distance—or as Hortense Powdermaker (1966) put it, left as both "stranger and friend."

However, one thing no longer seems irreconcilable. Returning to the beginning here at the conclusion, his enigmatic statement becomes clearer. "Let's make a film about going back to Country, about the future. Let's make the real film." Mark's declaration was born of one night's sleep and a lifetime of heartbreak and renewal. It was in revisiting Mark's footage and spending time with his family that I got a glimpse of why keeping the story alive beyond his own life was what "real" meant to him. It was only at the end of this process that I began to understand that making these films was more than an arc of awakenings and envisionings for Mark. It was also one of redemption following a series of profound losses. In my last visit with him in Balgo, he increasingly alluded to his future passing. He would often half-jokingly say, "I'm an old man now. I'm getting cranky and it's time for me to settle down. It's up to young fellas to decide." In such moments, I thought back to his response to the option of traveling to New York and Toronto for film festival screenings of *Tjawa Tjawa*. With definitive clarity he had stated, "I want to die in my own Country."

Throughout his filmmaking, Mark was not interested in conceptual futures, but in the process of returning to Country with his family. Each envisioning was specific, of people in places. Mangkayi called Mark and his family back home to a place that has protected and continues to protect them. While living there was important to Mark, he often emphasized that so too was the calling itself. Mangkayi was not only calling Mark to be there; it was also calling for him to move through it, to engage with it, and to be of it. As he once told me, "Dreaming is about the future. It's about going back to Country and waking it up." *Kurrarlkatjanu, Tjawa Tjawa, Mangkayi Calling,* and the other films Mark worked on represent an envisioned place-making that asserts to Australians, Mark's relations, and himself that even though his family lives in Balgo, they are not bound by it. That their Country continues to be visited, thought about, and cared for. That it is still calling.

Twilights

Twilight serves as a cinematic mirror that is unlike sunrise and sunset. As opposed to dawn and dusk, which imply rising and setting, twilight is ambiguous. Defined as "the soft glowing light from the sky when the sun is below the horizon," it provides a luminous metaphor for Mark's many envisionings. Often associated with nighttime's preamble, it applies equally to its coda. While it would be more than understandable to become disheartened about the future amid widespread policies of cultural annihilation, Mark envisaged otherwise. Rather than the end, he imagined beginnings, bolstered by the portal of cinema and the expansiveness of its process.

After a lifetime of setbacks, Mark was not immune to despair. The first recording of "Ngurra Yulparirra" was steeped in it. Yet upon listening to it again, the tone did not ring true to him. It did not match what he saw and heard along the horizon, in the future, in the real, in his Country. This was no mirage, but a vision born of struggle and renewal. He insisted on Larry weeping, not to mourn the death of their connection to Country, but because sorrow was part of the process of returning.

Unlike sunrise and sunset, twilight is difficult to convey through cinema. It eludes the moving image, though it may be delicately captured through still photography with a wide aperture and slow shutter speed. It requires imagination, but more than that, patience—the care to look *slowly, slowly*. Twilights, while dim and potentially gloomy, are spaces between, illuminated with possibility for those who know how to see. Reflecting on his childhood memories from before the Old Balgo Mission, Mark often said, "That's how we would walk through Country, under stars." Navigating by the faintest of light, as he did in the numerous nights of his youth, Mark beheld the current twilight not as dusk, but as a new dawn.

"Almost," Mark says as he gazes along the horizon, toward his birthplace. With another flat and a single spare to make it back to Balgo, he smiles to himself as we finish the process of changing the tire. "I know how to walk there, though driving is a different story," he muses. "I have an idea. Next trip." Putting the troopy into gear, we backtrack as he envisions trying again, forging new tracks along old pathways leading home.

Acknowledgments

I want to thank, more than anyone, Mark Moora, whose dreams animate this book. I hope that these pages convey his generosity of spirit, strength of vision, and enduring legacy. Thank you to his children, Eric, Andrea, and Sophie Moora, who have been so welcoming over the years and who carry his memory and hopes into the future.

With deep gratitude, I would like to express my appreciation to everyone who has so graciously shared with me over the decades, especially those at PAKAM and Goolarri and in Balgo. This project was serendipitously inspired by Peter Brennan, who connected me with Kira Fong. Kira brought me into the world of Goolarri and Broome in 2006, leading to several late-night backyard jams with Steve Pigram and many other talented musicians in Broome. Thank you to everyone at Goolarri who graciously worked with me over the years, many of whom became mates, including Arthur Hunter, Mark Cochrane, Nigel Abbott, Kimberley West, Kira Fong, Sandy Dann, Renee Aharon, Mikaela Carter, Jodie Bell, Dot West, Koiki Hamaguchi, Elaine Rabbit, and the late Baamba Albert.

This project would not have been possible without Neil Turner's kindness and generosity. Neil welcomed me into PAKAM, throwing me into "the deep end" in 2013, when I drove an old troopy out to Balgo for *Kurrarlkatjanu*, leading to the many other films I was fortunate enough to collaborate on. I want to thank everyone else involved with PAKAM, including Trevor Ishiguchi, Henry Augustine, Dunba Nunju, Anna Cadden, Micah Bartlett, Anne Bennett, Bernadette Angus, Joe Pickering, Micha Bartlett, Jan Cattoni, and the late Clint Dixon, whose skill and laughter I will never forget. I also want to thank Rosemarie Colosi and Billy Watson, who welcomed me into Yungngora Community.

My fieldwork took me to many unexpected places, but none was more meaningful than Balgo. I want to deeply thank Warwick Nieass, who shared innumerable hopes, dreams, and meals with me over many journeys. Thank you to those involved in PAKAM projects in Balgo, including David “Shorty” Young, Allison Gill, Jimmy Tchooga, Larry Gundora, Ribnga Green, Bob Dingle, Helicopter Tjungurrayi, William Mandijarra, and David Banjo. I especially want to thank the Elders at the Kapululangu Women’s Law and Culture Centre, most of whom have passed away, including Payi Payi Sunfly Napangarti, Linda Charmawina Napangarti, Manaya Sarah Daniels Napanangka, Mayan Kathleen Padoon Napanangka, and Marti Maude Napanangka. I also want to thank the other Balgo women I worked with, including Marie Mudgedell, Eva Nagamora, Sadie Padoon, Lady Gordon, Brenda Brown, Tossie Baadjo, Frances Nowee, Jane Gimme, and Latoya Moody. I want to thank Quinton Milner and the many other multitalented Balgo musicians, including Aaron Milner, Delton Galova, Deryl Yumarrie, Bobby Daniels, and the late Ronald Mosquito, who was also a gifted and beloved translator. Thank you to the multitude of other project collaborators in Balgo, including Zohl de Ishtar, Suzie Thomas, Sheryl Anderson, Nick Withers, Poppy Lever, Helen Puckey, Katja Nedoluha, Angela Berry, Camille Berthelier, Jamie Hayden, Jaz Brooks, Rowena Potts, Staf Smith, Angie Reid, Tom Vidot, Giancarlo Mazzella, and Tibor Hegedis.

I thank everyone at the Indigenous Remote Communications Association (now First Nations Media), including Daniel Featherstone, Liam Campbell, and Maor Lambert, as well as everyone at Indigenous Community Television, especially Rita Cattoni, David Slowo, and Ciara Buckley. I also wish to thank the many people in Broome who helped to make it feel like home, including Sarah and Barbara Keenan, Sandy Faber, Sister Pat Rhatigan, Lachie Fraser, Mark Bin Bakar, Mitch Torres, and Kylie Jennings.

This project could not have been carried out without generous grants from the Wenner-Gren Foundation for Anthropological Research, the Fulbright IIE U.S. Scholar Program, the Lois Roth Endowment, the Andrew W. Mellon Foundation, the American Council of Learned Societies, and Bowdoin College. I want to express my appreciation to everyone at the Australian-American Fulbright Commission, including Tangerine Holt, Alex Maclaurin, Pablo Jiménez, and Cynthia Griffin.

I thank all of the academics who provided me with generous feedback, especially my PhD adviser, Jennifer Shannon, who encouraged me from day one and believed that this process was possible, even and especially when I doubted it myself. None of it would have happened without her, and I remain grateful for her years of support in a thousand moments, big and small, through which her brilliant and ethically nuanced guidance made all of the difference. I could not have asked for a better adviser. I also want to thank the rest of my committee for their generous feedback, including Carla Jones and her penchant for identifying and elevating the best in students and for our many inspiring chats, which among other insights led specifically to the structure of chapter 6; Donna Goldstein for her many encouragements and for helping me to step back to see the bigger picture; Faye Ginsburg for her years of support, repeatedly going out of her way to provide me with incisive feedback, as well as helping to orient me within the larger scholarly debates and social networks relating to Indigenous media; and John Carty for his cheerful and grounded wisdom based on his years of fieldwork in and around Balgo. Each of my committee members generously made time to regularly engage with me in critical and earnest ways, and I will remain forever grateful.

I thank other U.S. faculty who provided invaluable feedback and support over the years, including Paul Shankman, Kira Hall, Kaifa Roland, Danika Medak-Saltzman, Matt Sponheimer, Carole McGranahan, Chris Hammons, Clint Carroll, Angelica Lawson, Sylvie Poirier, Jennifer Deger, Fred Myers, Elizabeth Povinelli, Audra Simpson, Lisa Messeri, Daniel Fisher, Lisa Stefanoff, Kristen Dowell, Christina Leza, Chloe Ahmann, Salma Monani, Joseph Weiss, and Justin Latici. I appreciate the tireless work of the administrators in the University of Colorado Boulder Anthropology Department, including Valerie McBride, Lesa Morris, Diana Wilson, and Alison Davidson.

I thank all of the scholars at the University of Notre Dame Australia and the Nulungu Research Institute in Broome, including Bruce Gorring, Sandra Wooltorton, Maya Haviland, Patrick Sullivan, Stephen

Kinnane, Anna Dwyer, Kathryn Thorburn, Melissa Marshall, Stephen Muecke, Renata Cetinich, and Bobbie Chew Bigby. I also want to thank everyone at the National Centre for Indigenous Studies at Australian National University, who generously hosted me in Canberra, including Mick Dodson, Cressida Fforde, Corinne Walsh, Annie Te One, Ed Wensing, Magali McDuffie, and Diana Anderssen. I thank the other scholars in Canberra who provided valuable feedback on my developing ideas, including David MacDougall, Kaely Woods, Inge Kral, Nicolas Peterson, Howard Morphy, Francesca Merlan, and Vince Redhouse. I am also grateful for the generous feedback from other Australian scholars, including David Kelly, Emma Kowal, Sarah Pink, Sandy Toussaint, Jackie Healy, Michael McCall, and Richard Davis. This project would not have been possible without my past mentors, including Muriel Blaisdell, Mark McPhail, John Cinnamon, Linda Marchant, Rob Tolley, Richard Clemmer-Smith, Bonnie Clark, Christina Kreps, and Peter van Arsdale.

While I was reimagining this book at the height of both the pandemic and my own writing challenges, several people helped to guide me in this crucial period through manuscript workshopping, including Melinda Hinkson, Yasmine Musharbash, Bunny McBride, and Harald Prins. I am particularly grateful to Lucas Bessire, who provided the deepest insights when I needed them most, and without whom the form of this book would not exist. I also wish to express my appreciation to Bowdoin College, which has provided generous financial support and a community of many brilliant colleagues and students who challenge me to think in new ways.

I express a heartfelt thank you to Jason Weidemann, who believed in this book from our first meeting amid the AAA conference book room bustle. He and Zenyse Miller guided it throughout the publication process with such care and professionalism. I appreciate the time and labor that everyone else at the University of Minnesota Press devoted to this project, including Shelby Connelly, Eric Lundgren, Rachel Moeller, Terence Smyre, Michael Stoffel, cover designer Adrianna Sutton, the external readers, and the faculty board. I also thank Laura Portwood-Stacer for supporting my book proposal.

I am grateful to my graduate school colleagues and friends in Colorado for their support and feedback, including Allison Formanack, Dani

Merriman, Dawa Lokyitsang, Kathryn White, Meryleen Mena, Chris Morris, Erin Baxter, Ben Joffe, Magda Stawkowski, Marnie Thomson, Michaela Howells, James Loudon, Kate Fischer, Rachel Fleming, Richard Bender, Morgan Seamont, Teresa Montoya, Dave Bailey, Erik Reinhart, and Ethan Raath. Finally, I could not have done any of this without my wife, Anna, our daughter, Zelda, and my mom, dad, and sister: Judy, Barry, and Sarah.

While I am listed as the sole author of this book (and all errors are mine alone), countless people helped to bring it to fruition. Anything that it has to offer is due to their generosity.

Notes

Introduction: Awakenings

1. A true story, or *trustori* in the regional Kriol language, is roughly translated as a "legend" that contains deeper truths. It describes a story in which human characters can be located in time, space, and memory. This is distinctive from Tjukurrpa (Dreaming) stories about supernatural beings (Roe and Muecke 1983, 11).

2. While the projects I collaborated on did not involve physical film, I use the terms *film* and *video* interchangeably (though mostly *film*) as this reflects how the medium was commonly discussed throughout my fieldwork.

3. "Dreaming" is an English shorthand for the diverse and complex interweavings of metaphysical, cosmological, and symbolic ancestral connections that Aboriginal people across Australia have to their Country. I refer to this as either Dreaming or the more direct Kukatja word, *Tjukurrpa* (Carty 2021, 53; Myers 1986, 47; Poirier [1996] 2005, 244). It was originally translated into English as the "dream-time" by Spencer and Gillen (1899). This naming implied a mythical distant past, which Alfred Radcliffe-Brown drew upon to develop the idea of the ethnographic present. Intervening in this temporal bias, William Stanner (1969) reframed the Dreamtime into the present tense of the Dreaming, set within the larger context of the "everywhen." Jennifer Deger offers the alternative of the "Ancestral Always" to emphasize how the past permeates the present for Yolngu people (2006, 81). Like other such metaphysical terms, including Songlines and Country, the conceptualization of Dreaming is not its reality. As one community filmmaker told me, "I hate using the word Dreamtime. It makes it seem unreal. It's not a dream. It's our creation. You can't tell me it's not true, the way you try to shoot things to capture the spirits. It's real to us." Like the future, the Dreaming is not an ephemeral metaphor, and its totalizing English construction remains in tension with its expression in Aboriginal languages.

The concept of Songlines (Neale and Kelly 2020)—also described as Dreaming tracks, paths, or song cycles—was popularized through Bruce Chatwin's controversial 1988 book *The Songlines*. Songlines are described by Jan Wositsky and Yidumduma Bill Harney as "epic creation songs passed to present generations by a line of singers continuous since the Dreamtime. These songs, or songcycles, have various names according to which language group they belong to, and tell the story of the creation of the land, provide maps for the country, and hand down law as decreed by the creation heroes of the dreamtime" (1999, 301). Songs and maps are embedded within both land and stars, and some Songlines span across the continent. For a nuanced engagement with Kukatja Songlines and Dreaming, see Sylvie Poirier's ethnography, *A World of Relationships* ([1996] 2005).

4. Country, capitalized, refers to the matrix of complex meanings and beings that interconnect land with self, relations, tribal Law, Songlines, and Dreaming (Carty 2021; Gammage and Pascoe 2021). In Balgo and regional communities, this is described as Ngurra (Musharbash 2008a, 5; Myers 1986, 92). It is important to emphasize that Tjukurrpa (Dreaming), Ngurra (Country), and walytja (family) are themselves not isolated realms, and are interwoven through kanyininpa (holding), the Kukatja integration of each of these (McCoy 2008, 21).

5. Throughout this book I use the present tense within ethnographic vignettes. Inspired by ethnographers such as Melinda Hinkson (2021), this approach aims to add a sense of vitality and presence to these sections. Through present tense and a sans-serif font, I seek to provide clear signals for transitioning between narrative and analytical modes of writing. To mitigate the potential of conveying a detemporalized ethnographic present (Fabian 1983), these vignettes are not generalized, and are situated within the context of specific individuals and projects, including myself as an active and present subject.

6. As I have written elsewhere, "Despite its Christian connotations, the concept of apocalypse serves a critical role in theorizing Indigenous futurity, uniquely capturing the world-altering histories of colonial brutality" (Lempert 2018a, 202). Unlike a dystopia, a postapocalypse is not defined by resignation, but rather leaves future possibilities open amid a challenging backdrop.

7. For a detailed history of Yagga Yagga, see Cane (2016) and Poirier ([1996] 2005, 46, 86).

8. "Calling" is an Aboriginal expression describing the beckoning feeling from one's Country to return home. It takes on a double meaning in *Gapuwiyak Calling* (2014), a Miyarrka Media film engaging the use of cell phone video in the Arnhem Land community of Gapuwiyak.

9. Law, capitalized, has a substantially different, though related, meaning from what is usually understood by the law (Langton and Corn 2023). It is used as a shorthand for the totality of the rules and mores of Aboriginal codes,

including interpersonal social norms, rites of passage, kinship relations, and appropriate "payback" consequences in relation to Dreaming cosmologies (Poirier [1996] 2005, 56).

10. Hand sign meanings are highly contextual. Palya can mean "good one," "that is correct," or "proper process," while wiya generally conveys that something cannot happen, depending on the question it responds to. The most used sign, nganaku, is a flexible signifier asking the question that the signer does not need to even ask due to the density of context. Its most common response is wiya, which roughly means "nothing" or "that can't happen right now," which is invaluable for indirect declining in contexts where saying no is inappropriate.

11. After being developed by Nelson Mandela and others in the 1990s aftermath of South African apartheid, reconciliation has become an increasingly common framework for Indigenous relations with settler state governments around the world. Beyond Australia, this has been most notable in Canada, where a Truth and Reconciliation Commission was formed in 2008 to address the layers of trauma caused by residential schooling policies. In ways that parallel its deployment in Australia, Joseph Weiss (2025) articulates the limits of reconciliation as a framework of meaningful justice for Canadian First Nations.

12. *Terra nullius* has its origin in Roman law and means "land deriving from no one." Under colonial British law, it was illegal to annex occupied land. However, definitions of occupation were narrow and selective during the Australian colonial era, so much so that many farmers in England would build unnecessary structures simply to comply with occupation standards. Bruce Pascoe (2014) articulates how British colonizers misunderstood and mischaracterized Aboriginal land use in order to declare the continent as unoccupied and therefore claimable. The legal standing of *terra nullius* was not technically overturned in Australia until the 1992 *Mabo* case, though practically speaking, it endures through the sustained lack of Indigenous treaties.

13. The 1993 Native Title Act was passed following the 1992 *Mabo* case. Native Title provided a new legal foundation for Aboriginal land rights. This was challenged by pastoral lease holders who were concerned about its impact on their interests. The 1996 case *Wik Peoples v. The State of Queensland* settled this, declaring that Native Title could coexist with pastoral leases. The conservative Liberal government led by John Howard responded to this decision by passing the 1998 Native Title Amendment Act, which heavily curtailed the scope and power of Native Title and represented a significant setback for Aboriginal land rights (Bauman and Glick 2012; E. Vincent 2017).

14. Many anthropologists have analyzed the impacts of multiculturalism, an influential discourse in settler societies. This framework is an extension of neoliberal logic that—despite its inclusive rhetoric on diversity—serves to construct an elite rootless Anglo-European subject position that is implicitly

superior to a variety of recognized but "tiered" (Silverstein 2003, 535) ethnic others (Turner 1993; Žižek 1997). Its discourse allows the dominant majority to claim a moral high ground without having to acknowledge or address persisting structural inequalities (Ramzan, Pinib, and Bryant 2009). Povinelli (1998) establishes Australia as the global bellwether for multiculturalism due to its particular combination of colonialism, xenophobia, and the early adoption of this rhetoric at a national level.

15. There is an extensive lineage of anthropologists engaged in understanding fundamental incommensurability between human societies (Povinelli 2001), including ontologically focused debates in recent decades (Bessire and Bond 2014; Descola 2013; de Castro 1998).

16. Alfred Gell (1992) provides a broader genealogy of anthropological understandings of time as culturally mediated.

17. In recent years, the confident archeological dates for the human occupation of Australia have been pushed back further to at least 65,000 years ago (Clarkson et al. 2017).

18. While the terms *whitefella* and *kartiya* are often used interchangeably, a key difference is that *whitefella* has a relatively neutral connotation, whereas *kartiya* has more negative implications, outside of joking exceptions.

19. Throughout this book, I italicize Kukatja words such as *palya* when I use them in a conceptual sense. I do this to emphasize the analytical aspects of Kukatja concepts.

20. While it is standard practice to list the director's name along with the year in the in-text citation, I break from this convention as it does not align with the collaborative and nonhierarchical practices of the community film projects that I worked on.

1. The First Film, *The Last Generation*

1. In many desert Aboriginal societies there is a strong prohibition against speaking the name of the recently deceased, which also applies to viewing their image. As described in chapter 5, attitudes around this issue are changing.

2. The broader Western Desert kinship system is Dravidian and includes sixteen social categories called "skin names," through which every individual in a community is connected. These apply not only to blood relations but also extend to other people in the community. It is critical for anyone who is going to stay in community for the long term to have a skin name so that they will have clearly defined roles of relationality and general behavior with everyone else. This is succinctly summarized by Laurent Dousset (2011) and has been the subject of many early anthropological studies of Aboriginal Australian people. There is also a great deal of variation in the perceived meaning of whitefellas receiving a skin name. On the one hand, outsiders are often ecstatic to have been "accepted" into an Aboriginal family, while some describe this "fictive kinship" as a cynical attempt by community members to "claim"

outsiders to gain access to their resources. In my experience, the receiving of a skin name is simply as meaningful (or not) as the relationship is in practice. On balance, the significance of outsider skin names seems to be more often overstated than understated.

3. I capitalize *Elders* throughout as this was widely seen as a sign of respect in Balgo, especially at Kapululangu.

4. The Seven Sisters Dreaming is explained in thoughtful depth by Sylvie Poirier ([1996] 2005), who lived for years in Balgo and Yagga Yagga.

5. PAKAM has since become more independent from Goolarri. It is also important to note here that in recent years PAKAM has moved into another area on the same property, out of the large shed and into a house-style building with a large central room surrounded by offices. Here, I describe PAKAM as it was structured and located during my primary fieldwork.

2. Laughing with the Camera

1. Keith Basso (1979) provides an exception, with his in-depth analysis of Western Apache comedy about "The Whiteman."

2. The truism about "missionaries, mercenaries, and misfits" became part of the title for *8MMM* (Curtis 2015), an ABC series that engaged many of the white/black dynamics discussed throughout this chapter, with more than a little bit of comedy and satire. One of its key collaborators, Anna Cadden, was the director of *Kurrarlkatjanu* (2013) and a whitefella collaborative filmmaker who served as a model for my own collaborative relationships.

3. This dynamic and stereotype can be partly traced back to the laws around fair wages that were passed in 1968, which led to most Aboriginal workers being fired from cattle stations and forced to move to the outskirts of regional towns. Alongside such welfare programs, various individual payment schemes are often described as "sit-down money" by community members.

4. "Growling" is a local slang term for arguing, which is often used ironically in relation to partner disputes and carries a similar register to "grumpy." Growling is closely connected with dogs barking at each other, with the hand sign for barking consisting of miming an angry dog. However, it does not carry connotations of comparing someone to a dog in a pejorative way.

5. Also see Zajdman (1995) on "saving face," which is closely related to dignity, though more defined by what to do in the case of something potentially undignified happening, as opposed to appropriate behavior in general.

6. This change was furthered by the former magistrate Antoine Bloemen, who was one of the first judges to try to integrate Aboriginal systems of justice into the Australian system. He supported the inclusion of Elder input in traveling circuit courts to help the magistrate understand the local context, including previous payback and what would happen to a broader family if someone went to prison. This is described in Bloemen's (2014) book on the subject—containing several stories in Balgo—which I discussed with him at the Broome

weekend markets where he sold them. His story was an inspiration for the ABC series *The Circuit* (2007), which dramatized this period within the Kimberley circuit court.

7. While getting bogged specifically referred to sinking down into mud or sand, it was often used to described people getting stranded for a variety of reasons.

8. Part of the purpose of one trip was to leave the old PAKAM troopy permanently in Balgo. The bottom was severely rusted and it would not last many more coastal wet seasons, through could endure for years in the dry desert. It would no longer need to be registered or pass an emissions test, as it would never again return to a highway or town.

9. Troopys run on diesel, which is less prone to catching on fire than petrol (gasoline). Thus, we could safely drive through even large fires for short periods if required.

10. Grinding stones were, and are, used to grind bush flour into damper bread. Because of their weight, their importance, and the immense amount of time they take to create, they are often left in one particular place.

11. *Basically Black* (1973) was a pilot episode put on by the revolutionary National Black Theatre, led by Bob Maza, which was inspired directly by the Black Panther Party and their theater work in the United States. Its pilot episode was produced in 1973, and its larger context and history are chronicled in *The Redfern Story* (2014), a documentary by Darlene Johnson.

3. Social Editing and Screening

1. I focus on film projects, not only because they were the media I was most deeply involved with but also because their long, complex, and social processes match the process-oriented method of tracing the social life of media. However, radio was ever-present throughout my fieldwork. Radio hubs were central and formative for PAKAM and Goolarri in Broome, in addition to the remote radio stations at each of the PAKAM network remote communities I spent time in, including Balgo. For decades, radio has formed the bedrock of Aboriginal media organizations, both in terms of funding and labor (Bessire and Fisher 2013; Hinkson 2012; Morrison 2000). Unlike video, radio can be taught quickly, and it served as the point of first contact for most people joining these organizations.

2. A similar situation occurred while filming *Jimmy Tchooga: Painting Two Snakes*. Like Dunba, Jimmy was a strong storyteller, though somewhat soft-spoken in front of the camera. When we reviewed the footage, it seemed that it might not be quite clear enough for non-subtitled broadcasting standards. When we explained the issue, he agreed that we should make sure to avoid the need for subtitles. The next day we sat down in the Balgo art center to record a narration of the documentary in a quiet space with a high-quality microphone. Despite the troopy getting stuck during this shoot and having arrived home

only the previous night, our collective effort to avoid using subtitles seemed to provoke a renewed energy in the project. As a PAKAM worker in Balgo explained, our concern for upholding Jimmy's dignity in the film was noted by him as prioritizing palya production values.

3. "Singing" someone refers to that person being the target of an act of sorcery, which is often subtle, deadly, and done from a distance (McKnight 1981). This is one of many ways in which songs and the act of singing are demonstrated to be powerful forces in Aboriginal life, with the capability for healing and injuring as well as navigating and relating with Country.

4. While this might seem to contradict the relative success in Indigenous media funding, the differences here are that the media center was housed within an art center, which was not set up to prioritize media production, and that there was no long-term organizational infrastructure set up to support these centers. Rather, they were extensions of the art center and dependent on its ability to fund them through intermittent grants.

5. The peak body later transitioned from IRCA to First Nations Media Australia.

6. Neil did not seem motivated by prestigious festival awards or winning large grants. For example, he discussed the challenges of participating in the Songlines on Screen program, which diverted significant resources from smaller community projects. He described being ultimately pleased for PAKAM to participate because of the potential positive implications of such a public program on the sector more broadly. What seemed to make Neil most excited were community-focused goals, such as when a remote radio station went back online, when community workers completed training workshops in Broome, and when ICTV was launched in Broome so that more people could watch community Aboriginal media.

7. For relevant scholarship on film stock and skin tone see Winston (1985, 1996) and Roth (2009).

8. Such restricted recordings occurred frequently in Balgo with Mark and the women Elders, who received copies of this footage. Password-protected files were also archived in the Balgo culture center.

4. Fires, Tires, and Paper

1. For many thousands of years, Aboriginal people across much of Australia have strategically lit bush fires throughout the year. Researchers have often described this as "fire-stick farming" (Jones [1969] 2012), done for a variety of reasons including facilitating ease of travel and encouraging new growth to attract game animals (Garde 2009). Bill Gammage and Bruce Pascoe (2021) make the case that these fires are part of deeper understandings around environmental balance, cultivating seedlings that require small-scale fires to germinate but are killed by the high heat of destructive mass-scale fires. As they detail, ever since the profound colonial disruption of Aboriginal life, there have

been increasingly devastating fires, starting only years after major land dispossession, and continuing through to Australia's deadliest fire in the "Black Summer" of 2019–20. There are currently a variety of programs integrating Aboriginal fire practices to not only reduce deadly fires but also to curb their globally significant carbon emissions (Russell-Smith et al. 2013). One of the most sought-after job programs in Balgo is the Bush Ranger program, with Aboriginal Rangers working on fire projects as part of the process of taking care of Country.

2. My initial impetus for reframing creative production was in response to disparaging comments toward Balgo community members, such as "Well, you know how blackfellas are. They are lazy. They show up late or not at all. I'm not trying to judge them. They make beautiful paintings. They just aren't cut out for real jobs." I overheard this comment by a visiting bureaucrat who was walking through the art center, though similar remarks were commonplace by whitefellas. Without an alternative framework, the refutation of laziness runs into the problem of accepting and reinforcing the capitalist premises built into "lazy," which, in addition to negating collective creative rhythms, also ignores the myriad social obligations that are simply more important than a work shift.

3. Australian rules football is a popular sport in Western Australia. Described in communities as "footy" and nationally through the acronym AFL (Australian Football League), this sport is often contrasted with rugby, which is relatively more popular on the east coast of Australia. In recent years, increasing evidence suggests that the sport's origins are intertwined with the Mukjarrawaint ball game of Marngrook (Hocking and Reidy 2016).

4. This included IndigiTube, whose video streaming would later largely migrate to ICTV Play.

5. As a counterpoint, another manager noted that while this was a common sentiment, they disagreed that it should be. She viewed the "air filter" metaphor of accepting all of the blame as paternalistic and lacking proper boundaries.

6. While many love to paint, community members tend to stop if they begin receiving other income streams, such as mining royalties (Carty 2011, 88).

7. CDEP is an acronym for Community Development Employment Projects, a complex governmental system that focused on skill building and employment in Aboriginal communities. Mary G alludes here to programs that provide relatively small amounts of money while exerting intensive bureaucratic surveillance.

8. Linda Tuhuwai Smith's (Ngāti Awa and Ngāti Porou, Māori) *Decolonizing Methodologies* (1999) and Leanne Simpson's (Michi Saagiig Nishnaabeg) *Dancing on Our Turtle's Back* (2011) are foundational texts in such frameworks and practices. Simpson—similarly to Ngũgĩ wa Thiong'o (1993)—argues for the importance of centering Nishnaabeg language itself within analyses of Indigenous sovereignty.

9. One of these two films, the *Hand Talk Trilogy* (2016), featured shorts showing signs being used to describe cultural objects, the relationship between gestures and animal tracks, and a comedy skit satirizing money morning through subtitled hand signs. *Bush Hunt Hand Talk* (2016) featured women Elders as they hunted for food while communicating with one another primarily through hand signs, subtitled into English. Over the course of a long day, the women planned and carried out the trip in their trusty troopy, then returned to eat bush food and kangaroo tails in the evening. The full story of this process could fill another book. Here, it is sufficient to say that this trinity was useful within, and refined through, practicing it throughout the social lives of these projects.

5. After-Images

1. For an in-depth engagement with the changing protocols regarding images of the deceased in Aboriginal Australian communities, see Deger (2006).

2. Like "sorry business," saying sorry is not meant apologetically, but rather as a way of expressing condolences around a recent death to the close family members.

3. A parallel situation happened with the documentary *Gurrumul* (2017), about the acclaimed blind Yolngu singer by the same name. He passed away just three days after approving the final cut, and the Elders in his Yolngu community of Galiwin'ku on Elcho Island decided to allow the film to be released.

4. As part of First Nations Media's Our Archives, Our Stories program, PAKAM began adding to a high-quality digital repository for their media. Depending on cultural protocols, some media are available to the general public and some are password protected for individuals or communities.

5. As Benjamin Smith notes, the circulation of meaningful photographs leads to unexpected outcomes. This often includes interest in contributing to an archive, involving dynamic storytelling about the people being remembered (2003, 18).

6. While contemporary narrative history following individual characters has become commonplace (e.g., Wilkerson 2010), the inclusion of biography within history is the result of decades of long disciplinary debates, largely led by feminist historians (Banner 2009; Jackson 2004; Salvatore 2004; Wolpert 2010). There is also a rich tradition of life history in anthropology (Langness and Frank 1981; Mintz 1960; Myerhoff 1974; Nash 1992; Neihardt 1932). Given the relatively succinct nature of this section, it is more accurate to categorize this short life story of Mark Moora as biographical rather than biography—akin to the distinction between ethnographic and ethnography. Contextually, it does not approach the depth of several extensive histories of Balgo and Yagga Yagga communities (e.g., Cane 2016; de Ishtar 2005; McCoy 2008; Poirier [1996] 2005). Rather, I provide historical scaffolding to engage the primary

events in Mark's life and the ways in which his own story interweaves these regional histories.

7. While often misunderstood as an Aboriginal impulse to wander aimlessly, the walkabout is a rite of passage in which a young person goes off to live by themselves in Country for an extended period of time, after which they return transformed.

8. Jean Rouch (1974) developed the idea of *anthropologie partagée,* or "shared anthropology," a prescient precursor to anthropological reflexivity. This collaborative orientation was interwoven with his development of the documentary style of cinema vérité. Rather than attempting to make the camera and filmmaker invisible—as practiced in observational and direct documentary—Rouch appeared on-screen and was heavily involved in shaping creative narratives (Henley 2010). This approach led him to pioneer *ethnofiction,* in which he encouraged his co-creators to self-consciously act and create narratives. Rouch considered filmmaking to be a provocation, which often led to moments of *ciné-trance* that transformed subject and object toward the ends of revealing deeper truths (Rouch 2003).

6. The Visibility Paradox

1. I use the term "golden age" in a very relative sense. While Indigenous Australian media funding, infrastructure, and circulation are expansive in comparison with the past and to most other nations, it remains paltry in comparison with non-Indigenous media sectors. Furthermore, I compare Australia with the United States, Canada, and New Zealand, as they provide the closest analogs in light of their current first-world status as well as their relatively similar scale and historical dynamics in relation to European settler colonialism and Indigenous people. While I could certainly understand some pushing back on the utopian and potentially overstated connotations of "golden age," I use it to emphasize its marked contrast with other Aboriginal funding policy trends during this era.

2. To the dismay of many Indigenous filmmakers, the Native American Film + Video Festival at the National Museum of the American Indian Festival (1995–2011) in New York City was discontinued primarily due to a lack of funding, and its archives were secured only through an accessioning program assisted by Faye Ginsburg and New York University. This is part of a broader dearth of public funding for Indigenous (or other) media within the United States, where there is no equivalent organization to Screen Australia or the Indigenous Screen Office in Canada. Rather, there is a patchwork of funding from Native nations including the Cherokee Nation Film Office, OsiyoTV, and Chickasaw TV; private organizations such as the Sundance Indigenous Institute; and VisionMaker Media, which was founded in 1976 and previously known as Native American Public Telecommunications.

3. Australia has a long disciplinary history of cutting-edge mediation including Aboriginal people. Less than two decades after the first ever film was made—Eadweard Muybridge's *The Horse in Motion* (1878)—Félix-Louis Regnault took footage of Wolof women in Africa making pots as part of the first cross-cultural visual study of movement (Hockings 2003, 15). Just a few years later, on April 4, 1901, Baldwin Spencer became the first anthropologist to attempt either photography or filmmaking in the field, shooting ceremonial Aboriginal dances in Northern Australia, though his film aspirations never came to full fruition due to technical setbacks (17). In Spencer's work with Gillen (1899) they argued that photography helped to capture performative acts such as ceremonial dance that could not be fully understood through words alone, though Nicolas Peterson (2006) argues that this photographic reliance was also due to their lack of language mastery. Interestingly—and supporting Mead's argument for the objectivity of photographic evidence—many of their conclusions were contradicted by their own photographs, illuminating the difficulty for anthropologists at this time to engage different worldviews (Hockings 2003, 20). Furthermore, Jane Lydon (2006) articulates how Aboriginal people have used photography to convey their own messages since the 1860s. As she argues, rather than being victims of this colonial technology, Aboriginal people in communities in places such as Coranderrk Station actively presented strategically advantageous representations, acutely aware of how these images would be framed within the Western world. Eric Michaels's (1986) work on self-expression in Aboriginal television of Central Australia was a watershed moment in the study of Indigenous media and self-representation. Working contemporaneously with him, Neil Turner often discussed Michaels's importance in the early days of Aboriginal video production.

4. See Stefanoff (2009) for an in-depth history and ethnographic engagement with CAAMA and how it fits within the Indigenous Australian mediascape.

5. For more on how Aboriginal media articulate with the Australian imaginary, see Ginsburg (1993).

6. There is a constellation of reasons why Aboriginal Australians do not have treaties. One has to do with their low population density in much of the continent and their social structure at the time of contact, which made it impractical to organize the large-scale armed resistance that occurred in New Zealand and North America. That said, there were a variety of regional resistance movements.

7. The first two minutes of "Remote Hope" are particularly revealing and may be found in various places online.

8. Along similar lines, Māori filmmaker Barry Barclay developed the idea of "Fourth Cinema," that exists beyond the nation-state orientation of first, second, and third cinemas. The "Fourth Eye" (Hokowhitu and Devadas 2013)

further theorizes this line of thinking by centering the productive, rather than the resistant, potential of Indigenous media.

9. As with the much-debated "suffering slot" (Robbins 2013) in anthropology, such depictions can unintentionally serve to dispossess Indigenous futures through what Sherry Ortner describes as "dark anthropology" (2016). Framing this in the positive sense, Robbins argues for the importance of instead critically engaging an "anthropology of the good."

10. In 2017 the "Statement of Eminent Australians" was released, signed by two hundred prominent Australians. This included many Aboriginal Elders and university professors such as Jon Altman and Gillian Triggs, who was the Australian Human Rights Commissioner at the time. This statement not only summarizes the negative impact of the intervention but also calls for the repeal of ongoing related measures. For more on anthropological engagements with Aboriginal politics see Altman and Hinkson (2010).

11. The IAS amalgamated 150 programs and cut a total of $534 million (approximately 40 percent) from the overall budget for Indigenous services. Ultimately only 41 percent of the applications were successful, less than half of which (45 percent) were Indigenous organizations.

12. While the Indigenous media sector was funded *relatively* well through the IAS, it did receive some cuts under the banner of reducing bureaucracy at the level of larger organizations. For example, the urban-focused Australian Indigenous Communications Association was defunded and absorbed by the remote media peak body, the Indigenous Remote Communications Association (IRCA). In addition, around this time NITV's funding was cut significantly, making it more difficult for them to fund their own in-house content beyond the news.

13. For Goolarri, this funding shift was more complex in practice. While their baseline funding continued at about the same levels, the restructuring represented by the IAS also reduced the amount of funding sources that they were able to apply for throughout the year. Goolarri has in recent years been increasingly pressured to supplement government funding with private money. The only consistent funding that they receive is $280,000 annually that is specifically for radio, which has not increased in over a decade. For example, when expected government funds for the 2015 Pilbara and Kimberley Girl competitions were unexpectedly cut, they made up the difference with funding from multiple mining companies with interests in the region. Receiving support from such sources was a controversial decision. As Kira Fong noted about the situation, "these are not easy decisions, and sometimes you almost feel like you have to sell your soul to keep an important program alive." Such "Faustian contracts" (Ginsburg 1991) around funding were common. For example, Noonkanbah Station, just outside of Yungngora, had their first major rodeo since the 1980s in 2014, which Trevor Ishiguchi and I recorded for PAKAM. However, it was funded through a deal with Buru Energy to frack the

lands in the region. This was especially painful for many in this area in light of the important protests at Noonkanbah Station in 1978 to prevent the AMAX company from drilling near sacred sites.

14. Managers and directors of Aboriginal organizations commonly used the phrase "checking boxes" to express bureaucratic frustration at having to fulfill long lists of requirements that were perceived as unimportant.

15. This history makes up and underlies much of the explicit and implicit textures of Australian national identity. Much early settlement was founded upon the British dispossession of Irish land and the loss of Georgia as a colony to send convicts to. Many of the Irish people who were forcibly deported as criminals to Australia had been evicted from their land and then convicted of minor offenses, including stealing food during times of famine.

16. As described in the introduction, despite its early promise to deliver meaningful land rights, the efficaciousness of Native Title claims was significantly watered down over the years and the process was enacted in ways that often created more problems than they solved (Bauman and Glick 2012; E. Vincent 2017).

Bibliography

Ahmann, Chloe. 2019. "Waste to Energy: Garbage Prospects and Subjunctive Politics in Late-Industrial Baltimore." *American Ethnologist* 46 (3): 328–42.

Altman, Jon, and Melinda Hinkson, eds. 2010. *Culture Crisis: Anthropology and Politics in Aboriginal Australia.* Sydney: University of New South Wales Press.

Appadurai, Arjun, ed. 1986. *The Social Life of Things: Commodities in Cultural Perspective.* Cambridge: Cambridge University Press.

Appadurai, Arjun. 1994. "Introduction: Commodities and the Politics of Value." In *The Social Life of Things: Commodities in Cultural Perspective,* edited by Arjun Appadurai, 76–91. Cambridge: Cambridge University Press.

Apte, Mahadev. 1983. "Humor Research, Methodology, and Theory in Anthropology." In *Handbook of Humor Research,* edited by Paul E. McGhee, 183–212. New York: Springer-Verlag.

Apte, Mahadev. 1988. "Disciplinary Boundaries in Humorology: An Anthropologist's Ruminations." *Humor-International Journal of Humor Research* 1 (1): 5–26.

Aston, Judith, and Stefano Odorico. 2022. "Interactive Documentary: Its History and Future as a Polyphonic Form." In *Interactive Documentary: Decolonizing Practice-Based Research,* edited by Kathleen M. Ryan and David Staton, 20–37. New York: Routledge.

Attwood, Bain. 2005. *Telling the Truth about Aboriginal History.* Sydney: Allen & Unwin.

Aufderheide, Patricia. 1995. "The Video in the Villages Project: Videomaking with and by Brazilian Indians." *Visual Anthropology Review* 11 (2): 83–93.

Bach, J. P. S. 1962. "The Pearlshelling Industry and the 'White Australia' Policy." *Australian Historical Studies* 10 (38): 203–13.

Banner, Lois. 2009. "Biography as History." *American Historical Review* 114 (3): 579–86.

Basso, Keith. 1979. *Portraits of "The Whiteman": Linguistic Play and Cultural Symbols among the Western Apache.* Cambridge: Cambridge University Press.

Bateson, Gregory. (1936) 1958. *Naven: A Survey of the Problems Suggested by a Composite Picture of the Culture of a New Guinea Tribe Drawn from Three Points of View*. Palo Alto: Stanford University Press.

Bauman, Toni, and Lydia Glick, eds. 2012. *The Limits of Change: Mabo and Native Title 20 Years On*. Canberra: AIATSIS Research Publications.

Beeman, William. 1999. "Humor." *Journal of Linguistic Anthropology* 9 (1/2): 103–6.

Behar, Ruth. 1996. *The Vulnerable Observer: Anthropology That Breaks Your Heart*. Boston: Beacon Press.

Bell, Wendy. 2008. *A Remote Possibility: The Battle for Imparja Television*. Canberra: IAD Press.

Berlant, Lauren. 2018. "Genre Flailing." *Capacious: Journal for Emerging Affect Inquiry* 1 (2): 156–62.

Berndt, Ronald Murray. 1974. *Australian Aboriginal Religion*. Brill Book Archive.

Bessire, Lucas. 2017. "Glimpses of Emergence in the Ayoreo Video Project." *Visual Anthropology Review* 33 (2): 119–29.

Bessire, Lucas, and David Bond. 2014. "Ontological Anthropology and the Deferral of Critique." *American Ethnologist* 41 (3): 440–56.

Bessire, Lucas, and Daniel Fisher. 2013. "The Anthropology of Radio Fields." *Annual Review of Anthropology* 42 (1): 363–78.

Biddle, Jennifer Loureide. 2016. *Remote Avant-Garde: Aboriginal Art under Occupation*. Durham: Duke University Press.

Biehl, João. 2013. *Vita: Life in a Zone of Social Abandonment*. Berkeley: University of California Press.

Biehl, João, and Peter Locke. 2017. *Unfinished: The Anthropology of Becoming*. Durham: Duke University Press.

Bloemen, Antoine. 2014. *No Regrets: A Bicycle Dreaming from Belgium to Broome*. Carlisle: Hesperian Press.

Bombeck, Erma. 2013. *If Life Is a Bowl of Cherries, What Am I Doing in the Pits?* New York: Open Road Media. Kindle.

Bonilla, Yarimar. 2015. *Non-Sovereign Futures: French Caribbean Politics in the Wake of Disenchantment*. Chicago: University of Chicago Press.

Bourdieu, Pierre. 1977. *Outline of a Theory of Practice*. Cambridge: Cambridge University Press.

Boyer, Dominic. 2008. "Thinking Through the Anthropology of Experts." *Anthropology in Action* 15 (2): 38–46.

Campbell, Anita, Sivasankaran Balaratnasingam, Catherine McHugh, Aleksandar Janca, and Murray Chapman. 2016. "Alarming Increase of Suicide in a Remote Indigenous Australian Population: An Audit of Data from 2005 to 2014." *World Psychiatry* 15 (3): 296–97.

Cane, Scott. 2016. "People and Policy in the Development and Destruction of Yagga Yagga Outstation, Western Australia." In *Experiments in Self-Determination: Histories of the Outstation Movement in Australia*, edited by Nicolas Peterson and Fred Myers, 253–78. Canberra: ANU Press.

Carty, John. 2010. "Drawing a Line in the Sand: The Canning Stock Route and Contemporary Art." In *Yiwarra Kuju: The Canning Stock Route*, edited by John Carty, Carly Davenport, and Monique Lafontaine, 23–77. Canberra: National Museum of Australia Press.

Carty, John. 2011. "Creating Country: Abstraction, Economics and the Social Life of Style in Balgo Art." PhD diss., Anthropology, Australia National University.

Carty, John. 2021. *Balgo: Creating Country*. Perth: UWA Publishing.

Carty, John, and Yasmine Musharbash. 2008. "You've Got to Be Joking: Asserting the Analytical Value of Humour and Laughter in Contemporary Anthropology." *Anthropological Forum* 18 (3): 209–17.

Cattelino, Jessica R., and Audra Simpson. 2022. "Rethinking Indigeneity: Scholarship at the Intersection of Native American Studies and Anthropology." *Annual Review of Anthropology* 51:365–81.

Chang, Anita Wen-Shin. 2022. "Decolonizing Transmedia Practices: An Essay on Editing." In *Interactive Documentary: Decolonizing Practice-Based Research*, edited by Kathleen M. Ryan and David Staton, 126–44. New York: Routledge.

Chatwin, Bruce. 1988. *The Songlines*. New York: Penguin Books.

Clarkson, Chris, Zenobia Jacobs, Ben Marwick, Richard Fullagar, Lynley Wallis, Mike Smith, Richard G. Roberts, Elspeth Hayes, Kelsey Lowe, and Xavier Carah. 2017. "Human Occupation of Northern Australia by 65,000 Years Ago." *Nature* 547 (7663): 306–10.

Cosgrove, Laurie, and Beverley Kliger. 1997. "Planning with a Difference: A Reflection on Planning and Decision Making with Indigenous People in Broome, Western Australia." *Urban Policy and Research* 15 (3): 211–17.

Coulthard, Glen Sean. 2014. *Red Skin, White Masks: Rejecting the Colonial Politics of Recognition*. Minneapolis: University of Minnesota Press.

Cruikshank, Julie. 1998. *The Social Life of Stories: Narrative and Knowledge in Northern Canada*. Vancouver: University of British Columbia Press.

de Castro, Eduardo Viveiros. 1998. "Cosmological Deixis and Amerindian Perspectivism." *Journal of the Royal Anthropological Institute* 4 (3): 469–88.

Deger, Jennifer. 2006. *Shimmering Screens: Making Media in an Aboriginal Community*. Minneapolis: University of Minnesota Press.

de Ishtar, Zohl. 2005. *Holding Yawulyu: White Culture and Black Women's Law*. North Geelong: Spinifex Press.

Deleuze, Gilles. 1989. *Cinema 2: The Time-Image*. Translated by Hugh Tomlinson and Robert Galeta. Minneapolis: University of Minnesota Press.

Deleuze, Gilles. 2019. "Cinema II: The Time-Image." In *Philosophers on Film from Bergson to Badiou: A Critical Reader*, edited by Christopher Kul-Want, 177–99. New York: Columbia University Press.

Deloria, Vine, Jr. 1969. *Custer Died for Your Sins: An Indian Manifesto*. Norman: University of Oklahoma Press.

Derrida, Jacques. (1967) 1993. "Structure, Sign, and Play in the Discourse of the Human Sciences." In *A Postmodern Reader*, 223–42. Albany: SUNY Press.

Derrida, Jacques. 1995. *Archive Fever: A Freudian Impression*. Chicago: University of Chicago Press.

Descola, Philippe. 2013. *Beyond Nature and Culture*. Chicago: University of Chicago Press.

Dillon, Grace. 2012. *Walking the Clouds: An Anthology of Indigenous Science Fiction*. Tucson: University of Arizona Press.

Dodson, Michael. 2007. "Bully in the Playground: A New Stolen Generation?" In *Coercive Reconciliation: Stabilise, Normalise, Exit Aboriginal Australia*, edited by Jon Altman and Melinda Hinkson, 85–96. Melbourne: Arena Publications.

Donaldson, Mike. 1996. "The End of Time? Aboriginal Temporality and the British Invasion of Australia." *Time & Society* 5 (2): 187–207.

Douglas, Mary. (1966) 2003. *Purity and Danger: An Analysis of Concepts of Pollution and Taboo*. New York: Routledge.

Dousset, Laurent. 2011. *Australian Aboriginal Kinship: An Introductory Handbook with Particular Emphasis on the Western Desert*. Marseilles: Pacific-Credo Publications.

Dowell, Kristin. 2013. *Sovereign Screens: Aboriginal Media on the Canadian West Coast*. Lincoln: University of Nebraska Press.

Dowell, Kristin. 2018. "Digital Sutures: Experimental Stop-Motion Animation as Future Horizon of Indigenous Cinema." *Cultural Anthropology* 33 (2): 189–201.

Drazin, Adam, and Susanne Küchler, eds. 2015. *The Social Life of Materials: Studies in Materials and Society*. London: Bloomsbury.

Driessen, Henk. 2015. "Anthropology of Humor." In *International Encyclopedia of the Social and Behavioral Sciences*, 2nd ed., edited by J. D. Wright, 416–19. Amsterdam: Elsevier.

Elder, Sarah. 1995. "Collaborative Filmmaking: An Open Space for Making Meaning, a Moral Ground for Ethnographic Film." *Visual Anthropology Review* 11 (2): 94–101.

Estes, Nick. 2019. *Our History Is the Future: Standing Rock versus the Dakota Access Pipeline, and the Long Tradition of Indigenous Resistance*. New York: Verso.

Fabian, Johannes. 1983. *Time and the Other: How Anthropology Makes Its Object*. New York: Columbia University Press.

Finnane, Mark. 2001. "'Payback,' Customary Law and Criminal Law in Colonised Australia." *International Journal of the Sociology of Law* 29 (4): 293–310.

Fisher, Daniel. 2016. *The Voice and Its Doubles: Media and Music in Northern Australia*. Durham: Duke University Press.

Forde, Susan, Kerrie Foxwell, and Michael Meadows. 2009. *Developing Dialogues: Indigenous and Ethnic Community Broadcasting in Australia*. Chicago: University of Chicago Press.

Forster, Edward Morgan. 1927. *Aspects of the Novel*. London: Edward Arnold.

Franks, Travis. 2023. "Uncanny Encounters and Haunting Colonial Histories in Australia's Reconciliation-Era Narratives." *Settler Colonial Studies* 13 (3): 398–418.

Gal, Susan. 2015. "Politics of Translation." *Annual Review of Anthropology* 44 (1): 225–40.

Gammage, Bill, and Bruce Pascoe. 2021. *Country: Future Fire, Future Farming.* Melbourne: Thames & Hudson Australia.

Ganter, Regina. 2006. *Mixed Relations: Asian-Aboriginal Contact in North Australia.* Crawley: University of Western Australia Press.

Ganti, Tejaswini. 2012. *Producing Bollywood: Inside the Contemporary Hindi Film Industry.* Durham: Duke University Press Books.

Garde, Murray. 2009. "The Language of Fire: Seasonality, Resources, and Landscape Burning on the Arnhem Land Plateau." In *Culture, Ecology, and Economy of Fire Management in North Australian Savannas: Rekindling the Wurrk Tradition,* 85–164. Collingwood: CSIRO Publishing.

Geddarrdyu, Mary. 2003. "Poorbala Poorbala Me." *Whaddayow.* Whaddayow Music.

Gell, Alfred. 1992. *The Anthropology of Time: Cultural Constructions of Temporal Maps and Images.* Oxford: Berg.

Ginsburg, Faye. 1991. "Indigenous Media: Faustian Contract or Global Village?" *Cultural Anthropology* 6 (1): 92–112.

Ginsburg, Faye. 1993. "Aboriginal Media and the Australian Imaginary." *Public Culture* 5 (3): 557–78.

Ginsburg, Faye. 1994. "Embedded Aesthetics: Creating a Discursive Space for Indigenous Media?" *Cultural Anthropology* 9 (3): 365–82.

Ginsburg, Faye. 1995. "Production Values: Indigenous Media and the Rhetoric of Self-Determination." In *Rhetorics of Self-Making,* edited by Debbora Battaglia, 121–38. Berkeley: University of California Press.

Ginsburg, Faye. 1997. "'From Little Things, Big Things Grow': Indigenous Media and Cultural Activism." In *Between Resistance and Revolution: Cultural Politics and Social Protest,* edited by Richard G. Fox and Orin Starn, 118–44. New Brunswick: Rutgers University Press.

Ginsburg, Faye. 2002. "Screen Memories: Resignifying the Traditional in Indigenous Media." In *Media Worlds: Anthropology on New Terrain,* edited by Faye Ginsburg, Lila Abu-Lughod, and Brian Larkin, 39–57. Berkeley: University of California Press.

Ginsburg, Faye. 2011. "Native Intelligence: A Short History of Debates on Indigenous Media and Ethnographic Film." In *Made to Be Seen: Perspectives on the History of Visual Anthropology,* edited by Marcus Banks and Jay Ruby, 234–55. Chicago: University of Chicago Press.

Ginsburg, Faye. 2012. "Australia's Indigenous New Wave: Future Imaginaries in Recent Aboriginal Feature Films." Adrian Gerbrands Annual Lecture, Leiden.

Ginsburg, Faye. 2018. "The Indigenous Uncanny: Accounting for Ghosts in Recent Indigenous Australian Experimental Media." *Visual Anthropology Review* 34 (1): 67–76.

Ginsburg, Faye, and Fred Myers. 2006. "A History of Aboriginal Futures." *Critique of Anthropology* 26 (1): 27–45.

Goldstein, Donna. 2003. *Laughter out of Place: Race, Class, Violence, and Sexuality in a Rio Shantytown*. Berkeley: University of California Press.

Gordillo, Gastón. 2014. *Rubble: The Afterlife of Destruction*. Durham: Duke University Press.

Gourevitch, Philip. 1998. *We Wish to Inform You That Tomorrow We Will Be Killed with Our Families*. New York: Picador.

Gross, Lawrence. 2007. "Silence as the Root of American Indian Humor: Further Meditations on the Comic Vision of Anishinaabe Culture and Religion." *American Indian Culture and Research Journal* 31 (2): 69–85.

Guster, Christine. 2011. *Keeping Our Story: The Growth of First Nation Media*. Canberra: National Film and Sound Archives of Australia website. https://www.nfsa.gov.au/latest/keeping-our-story.

Halkin, Alexandra. 2008. "Outside the Indigenous Lens: Zapatistas and Autonomous Videomaking." In *Global Indigenous Media: Cultures, Poetics, and Politics*, edited by Pamela Wilson and Michelle Stewart, 160–80. Durham: Duke University Press.

Haraway, Donna Jeanne. 2016. *Staying with the Trouble: Making Kin in the Chthulucene*. Durham: Duke University Press.

Haviland, Maya. 2016. *Side by Side? Community Art and the Challenge of Co-creativity*. New York: Routledge.

Healy, Jacqueline. 2014. *Warlayirti: The Art of Balgo*. Melbourne: RMIT Gallery.

Heidegger, Martin. 1977. *Basic Writings: From* Being and Time *(1927) to* The Task of Thinking *(1964)*. Edited by David Krell. New York: Harper & Row.

Henley, Paul. 2010. *The Adventure of the Real: Jean Rouch and the Craft of Ethnographic Cinema*. Chicago: University of Chicago Press.

Hennessy, Kate. 2009. "Virtual Repatriation and Digital Cultural Heritage: The Ethics of Managing Online Collections." *Anthropology News* 50 (4): 5–6.

Henry, Rosita. 2012. *Performing Place, Practising Memories: Aboriginal Australians, Hippies, and the State*. New York: Berghahn Books.

Hinkson, Melinda. 2012. "The Cultural Politics of Radio: Two Views from the Warlpiri Public Sphere." In *Radio Fields: Anthropology and Wireless Sound in the 21st Century*, edited by Lucas Bessire and Daniel Fisher, 142–59. New York: New York University Press.

Hinkson, Melinda. 2021. *See How We Roll: Enduring Exile between Desert and Urban Australia*. Durham: Duke University Press.

Hocking, Jenny, and Nell Reidy. 2016. "Marngrook, Tom Wills, and the Continuing Denial of Indigenous History: On the Origins of Australian Football." *Meanjin* 75 (2): 83–93.

Hockings, Paul. 2003. *Principles of Visual Anthropology*. 3rd ed. Berlin: Walter de Gruyter.

Hokowhitu, Brendan, and Vijay Devadas, eds. 2013. *The Fourth Eye: Māori Media in Aotearoa New Zealand*. Minneapolis: University of Minnesota Press.

Hope, Alastair. 2012. *State Coroner Annual Report, 2011–2012*. Office of the State Coroner. Perth.

Horner, Jack, and Marcia Langton. 1987. "The Day of Mourning." In *Australians: A Historical Library*, edited by Bill Gammage and Peter Spearitt, 28–35. Fairfax: Syme & Weldon Associates.

Huhndorf, Shari. 2003. "*Atanarjuat, the Fast Runner*: Culture, History, and Politics in Inuit Media." *American Anthropologist* 105 (4): 822–26.

Hull, Matthew. 2012. *Government of Paper: The Materiality of Bureaucracy in Urban Pakistan*. Berkeley: University of California Press.

Humboldt, Wilhelm von. 1796. "Plan einer vergleichenden Anthropologie." *Werke in fünf Bänden* 1:337–75.

Hurston, Zora Neale. (1937) 1998. *Their Eyes Were Watching God*. New York: HarperCollins First Perennial Classics.

Hurston, Zora Neale. (1938) 1991. *Tell My Horse*. New York: HarperCollins.

Jackson, Mark. 2004. "Biography as History." *Journal of Medical Biography* 12 (2): 63–65.

Jebb, Mary Anne. 2002. *Blood, Sweat and Welfare: A History of White Bosses and Aboriginal Pastoral Workers*. Crawley: University of Western Australia Press.

Jones, Rhys. (1969) 2012. "Fire-Stick Farming." *Fire Ecology* 8:3–8.

Keane, Webb. 2003. "Semiotics and the Social Analysis of Material Things." *Language & Communication* 23 (3): 409–25.

Kendon, Adam. 1988. *Sign Languages of Aboriginal Australia: Cultural, Semiotic and Communicative Perspectives*. Cambridge: Cambridge University Press.

Kirk, Geoffrey Stephen. 1962. *Heraclitus: The Cosmic Fragments*. Cambridge, Mass.: CUP Archive.

Kopytoff, Igor. 1986. "The Cultural Biography of Things: Commoditization as Process." In *The Social Life of Things: Commodities in Cultural Perspective*, edited by Arjun Appadurai, 64–91. Cambridge: Cambridge University Press.

Kowal, Emma. 2015. *Trapped in the Gap: Doing Good in Indigenous Australia*. New York: Berghahn Books.

Kuckles. 1993. "Listen to the News." In *Bran Nue Dae: Original Cast Recording*: BND Records.

Langness, Lewis, and Gelya Frank. 1981. *Lives: An Anthropological Approach to Biography*. Novato: Chandler & Sharp.

Langton, Marcia, and Aaron Corn. 2023. *First Knowledges Law: The Way of the Ancestors*. Melbourne: Thames & Hudson Australia.

Larkin, Brian. 2008. *Signal and Noise: Media, Infrastructure, and Urban Culture in Nigeria*. Durham: Duke University Press.

Latour, Bruno. 1996. *Aramis, or the Love of Technology*. Translated by Catherine Porter. Cambridge, Mass.: Harvard University Press.

Lea, Tess. 2008. *Bureaucrats and Bleeding Hearts: Indigenous Health in Northern Australia*. Sydney: University of New South Wales Press.

Lea, Tess, and Elizabeth Povinelli. 2018. "Karrabing: An Essay in Keywords." *Visual Anthropology Review* 34 (1): 36–46.

Lempert, William. 2014. "Decolonizing Encounters of the Third Kind: Alternative Futuring in Native Science Fiction Film." *Visual Anthropology Review* 30 (2): 164–76.

Lempert, William. 2018a. "Generative Hope in the Postapocalyptic Present." *Cultural Anthropology* 33 (2): 202–12.

Lempert, William. 2018b. "Indigenous Media Futures: An Introduction." *Cultural Anthropology* 33 (2): 173–79.

Lepselter, Susan. 2016. *The Resonance of Unseen Things: Poetics, Power, Captivity, and UFOs in the American Uncanny*. Ann Arbor: University of Michigan Press.

Liboiron, Max. 2021. *Pollution Is Colonialism*. Durham: Duke University Press.

Lorde, Audre. 1984. "The Master's Tools Will Never Dismantle the Master's House." In *Sister Outsider: Essays and Speeches*, edited by Audre Lorde, 110–13. Santa Cruz: The Crossing Press.

Lydon, Jane. 2006. *Eye Contact: Photographing Indigenous Australians*. Durham: Duke University Press.

Lydon, Jane. 2010. "'Behold the Tears': Photography as Colonial Witness." *History of Photography* 34 (3): 234–50.

Lydon, Jane. 2014. *Calling the Shots: Indigenous Photographies*. Canberra: Aboriginal Studies Press.

MacDougall, David. 2006. *The Corporeal Image: Film, Ethnography, and the Senses*. Princeton: Princeton University Press.

Mahood, Kim. 2012. "Kartiya Are Like Toyotas: White Workers on Australia's Cultural Frontier." *Griffith Review* 1 (36): 26–46.

Mahood, Kim. 2016. *Position Doubtful: Mapping Landscapes and Memories*. Melbourne: Scribe Publications.

Marcus, George. 1995. "Ethnography in/of the World System: The Emergence of Multi-sited Ethnography." *Annual Review of Anthropology* 24 (1): 95–117.

Mayer, Vicki. 2011. *Below the Line: Producers and Production Studies in the New Television Economy*. Durham: Duke University Press Books.

Mazzarella, William. 2004. "Culture, Globalization, Mediation." *Annual Review of Anthropology* 33 (1): 345–67.

McCarthy, Theresa. 2016. *In Divided Unity: Haudenosaunee Reclamation at Grand River*. Tucson: University of Arizona Press.

McCoy, Brian. 2008. *Holding Men: Kanyirninpa and the Health of Aboriginal Men*. Canberra: Aboriginal Studies Press.

McKnight, David. 1981. "Sorcery in an Australian Tribe." *Ethnology* 20 (1): 31–44.

Medak-Saltzman, Danika. 2017. "Coming to You from the Indigenous Future: Native Women, Speculative Film Shorts, and the Art of the Possible." *Studies in American Indian Literatures* 29 (1): 139–71.

Michaels, Eric. 1986. *The Aboriginal Invention of Television in Central Australia, 1982–1986: Report of the Fellowship to Assess the Impact of Television in Remote Aboriginal Communities.* Canberra: Australian Institute of Aboriginal Studies.

Michaels, Eric. 1994. *Bad Aboriginal Art: Tradition, Media, and Technological Horizons.* Minneapolis: University of Minnesota Press.

Miller, Daniel. 2008. *The Comfort of Things.* Cambridge: Polity.

Mintz, Sidney W. 1960. *Worker in the Cane: A Puerto Rican Life History.* New Haven: Yale University Press.

Miyarrka Media. 2019. *Phone & Spear: A Yuṯa Anthropology.* London: Goldsmiths Press.

Molnar, Helen. 1990. "Aboriginal Broadcasting in Australia: Challenges and Promises." *Howard Journal of Communications* 2 (2): 149–69.

Monani, Salma, Renata Ryan Burchfield, Danika Medak-Saltzman, and William Lempert. 2021. "Indigenous Media: Dialogic Resistance to Climate Disruption." In *The Routledge Companion to Contemporary Art, Visual Culture, and Climate Change,* edited by T. J. Demos, Emily Eliza Scott, and Subhankar Banerjee, 182–93. New York: Routledge.

Montoya, Teresa. 2016. "Violence on the Ground, Violence below the Ground." *Cultural Anthropology,* in the Hot Spots collection "Standing Rock, #NoDAPL, and Mni Wiconi."

Mookherjee, Nayanika. 2022. "Introduction: On Irreconciliation." *Journal of the Royal Anthropological Institute* 28 (51): 11–33.

Moreton-Robinson, Aileen. 2015. *The White Possessive.* Minneapolis: University of Minnesota Press.

Morrison, Joy. 2000. "Dreamtime Radio: Remote Aboriginal Communities in Australia Create a Voice of Their Own." *Journal of Radio Studies* 7 (1): 136–52.

Mudrooroo. 1995. "White Forms, Aboriginal Content." In *The Post-colonial Studies Reader,* edited by Bill Ashcroft, Gareth Griffiths, and Helen Tiffin, 228–31. London: Routledge.

Muecke, Stephen, and Paddy Roe. 2020. *The Children's Country: Creation of a Goolarabooloo Future in North-West Australia.* London: Rowman & Littlefield.

Musharbash, Yasmine. 2007. "Boredom, Time, and Modernity: An Example from Aboriginal Australia." *American Anthropologist* 109 (2): 307–17.

Musharbash, Yasmine. 2008a. "Perilous Laughter: Examples from Yuendumu, Central Australia." *Anthropological Forum* 18 (3): 271–77.

Musharbash, Yasmine. 2008b. *Yuendumu Everyday: Contemporary Life in Remote Aboriginal Australia.* Canberra: Aboriginal Studies Press.

Myerhoff, Barbara. 1974. *Peyote Hunt: The Sacred Journey of the Huichol Indians.* Ithaca: Cornell University Press.

Myers, Fred. 1986. *Pintupi Country, Pintupi Self: Sentiment, Place, and Politics among Western Desert Aborigines*. Berkeley: University of California Press.

Myers, Fred. 2004. "Unsettled Business: Acrylic Painting, Tradition, and Indigenous Being." *Visual Anthropology* 17 (3–4): 247–71.

Myers, Fred. 2016. "History, Memory, and the Politics of Self-Determination at an Early Outstation." In *Experiments in Self-Determination: Histories of the Outstation Movement in Australia*, edited by Nicolas Peterson and Fred Myers, 81–103. Canberra: ANU Press.

Myers, Fred, and Nicolas Peterson. 2016. "The Origins and History of Outstations as Aboriginal Life Projects." In *Experiments in Self-Determination: Histories of the Outstation Movement in Australia*, edited by Nicolas Peterson and Fred Myers, 1–22. Canberra: ANU Press.

Nash, June. 1992. *I Spent My Life in the Mines: The Story of Juan Rojas, Bolivian Tin Miner*. New York: Columbia University Press.

Neale, Margo, and Lynne Kelly. 2020. *Songlines: The Power and Promise*. Melbourne: Thames & Hudson Australia.

Neihardt, John. 1932. *Black Elk Speaks*. Woodstock, Ill.: Dramatic Publishing.

Ngũgĩ wa Thiong'o. 1993. *Moving the Centre: The Struggle for Cultural Freedoms*. London: James Currey.

Nichols, Bill. 1991. *Representing Reality: Issues and Concepts in Documentary*. Bloomington: Indiana University Press.

Niezen, Ronald. 2022. "Perpetration, Impunity, and Irreconciliation in Canada's Truth and Reconciliation Commission on Indian Residential Schools." *Journal of the Royal Anthropological Institute* 28 (1): 79–94.

Ortner, Sherry. 1995. "Resistance and the Problem of Ethnographic Refusal." *Comparative Studies in Society and History* 37 (1): 173–93.

Ortner, Sherry. 2016. "Dark Anthropology and Its Others: Theory since the Eighties." *HAU: Journal of Ethnographic Theory* 6 (1): 47–73.

Pandian, Anand. 2015. *Reel World: An Anthropology of Creation*. Durham: Duke University Press.

Pascoe, Bruce. 2014. *Dark Emu*. Broome: Magabala Books.

Peterson, Nicolas. 2003. "Myth of the 'Walkabout': Movement in the Aboriginal Domain." In *Population Mobility and Indigenous Peoples in Australasia and North America*, edited by John Taylor and Martin Bell, 239–54. New York: Routledge.

Peterson, Nicolas. 2006. "Visual Knowledge: Spencer and Gillen's Use of Photography in *The Native Tribes of Central Australia*." *Australian Aboriginal Studies* 1:12–22.

Peterson, Nicolas, and Fred Myers, eds. 2016. *Experiments in Self-Determination: Histories of the Outstation Movement in Australia*. Canberra: ANU Press.

Petryna, Adriana. 2022. *Horizon Work: At the Edges of Knowledge in an Age of Runaway Climate Change*. Princeton: Princeton University Press.

Poirier, Sylvie. (1996) 2005. *A World of Relationships: Itineraries, Dreams, and Events in the Australian Western Desert*. Toronto: University of Toronto Press.

Popa, Mihai. 2022. *The Anthropology of Poiesis*. Cambridge: Cambridge Scholars Publishing.

Povinelli, Elizabeth. 1993. *Labor's Lot: The Power, History, and Culture of Aboriginal Action*. Chicago: University of Chicago Press.

Povinelli, Elizabeth. 1998. "The State of Shame: Australian Multiculturalism and the Crisis of Indigenous Citizenship." *Critical Inquiry* 24 (2): 575–10.

Povinelli, Elizabeth. 2001. "Radical Worlds: The Anthropology of Incommensurability and Inconceivability." *Annual Review of Anthropology* 30:319–34.

Povinelli, Elizabeth. 2002. *The Cunning of Recognition: Indigenous Alterities and the Making of Australian Multiculturalism*. Durham: Duke University Press.

Povinelli, Elizabeth. 2011. *Economies of Abandonment: Social Belonging and Endurance in Late Liberalism*. Durham: Duke University Press.

Powdermaker, Hortense. 1966. *Stranger and Friend: The Way of an Anthropologist*. New York: Norton.

Provine, Robert R. 2001. *Laughter: A Scientific Investigation*. New York: Penguin.

Raheja, Michelle. 2010. *Reservation Reelism: Redfacing, Visual Sovereignty, and Representations of Native Americans in Film*. Lincoln: University of Nebraska Press.

Ramzan, Bebe, Barbara Pinib, and Lia Bryant. 2009. "Experiencing and Writing Indigeneity, Rurality, and Gender: Australian Reflections." *Journal of Rural Studies* 25 (4): 435–43.

Redmond, Anthony. 2008. "Captain Cook Meets General Macarthur in the Northern Kimberley: Humour and Ritual in an Indigenous Australian Life-World." *Anthropological Forum* 18 (3): 255–70.

Rickard, Jolene. 2011. "Visualizing Sovereignty in the Time of Biometric Sensors." *South Atlantic Quarterly* 110 (2): 465–86.

Rifkin, Mark. 2017. *Beyond Settler Time: Temporal Sovereignty and Indigenous Self-Determination*. Durham: Duke University Press.

Robbins, Joel. 2013. "Beyond the Suffering Subject: Toward an Anthropology of the Good." *Journal of the Royal Anthropological Institute* 19 (3): 447–62.

Roe, Paddy, and Stephen Muecke. 1983. *Gularabulu: Stories from the West Kimberley*. Crawley: University of Western Australia Press.

Roth, Lorna. 2005. *Something New in the Air: The Story of First Peoples Television Broadcasting in Canada*. Kingston: McGill-Queen's Press.

Roth, Lorna. 2009. "Looking at Shirley, the Ultimate Norm: Colour Balance, Image Technologies, and Cognitive Equity." *Canadian Journal of Communication* 34 (1): 111–39.

Rouch, Jean. 1974. "The Camera and Man." *Studies in Visual Communication* 1 (1): 83–102.

Rouch, Jean. 2003. *Ciné-Ethnography*. Translated by Stephen Feld. Minneapolis: University of Minnesota Press.

Russell-Smith, Jeremy, Garry D. Cook, Peter M. Cooke, Andrew C. Edwards, Mitchell Lendrum, C. P. Meyer, and Peter J. Whitehead. 2013. "Managing

Fire Regimes in North Australian Savannas: Applying Aboriginal Approaches to Contemporary Global Problems." *Frontiers in Ecology and the Environment* 11 (1): 55–63.

Ryan, Kathleen, and David Staton. 2022. "Agency through Co-Creation: Interactive Documentary as Decolonizing Practice." In *Interactive Documentary: Decolonizing Practice-Based Research*, edited by Kathleen M. Ryan and David Staton, 3–19. New York: Routledge.

Salvatore, Nick. 2004. "Biography and Social History: An Intimate Relationship." *Labour History* 87:187–92.

Scott, Geoff. 2015. "Close the Gap: Don't Just Do Something! The Indigenous Affairs Budget." *Australian Quarterly* 86 (1): 20.

Shannon, Jennifer. 2014. *Our Lives: Collaboration, Native Voice, and the Making of the National Museum of the American Indian*. Santa Fe: SAR Press.

Sheehi, Stephen. 2012. "The Nahḍa After-Image, or All Photography Expresses Social Relations." *Third Text* 26 (4): 401–14.

Silverstein, Michael. 2003. "The Whens and Wheres—As Well as Hows—Of Ethnolinguistic Recognition." *Public Culture* 15 (3): 531–57.

Simpson, Audra. 2014. *Mohawk Interruptus: Political Life across the Borders of Settler States*. Durham: Duke University Press.

Simpson, Audra. 2018. "'Tell Me Why, Why, Why': A Critical Commentary on the Visuality of Settler Expectation." *Visual Anthropology Review* 34 (1): 60–66.

Simpson, Leanne Betasamosake. 2011. *Dancing on Our Turtle's Back: Stories of Nishnaabeg Re-creation, Resurgence, and a New Emergence*. Winnipeg: Arbeiter Ring Publishing.

Simpson, Leanne Betasamosake. 2017. *As We Have Always Done: Indigenous Freedom through Radical Resistance*. Minneapolis: University of Minnesota Press.

Skyring, Fiona. 2012. "Low Wages, Low Rents, and Pension Cheques: The Introduction of Equal Wages in the Kimberley, 1968–1969." In *Indigenous Participation in Australian Economies II*, edited by Natasha Fijn, Ian Keen, Christopher Lloyd, and Michael Pickering, 153–69. Canberra: ANU Press.

Smith, Benjamin. 2003. "Images, Selves, and the Visual Record: Photography and Ethnographic Complexity in Central Cape York Peninsula." *Social Analysis* 47 (3): 8–26.

Smith, Linda Tuhiwai. 1999. *Decolonizing Methodologies: Research and Indigenous Peoples*. London: Zed Books.

Spencer, Baldwin, and Francis James Gillen. 1899. *The Native Tribes of Central Australia*. London: Macmillan.

Spitulnik, Debra. 2002. "Mobile Machines and Fluid Audiences: Rethinking Reception through Zambian Radio Culture." In *Media Worlds: Anthropology on New Terrain*, edited by Faye Ginsburg, Lila Abu-Lughod, and Brian Larkin, 337–54. Berkeley: University of California Press.

Stanner, William. 1969. "After the Dreaming: Black and White Australians—An Anthropologist's View." The 1968 Boyer Lectures, Sydney.

Stefanoff, Lisa. 2009. "© CAAMA Productions: Listening, Revelation, and Cultural Intimacy at the Central Australian Aboriginal Media Association." PhD thesis, Department of Anthropology, New York University.

Stokes, Geoffrey. 1997. *The Politics of Identity in Australia*. Cambridge: Cambridge University Press.

Strickland, April. 2013. "Barry Barclay's *Te Rua*: The Unmanned Camera and Māori Political Activism." In *The Fourth Eye: Māori Media in Aotearoa New Zealand*, edited by Brendan Hokowhitu and Vijay Devadas, 143–61. Minneapolis: University of Minnesota Press.

Sutton, Peter. 2009. *The Politics of Suffering: Indigenous Australia and the End of the Liberal Consensus*. Melbourne: Melbourne University Publishing.

Tatz, Colin. 2001. *Aboriginal Suicide Is Different: A Portrait of Life and Self-Destruction*. Canberra: Aboriginal Studies Press.

Taussig, Michael. 1993. *Mimesis and Alterity: A Particular History of the Senses*. New York: Routledge.

Taussig, Michael. 2015. *The Corn Wolf*. Chicago: University of Chicago Press.

Taylor, Drew Hayden. 2021. *Me Tomorrow: Indigenous Views on the Future*. Madeira Park: Douglas & McIntyre.

Taylor, Lucien. 1996. "Iconophobia." *Transition* 69:64–88.

Thorner, Sabra. 2010. "Imagining an Indigital Interface: Ara Irititja Indigenizes the Technologies of Knowledge Management." *Collections: A Journal for Museum and Archives Professionals* 6 (3): 125–46.

Tjama, Freda Napanangka, Payi Payi Napangarti, Martingale Mudgedel Napanangka, Kuninyi Rita Nampitjin, Nanyuma Rosie Napurrula, Millie Skeen Nampitjin. 1997. *Yarrtji: Six Women's Stories from the Great Sandy Desert*. Canberra: Aboriginal Studies Press.

Trouillot, Michel-Rolph. 1995. *Silencing the Past: Power and the Production of History*. Boston: Beacon Press.

Trudgen, Richard. 2000. *Why Warriors Lie Down and Die: Towards an Understanding of Why the Aboriginal People of Arnhem Land Face the Greatest Crisis in Health and Education since European Contact*. Darwin: Aboriginal Resource and Development Services.

Tuck, Eve. 2009. "Suspending Damage: A Letter to Communities." *Harvard Educational Review* 79 (3): 409–28.

Turner, Terence. 1993. "Anthropology and Multiculturalism: What Is Anthropology That Multiculturalists Should Be Mindful of It?" *Cultural Anthropology* 8 (4): 411–29.

Valentine, David, and Amelia Hassoun. 2019. "Uncommon Futures." *Annual Review of Anthropology* 48:243–60.

Vaughan, Dai. 1974. "The Space between Shots." *Screen* 15 (1): 73–86.

Vincent, Eve. 2017. *"Against Native Title": Conflict and Creativity in Outback Australia*. Canberra: Aboriginal Studies Press.

Vincent, Phil. 1983. "Noonkanbah." In *Aborigines, Land, and Land Rights*, edited by Nicolas Peterson and Marcia Langton, 327–38. Canberra: Australian Institute of Aboriginal Studies.

Vizenor, Gerald. 2008. "Aesthetics of Survivance: Literary Theory and Practice." In *Survivance: Narratives of Native Presence*, edited by Gerald Vizenor, 1–23. Lincoln: University of Nebraska Press.

Weiss, Joseph. 2018. *Shaping the Future on Haida Gwaii: Life beyond Settler Colonialism*. Vancouver: UBC Press.

Weiss, Joseph. 2025. *Irreconcilable: Indigeneity and the Violence of Colonial Erasure in Canada*. Durham: University of North Carolina Press.

Whittaker, Paul. 2016. "*The Australian* Defends Bill Leak Indigenous Cartoon." BBC, August 4.

Wilkerson, Isabel. 2010. *The Warmth of Other Suns: The Epic Story of America's Great Migration*. New York: Vintage.

Wilss, Wolfram. 1982. *The Science of Translation: Problems and Methods*. Tübingen: Gunter Narr Verlag.

Winston, Brian. 1985. "A Whole Technology of Dyeing: A Note on Ideology and the Apparatus of the Chromatic Moving Image." *Daedalus* 114 (4): 105–23.

Winston, Brian. 1996. *Technologies of Seeing: Photography, Cinematography and Television*. London: British Film Institute.

Wolfe, Patrick. 2006. "Settler Colonialism and the Elimination of the Native." *Journal of Genocide Research* 8 (4): 387–409.

Wolpert, Stanley. 2010. "Biography as History: A Personal Reflection." *Journal of Interdisciplinary History* 40 (3): 399–412.

Woods, Kaely. 2014. "Valuing Aboriginal Cultural Activity: Beyond Markets." In *Engaging Indigenous Economy: Debating Diverse Approaches*, edited by Will Sanders, 79–94. Canberra: ANU Press.

Wortham, Erica Cusi. 2013. *Indigenous Media in Mexico: Culture, Community, and the State*. Durham: Duke University Press.

Wositsky, Jan, and Yidumduma Bill Harney. 1999. *Born under the Paperbark Tree: A Man's Life*. Marlston: JB Books.

Yu, Peter. 1994. "Aboriginal Peoples, Federalism, and Self-Determination." *Social Alternatives* 13 (1): 19–21.

Yunkaporta, Tyson. 2019. *Sand Talk: How Indigenous Thinking Can Save the World*. Melbourne: Text Publishing.

Zajdman, Anat. 1995. "Humorous Face-Threatening Acts: Humor as Strategy." *Journal of Pragmatics* 23 (3): 325–39.

Zijderveld, Anton. 1983. "Introduction: The Sociology of Humour and Laughter—An Outstanding Debt." *Current Sociology* 31 (3): 1–6.

Žižek, Slavoj. 1997. *Multiculturalism, or, The Cultural Logic of Multinational Capitalism*. London: New Left Review.

Filmography

Accessibility note: Many of these films, including *Tjawa Tjawa* and the primary films discussed, may be found at ICTV's streaming site (ictv.com.au).

Basically Black. 1973. Directed by Nicholas Parsons. ABC.
Black Comedy. 2014. Directed by Beck Cole and Craig Anderson. ABC.
Brand New Day. 2010. Directed by Rachel Perkins. Roadshow Films.
Bush Hunt Hand Talk. 2016. Directed by William Lempert. PAKAM/NITV.
Bush Mechanics. 1998. Directed by Francis Jupurrula Kelly. PAW Media.
Catch and Cook. 2005. Directed by Mark Cochrane. Goolarri Media Enterprises.
The Circuit. 2007. Directed by Catriona McKenzie. SBS.
Crocodile Dundee. 1986. Directed by Peter Faiman. Rimfire Films.
Dunba. 2015. Directed by Henry Augustine. PAKAM/NITV.
8MMM Aboriginal Radio. 2015. Directed by Dena Curtis. ABC.
Footprints. 2014. Directed by Cornel Ozies. Wawili Pitjas.
For Young Futures. 2015. Directed by David Young and William Lempert. PAKAM.
Four Corners—"Remote Hope." 2015. Directed by Dave Everett. ABC.
Gapuwiyak Calling. 2014. Directed by Miyarrka Media Collective (Paul Gurrumuruwuy, Fiona Yangathu, Jennifer Deger, and David Mackenzie). Miyarrka Media.
Gurrumul. 2017. Directed by Paul Damien Williams. Madman Films.
Hand Talk Trilogy. 2016. Directed by William Lempert. PAKAM/NITV.
The Horse in Motion. 1878. Directed by Eadweard Muybridge.
Jimmy Tchooga: Painting Two Snakes. 2015. Directed by William Lempert. PAKAM.
Kurrarlkatjanu: The Last Generation. 2013. Directed by Anna Cadden. PAKAM/NITV.
Mangkayi Calling. Forthcoming. Directed by William Lempert and Mark Moora.
Marumpu Wangka: Kukatja Hand Talk. 2015. Directed by William Lempert and Zohl de Ishtar. PAKAM/ABC OPEN.

Naji. 2014. Directed by Kimberley West. Ramu Productions/NITV.

Painting Bush Potato. 2015. Directed by Mark Pindan and William Lempert. National Remote Indigenous Media Festival.

Putuparri and the Rainmakers. 2015. Directed by Nicole Ma. Sensible Films.

Rabbit-Proof Fence. 2002. Directed by Phillip Noyce. HanWay Films.

The Redfern Story. 2014. Directed by Darlene Johnson. Ronin Films.

Samson and Delilah. 2009. Directed by Warwick Thornton. Madman Entertainment.

Tjawa Tjawa. 2014. Directed by Mark Moora. Part of the Songlines on Screen Series. PAKAM/NITV.

Whirlpool. 2015. Directed by Kiefer Dann. PAKAM/NITV.

Yarra Ninytirri Kuurlta. 2015. Directed by Trevor Ishiguchi. PAKAM.

Index

WILLIAM LEMPERT is assistant professor of anthropology at Bowdoin College in Brunswick, Maine.